To George
From BAAL

Applied Linguistics and Communities of Practice

Selected papers from the
Annual Meeting of the British Association for Applied Linguistics
Cardiff University, September 2002

Edited by

Srikant Sarangi and
Theo van Leeuwen

Advisory Board: Srikant Sarangi, Goodith White, Celia Roberts and Gunther Kress

BRITISH ASSOCIATION FOR APPLIED LINGUISTICS
in association with

LONDON • NEW YORK

Continuum

The Tower Building, 11 York Road, London SE1 7NX
15 East 26th Street, New York, NY 10010

First published 2003

ISBN 0-8264-7280-X (paperback)

Production by Catchline, Milton Keynes
info@catchline.com

Typeset in Bembo 11/13

Printed and bound in Great Britain by MPG Books Ltd, Bodmin, Cornwall

Contents

1 Applied linguistics and communities of practice: gaining communality or losing disciplinary autonomy?

Srikant Sarangi and Theo van Leeuwen
Cardiff University

The 'what is' question revisited

Questions such as 'what is linguistics?' and 'what is applied linguistics?' continue to be asked with ontological and epistemological overtones (see Brumfit, 2001 for a recent overview). As an early statement, Crystal's (1968)'What is Linguistics?' devoted half the book's length to 'what is not linguistics'. The same would perhaps hold if one were to embark on a monograph on 'What is Applied Linguistics?'. A related issue concerns the potential barriers of communication between applied linguists and their target clients such as foreign language teachers (Kramsch, 1995). This can be extended to include aspects of research collaboration and dissemination among applied linguists and their counterparts in other disciplines and professions (Sarangi, 2002).

Like the term 'applied linguistics', the notion of community of practice (Lave and Wenger, 1991; Wenger, 1998) defies a precise definition with regard to its scope. Of relevance is Swales' (1988) concept of 'discourse communities', with its 'place' and 'focus' variations (Swales, 1998). While *place discourse communities* refer to local groups with shared communicative genres, *focus discourse communities* co-participate in discursive practices, although being separated by time, space and language (see Prior, 2003, for an insightful discussion of communities of practice and discourse communities). Both senses of discourse community are, however, manifest in the conduct of 'professional vision' (Goodwin, 1994).

In this year's Pit Corder lecture, Crystal (this volume) remembers discussing with Corder whether the now classic volume, *Introducing Applied Linguistics*, should deal only with forms of applied linguistics that presuppose linguistics ('one cannot apply what one does not possess') or also include the 'opposite, impure direction', where the cues come from real world problems, rather than from theoretical issues framed within the discipline of linguistics. In the 1970s the answer was 'yes, we should, but we can't think of any'. The papers in this volume, presented at BAAL 2002, demonstrate that such an answer could not be given today. They include much that is 'impure' or 'hybrid', and many report research cued by real world problems rather than e.g., by perceived lacunae in the specialist literature. As Crystal argues, applied linguistics will only grow and move on to the degree that problems of this kind are addressed, and as a result applied linguistics will never reach a complete account of its field: 'There is no final frontier. Applied linguists will continue to BAALdly go where no linguist has been before'.

This tension seems to be parallel to the langue/parole dichotomy in the Saussurian linguistics programme. Jakobson (1973:20) rightly critiques the Saussurian concepts of uniformity of the code within a speech community as 'a delusive fiction':

> As a rule, everyone belongs simultaneously to several speech communities of different radius and capacity; any overall code is multiform and comprises a hierarchy of diverse subcodes freely chosen by the speaker with regard to the variable functions of the message, to its addressee, and to the relation between the interlocutors.

For Jakobson (1973:21) applied linguistics 'is a natural and predictable offshoot of the modern goal-oriented linguistic thought'. Real world problems are 'the parole' of applied linguistic studies, hence new themes and new sites are the challenges awaiting applied linguists. Roberts (this volume) BOLDLY makes a case for applied linguistics to become more practically relevant and reflexively grounded not only in addressing real world concerns, but also in doing so collaboratively in a sustained way with practitioners involved.

Applied linguistic research on a cost-benefit scale

The 'impure', 'parole' approach has had its gains, but also its losses, at least in some linguists' views. Rather than discussing the papers one by one, we will here focus on some of these gains and losses. Perhaps we should come clean at the outset – as editors, we both believe they are gains, but we are aware that some members of BAAL see this differently, and we not only understand their concerns, we feel that there is a need for dialogue and give and take between the two viewpoints, based on a 'formative evaluation' of the achievements of applied linguistics as a disciplinary activity. They cannot always, as Widdowson has suggested, be seen as complimentary in an unproblematic way.

A key gain has been the way in which applied linguists interact with the people whose talk and texts they study. No longer are people treated as 'objects of study', who are left in the dark as to the effect that the research might have on their life and/or work. Increasingly they are becoming participants in the research (see Daborn and Miller, Roberts, Sarangi et al., as examples).

As a consequence the role of the applied linguistics also changes, and this counts as a gain. In the words of Strevens (1980:19), it 'redefines itself afresh for each task'. Here it is helpful to think along the lines of the theoretical formulation of 'perspective' – defined as 'a co-ordinate set of ideas and actions a person uses in dealing with a problematic situation' (Becker et al., 1961:34). Professional action follows previously elaborated perspectives until a new problematic situation requires the formation of a new perspective.

Applied linguists are no longer the scientific investigators of a phenomenon, but become, together with participants, part of a team, consultants in a process of production or reform, trading between reflexivity and relevance (see Sarangi and Candlin, 2003, for an overview). Such an enterprise adds contingency to application along the lines of Pit Corder's (1973:10) original formulation:

> The application of linguistic knowledge to some object – or, applied linguistics, as its name implies – is an activity. It is not a theoretical study. It makes use of the findings of theoretical studies. The applied linguist is a consumer, or user, not a producer of, of, theories.

In this sense, applied linguists come closer to the profession of medicine which selectively uses scientific knowledge for the benefit of an individual client – what Freidson (1970) captures as 'the clinical mentality'.

All this entails a certain loss of autonomy. The traditional hallmarks of the professional developed in the course of the 19th century, and include, next to specialist expertise, a number of autonomies: autonomy in relation to the state apparatus; autonomy in deciding what it is that needs to be produced and how, and for whom; autonomy in deciding who will be recruited into the profession and how they will be trained (legitimate peripheral participation); and autonomy in the sense that professionals make decisions on the basis of their professional expertise (based on knowledge and experience), and communicate this, in their own specialist code, through the traditional avenues of professional associations, conferences, journals and proceedings. All of this is today at the very least diluted, also here in our BAAL proceedings, however they are still a traditional professional medium.

It is important to note that applied linguistics should not be confined to dissemination via the traditional professional channels, such as this volume. Both the nature of the new research process and its dissemination require other channels and a mode of communication that works also with those who have not mastered the specialist registers of applied linguistics. Collaborative research and collaborative writing across professional communities remains a challenge. Again, this can be seen as a gain or a loss. It is equally important to invite non-applied linguists to write within a mainstream applied linguistics forum (e.g., Clarke, 2003).

It is no longer just the professional applied linguist who decides what will be studied and how. As shown in a number of papers in this volume, another model is coming up, in which this right/autonomy is in part given up, and shared with participants in the field that is being researched. To the degree in which this will influence the training of linguists, it will also affect the qualifications and expertise of future linguists, despite possessing and using sophisticated (applied) linguistic skills. Clearly this can be seen as a gain as well as a loss. Roberts passionately argues for a balance between theory and practice. For applied linguists to be relevant in solving real world problems, 'long-term relationships across professional boundaries' has to be seen as a pre-requisite. Such a working relationship will inevitably foster a sense of reflexivity – as a means by which a given professional group contextualises its intellectual practices (Bourdieu and Wacquant, 1992).

Dealing with real world problems can lead to methodological and analytic difficulties for the researcher. As Sarangi et al. show, categorisation – with its denotative and connotative meanings – is a community-specific practice. It is the evaluative nature of categories which can stand as a barrier to the accomplishment of analytic work across professional boundaries. It then becomes a matter of achieving a balance between expert knowledge and identity, leading to a self-reflexive mode. Through such self-reflexive activity, aided by collaborative interpretation of phenomena, new communities come into being. This amounts to taking applied linguistic work to other professional sites in relevant ways. Exploration of new areas will strengthen our tool-box and enhance new communality.

For the applied linguist, the new challenges include the learning of new ways of acting and seeing. Scaffolding is a core component of a given community of practice. Across professional sites, apprenticeship moves from the periphery to the centre through exposure, experience and practice. Participation – which implies knowledge, learning and competence – is central to this. Language plays a crucial role as a learning tool in this process, as socialisation occurs through language, although this is not to say that professional practice can be reduced to language. It is equally important to remember that shared practice is no guarantee for shared values and attitudes. Language (and discourse more generally to include other modalities) also becomes the means of displaying community practices.

Applied linguistics as a community of communities
We have in this volume the notion of community applied at various levels. We have already seen how Crystal talks about the new frontiers of applied linguistics as a disciplinary community, and how Roberts issues a call to arms to applied linguists to become more practically relevant. Swales goes beyond this to ask if the university can be regarded as a community. He illustrates how shared practices can be unevenly distributed within the university community, 'depending on whether the focus of inquiry falls upon *academic text* or *academic talk*'. While more differences are identifiable across academic disciplines with regard to the writing genre, there seems to be more sharedness as far as the spoken genres are concerned.

In a realistic sense applied linguistics is a community of communities, represented by different objects of study using different analytic frameworks. This becomes apparent from the diversity of studies included in this volume.

Daborn and Miller focus on the discourse of electrical engineering and show how linguistic resources are selectively used to construct positions of expertise – both as knower and as adviser. The taxonomic knowledge is both an indication of shared knowledge within a community, but it also provides a basis for shared meaning outside of the community.

Heydon looks at police-suspect interviews, and shows how police officers discursively accomplish their preferred version of events by orienting the suspects to such a version (to make it appear as volunteered confession by the suspect). Such practices are however institutionally regulated – both at the interactional level (e.g., turn types) and at the topical level (e.g., topic shifts and reformulations). These are useful tools for bringing off desirable conversational outcomes, while maintaining interactional authority.

Dray attempts to make sense of vernacular writing practices as expressed through billboard posters and graffiti. While her aim is to establish what these practices tell us about the constructions of literacy within a Jamaican society, as a researcher in the field she has to acquire and utilise local knowledge in the interpretation of such texts. The focus on identifying the relationships between Creole and English is illustrative of both 'pure' and 'impure' applied research.

Communities are indexed not just by different language families, or Creole and vernacular, but also by the institutional status given to a language. The distinctions drawn between ESL, EFL, EAL etc. are based on such institutional practices. Scott examines the proceedings of the literacy hour in the EAL context, and shows how collaborative, scaffolding work is accomplished at the level of negotiation of form rather than meaning. This focus on form demarcates this community of language users from many others.

Communities are formed historically, with changes in practice integrated over a period of time. Mitchell offers a context-specific account of foreign language education in the UK and outlines the stark challenges the profession faces at the current time. She draws our particular attention to the tensions arising out of instrumental rationales against the backdrop of the global English movement. It is a clear indication of how professional life and work is intricately tied up with government policies and priorities.

Harrison locates new practices in computer-mediated interaction which foreground multi-party, multi-topic asynchronous discussions. As such communication activities become a requirement for claiming membership of such discussion communities, the challenge is for the applied linguist to map such interactional complexities and find potential patterns.

How professions cope with new technologies is a defining moment. New technologies not only bring about new knowledge, but become integrated into professional practice. Marsden et al. illustrate how the tools of CHILDES – originally developed for first language acquisition – can be utilised for the study of second language acquisition. They also ask what the tools can offer the community of SLA researchers. Technology such as this helps to foster sharedness, and hence a sense of community.

Researching of communities of practice knows no limitations. Preferred or dispreferred use of titles can be a candidate topic. Schwarz focuses on the use of 'Ms' which functions remarkably for a sense of community of practice across age groups. There is something here to think about the identity of the researcher in investigating such phenomena.

Through this brief editorial we wish to reiterate that the study of language in its social context (the parole) will remain important as it always has been, and perhaps even grow in importance. But in the era of inter-disciplinarity this may not be the case with 'linguistics', at least in its 'pure' form, if the emphasis remained solely on 'langue'. If we take professions as constituted in discursive practices, then applied linguistics has a role to play in capturing the essence of a profession and in identifying changes within a professional community over time. All changes happen gradually, and the old continues to function alongside the new, as this volume demonstrates in the case of applied linguistics, with its 'pure' and its 'impure' aspects. It is one of the great strengths of BAAL that it has been able to be such an important and open-minded forum for issues of this kind, despite also being a wonderful and still thriving example of traditional professional association of fellow applied linguists.

References

Becker, H., Geer, B., Hughes, E. C. and Strauss, A. L. (1961) *Boys in White: Student Culture in Medical School*. Chicago: Chicago University Press.

Bourdieu, P. and Wacquant, L. (1992) *An Invitation to Reflexive Sociology*. Cambridge: Polity Press.

Brumfit, C. (2001) *Individual Freedom in Language Teaching*. Oxford: Oxford University Press.

Clarke, A. (2003) On becoming an object of research: reflections from a professional perspective. *Applied Linguistics*, 24,3:374–385.

Corder, S. P. (1973) *Introducing Applied Linguistics*. Harmondsworth: Penguin.

Crystal, D. (1968) *What is Linguistics?* London: Edward Arnold.

Freidson, E. (1970) *The Profession of Medicine: A Study of the Sociology of Applied Knowledge*. New York: Dodd, Mead and Company.

Goodwin, C. (1994) Professional vision. *American Anthropologist*, 96, 3: 606-633.

Jakobson, R. (1973) *Main Trends in the Science of Language*. London: George Allen & Unwin Ltd.

Kramsch, C. (1995) The applied linguist and the foreign language teacher: can they talk to each other? In G. Cook and B. Seidlhoffer (eds) *Principle and Practice in Applied Linguistics*. Oxford: Oxford University Press. pp. 43-56.

Lave, J. and Wenger, E. (1991) *Situated Learning: Legitimate Peripheral Participation*. Cambridge: Cambridge University Press.

Prior, P. (2003) *Are communities of practice really an alternative to discourse communities?* Paper presented at the American Association of Applied Linguistics, Washington, 22-25 March.

Sarangi, S. (2002) Discourse practitioners as a community of interprofessional practice: some insights from health communication research. In C. N. Candlin (ed.) *Research and Practice in Professional Discourse*. Hong Kong: City University Press. pp. 95-135.

Sarangi, S. and Candlin, C. N. (2003) Trading between reflexivity and relevance: new challenges for applied linguistics. *Applied Linguistics*, 24, 3: 271-285.

Strevens, P. (1980) Statement for AILA. In R. B. Kaplan (ed.) *On the Scope of Applied Linguistics*. Rowley, Mass.: Newbury House. pp. 17-20.

Swales, J. (1988) Discourse communities, genres, and English as an international language. *World Englishes*, 4: 211-220.

Swales, J. (1998) *Other Floors, Other Voices: A Textography of a Small University Building*. Mahwah, NJ: Lawrence Erlbaum.

Wenger, E. (1998) *Communities of Practice: Learning, Meaning and Identity*. Cambridge: Cambridge University Press.

2 Final frontiers in applied linguistics?

David Crystal
University of Wales, Bangor

Abstract

'I am enough of a purist', said Pit Corder, at the beginning of Introducing Applied Linguistics, *to believe that 'applied linguistics' presupposes 'linguistics'; that one cannot apply what one does not possess.' He would not, I think, have excluded the complementary view – cases where applied linguistic questions make linguists refine or rethink just what it is they possess. This process seems to be increasing, as applied linguistics continues to extend its boundaries. My paper cites some currently unanswerable questions, then illustrates from areas where applied questions are motivating a reappraisal of established linguistic concepts. Because Corder's focus was language teaching and learning, my main illustration is from this area. Global pedagogical reaction to the proliferation of 'new Englishes' requires the development of a domain of cultural linguistic studies which has hitherto been somewhat neglected and which does not sit comfortably within either semantics or pragmatics. I suggest some of the dimensions that a model of applied cultural linguistics would need to take into account.*

'I am enough of a purist', said Pit Corder, at the beginning of *Introducing Applied Linguistics*, to believe that 'applied linguistics' presupposes 'linguistics'; that one cannot apply what one does not possess.' I commissioned this hugely influential book for the short-lived Penguin Modern Linguistics series in 1970, and I remember discussing the range of the book with the author. What about the opposite, impure direction, as it were? Agreed, you need to know your linguistics before you can develop a mature and sophisticated applied linguistics; but should one not need to know applied linguistics before one can develop a mature and sophisticated linguistics? Should there not at least be a discussion of cases where applied linguistic questions make linguists refine or rethink just what it is they possess? There should, we agreed; but at the time, and given the focus of the study – language teaching and learning – we couldn't think of any. Nor was there much motivation to do the thinking: the climate of the time was against it. Even the pure direction had been recently questioned. A couple of years previously, Chomsky had stated very firmly that he was, 'frankly, rather sceptical' about the relevance of theoretical linguistics for language teaching (1966:43; see also Corder, 1973:143). He didn't rule it out; he simply said that it hadn't yet been demonstrated. But for Chomsky to express frank scepticism was enough. A generation of career linguists was turned off applied linguistics at that point.

That was 30 years ago. A lot has changed. We now know that a sense of what we need to possess, in linguistics, can partly come from a sense of the answers we are trying to provide in applied domains. So often we have found that linguistic models don't work well, or at all – that a linguistic description lets us down just at the point when we most need it. This was my repeated experience in the development of an applied clinical linguistics; it is, as I shall illustrate shortly, an ongoing experience in an applied Internet linguistics. In fact, I think most of my linguistic life has been devoted to worrying about applied linguistic questions, chiefly in clinical, educational, literary, and lexicographic domains, and finding the linguistics a bit leaky. I don't know about you, but I never had any particular career target in becoming an applied linguist. When I was little, and people asked me what I wanted to be when I grew up, I never said 'an applied linguist'. And when I did grow up, and became a linguist, the applied linguistic persona, like Topsy, just growed. People simply would not leave me alone, to get on with my first love, what Corder calls the 'first-order application of linguistics', the task of linguistic description. They kept asking fascinating questions, and expecting answers. Questions like 'what's linguistically wrong with that child?'. Or, in a different domain, I made a personal discovery of the crucial and still rather neglected role of English adverbials by trying to answer the question, 'Is it really true that the English present tense has 16 meanings, and if so how on earth do you teach them?' (Crystal, 1966). There is nothing worse than to see the facial expression of innocent hopeful expectation – the one that accompanies 'You're a linguist, you'll know!' – change to one of disillusioned disbelief on hearing the response 'Well I don't, actually.' We then try to salvage some face by offering to 'do some work on it'. That, I suspect, is how new communities of applied linguistics come to be born. The frontiers are ever widening.

The rate at which unanswerable questions continue to arise makes me wonder whether there will ever be a 'final frontier', as Trekkies put it, in applied linguistics. I get these questions perhaps more than most, because when you dare to write general encyclopedias about language, people assume you know everything – whereas in fact all you know is where to look things up – and ask you. Here are some of the questions which I have received in the past few months – and I identify the not-yet-existing community of applied linguists which should be answering them.

> A community of applied theatrical linguists. To answer questions like: Why are some actors' vocal performances more effective than others? What was it exactly that made John Gielgud's voice so memorable? And how can we use this information to improve the standards of acting? Is there any way we can improve the teaching of regional accents to actors? (I have a son who is an actor, and this was a repeated question from him and his friends in his training year. But there is not even a high-quality linguistically informed tape that one could recommend.)

> A community of applied musical linguists. To answer questions like: Why are some languages suitable to opera and not others? Why is English the language of pop music? Is there something about the structure of English which makes it suit rock-and-roll, or reggae? Could we devise a more linguistically representative and diverse (i.e. non-English) Eurovision song contest in the light of this information? A forthcoming television documentary by the (I kid you not) Cat-in-the-Hat production company will be elucidating this last question.

> And at a conference in Brussels in July on Internet security in the face of increased threats from hacking, fraud, and cyber-terrorism, a wide range of questions was being addressed to do with methods of spam exclusion, porn filtering, forensic linguistic identification of forged messages, and so on, all of which presupposed a descriptive linguistic frame of reference for what I have elsewhere called 'Internet linguistics', and which hardly yet exists. Applied Internet linguistics. Or rather, one branch of such a community – Applied Forensic Internet linguists.

And there are other branches of this last community, for other questions relating to other areas of application which have yet to be explored. What kind of language should we use on the Internet? How can Internet language be taught to children? How does the arrival of the Internet impact on children's abilities to read and write? Applied Educational Internet Linguists. There are others. This is an especially productive area. In fact I would hazard that, in a generation's time, Applied Linguistics as we know it will look very different, reflecting the range and ramifications of a technologically interactive world in which the options made available through the Internet (spoken, by then, as well as written) will become a primary linguistic force.

Linguists have hardly begun to look at these questions. And if they did they could not answer them because the relevant thinking has not been done. Let me take these three examples in turn. Linguists cannot address such questions as the difference between Gielgud's and Olivier's voices because they do not have a sufficiently well developed system of transcription to capture the full range of prosodic and paralinguistic features of the voice. Even the one Quirk and I devised for the Survey of English Usage back in the 1960s would not be able to handle everything we hear on stage (Crystal and Quirk, 1964). In clinical linguistics, there was indeed such a transcriptional development, a decade ago (Ball, Code, Rahilly and Hazlett, 1994), when a set of extensions to the IPA was proposed in order to handle the range of deviant phonetic effects encountered in speech and voice disorders. But nothing has happened on the theatrical side. The conventional phonetic system of transcription is inadequate to handle the contrasts of theatrical speech; but because it works well enough for everyday speech (with an exception I'll point out in a minute) phoneticians have no real motivation to develop new perspectives – at least, not without pressure from applied linguists.

Reflecting on what would be needed, transcriptionally, to investigate the musicological questions, reveals another area of ignorance. The overlap between music and speech has been another neglected topic. In the 1970s the Departments of Linguistics and Music at Reading held a series of joint seminars in which this question was discussed. It was motivated by the arrival for a term of a Canadian composer, Istvan Anhalt – a composer in the Berio, Stockhausen tradition of experimental acoustics – who was anxious to find ways of more accurately transcribing the full expressive potential of the voice in speech, and he hoped phoneticians would be able to help. I found my prosodic and paralinguistic transcriptions being used in ways never previously conceived of, as part of a musical score. I am not sure just how far this approach can go, but I know it has not gone very far. Even the most basic features of music encountered in speech are not yet capable of transcription in an agreed way. I am not here talking about intonation, sometimes described in a metaphorical way as the musical property of speech – 'metaphorical' because our voices do not need to be tuned to concert pitch before we begin a conversation. I said 'features of music' – musical quotations or catch-phrases would be a more accurate way of putting it – where a musical extract is given a generalized linguistic interpretation. A common contemporary example is the theme from Jaws. The jocular expression of an approaching dangerous social situation is often conveyed by its ominous low-pitched glissando quavers. Transcribe that. Or (to take other examples I have heard over the months in conversational settings – not always very well performed, but sufficiently recognizable for me to note them down): the theme from the *Twilight Zone, Dr Who, Dragnet*, the shower-room scene in *Psycho*, Laurel and Hardy's clumsy walk music, the riff in *Close Encounters of the Third Kind*, the opening motif of Beethoven's *Fifth Symphony*. The extract may be highly stereotyped and brief. Someone who arrives in a room with something special may accompany it with 'Ta-raa', or the racecourse riff, or the whistled motif from Clint Eastwood's Spaghetti Western films, or the chase music from a Keystone Kops film. Devotees of *The Prisoner* cult TV series introduce its musical motifs into their speech to the point of boredom. None of these are currently transcribable – not least because they presuppose an absolute musical scale, whereas speech presupposes a relativistic transcriptional scale (Crystal, 1971).

My third example is from Internet technology. I am delighted to see a focus on computer-mediated communication at this conference, the first major gathering I am aware of in this country. But isn't it interesting that this should be at an Applied Linguistics conference? If anything gives the lie to the principle that we must apply only what we possess, it is this domain. For the Internet raises a fundamental question for linguistic theory – namely, whether the binary model of linguistic communication which recognizes speech and writing only is valid. Elsewhere I have argued that it is not, that Netspeak is neither speech nor writing, but a unique medium (Crystal,

2001). It is not like traditional speech because, for example, it lacks the property of simultaneous feedback, cannot handle non-segmental sophistication (notwithstanding emoticons), and permits the monitoring of and contributing to multiple conversations (in chat rooms). Nor is it like traditional writing because, for example, it displays dynamic change (animation on screen, for example), it is primarily non-linear in character (through hypertext links), and its technology permits unprecedented graphic behaviour (such as email framing). Several notions from linguistic theory are going to require revision, in the light of what computer-mediated communication enables language to do. And we are only at the beginning of this technological revolution. We ain't seen nothing yet.

Pragmatics is a case in point. Anyone who operates with a Gricean notion of conversation – I believe there are still some around – knows that there are four maxims underlying the efficient cooperative use of language. Let me remind you – and please reflect, while I am doing so, on the extent to which these maxims characterize Internet linguistic behaviour as you have experienced it. My quotations are all from Grice (1975). The maxim of quality: try to make your contribution one that is true – specifically, do not say what you believe to be false, and do not say that for which you lack adequate evidence. The maxim of relevance: make your contributions relevant to the theme. The maxim of quantity: make your contribution as informative as is required for the current purposes of the exchange; do not make it more informative than is required. The maxim of manner: be perspicuous, and specifically, be orderly, be brief, and avoid ambiguity. This rosy view of pragmatic behaviour of course was only ever intended as a perspective within which actual utterances – often full of lies, irrelevance, ramblingness, and ambiguity – can be judged. But something fundamentally different seems to have happened on the Internet, where interactional anonymity has released conflicting notions of truth as norms, ranging from outright lying and fraud through harmless or harmful fantasy to mutually aware pretence and playful trickery. The phenomena known as spoofing and trolling, where messages are sent with the intention of causing communicative disruption (Crystal, 2001:52), undermine the maxim of quality. Lurking (entering a chatroom with no intention of contributing) and spamming (sending unwanted messages) undermine the maxim of quantity. Flaming (aggressive messaging) challenges the maxim of manner. The random nature of many chatgroup interactions challenge the maxim of relevance. The notion of 'conversational turn' needs to be fundamentally reappraised. It is difficult to know what to do with the egocentric sites known as blogs, Weblogs, which often break all four maxims at once. We have to deal here with a totally different world, for which we will need an empirically informed Internet pragmatics. Until that happens, those who are trying to answer applied questions are working in the dark.

But my main example here, in the context of a Pit Corder lecture, has to come from the field of language teaching and learning. It is now well known that the phenomenon of Global English has given rise to a range of new varieties and emergent regional standards which is causing teachers of EFL around the world not a little disquiet. 'At least I knew where I was when there was just British and American English' is a typical complaint. Traditional distinctions, such as that between first, second, and foreign language use, are breaking down faced with the immense number of new learning situations which have arisen – varieties of English that are so code-mixed now that it is difficult to know whether the label 'English' can continue to be accurately applied; partners who each learned English as a foreign language and who now use it as a lingua franca of their home, with the result that their children learn English as a foreign language as a somewhat unusual kind of mother tongue. Such scenarios were absent or unusual in Pit Corder's day, but are routine today. And to teach them – or, at least, to teach students how to cope with them – teachers require fresh models. Once again, we might expect them to turn to applied linguists for help, and for the applied linguists to switch on their linguistic personae to provide it. But if they do, they will be disappointed, for linguistic theory has only a primitive sense of the way language functions to express cultural identity

A primitive sense? I do not think I exaggerate, notwithstanding everything that has happened in sociolinguistics, ethnolinguistics, and anthropological linguistics over the past century. Here in Wales, people repeatedly ask the rather basic question, 'How much is language influenced by culture?'. This is a question Pit Corder explored in his book (p. 70), and I needed an answer to it too in order to help clarify the debate raging in the world of endangered language, when I was writing *Language Death* (2000). Here in Wales, virtually every edition of the *Daily Post* (a newspaper chiefly read in the north of the country, where the issue is high-profile and sensitive) has someone in the letters column arguing over the question of whether one needs to speak Welsh in order to be Welsh. Black-and-white answers are given: I can be Welsh without any Welsh at all; I can only be Welsh if I am fluent in Welsh. The reality, as we know, is somewhere in between, needing to recognize different kinds and degrees of bilingualism and the true complexity of linguistic functionality. There are aspects of Welsh – and we may now generalize, or of any – culture which are totally or heavily dependent on expression in the indigenous language, and there are aspects which are not. The indigenous language is intrinsic to such culturally distinctive domains as poetry and song; it is hardly so in such equally cultural domains as dance and cooking. I wanted an informed figure, a percentage estimate, of just how much of culture depends on an indigenous language for its expression. I found only one person daring to stick his neck out: a Mohawk leader, who said two-thirds (MacDougall, 1998:91). A guess, of course. We do not really know the answer to this rather basic question. That is why I use the word 'primitive'.

The reason for the difficulty, I suspect, is that linguistics has provided us with only two conceptual domains to get to grips with the 'language and culture' question – semantics and pragmatics – whereas we need a third. Indeed, the vast majority of traditional debate on it has been semantic in character, relating to such questions as mental categorization, the Sapir-Whorf hypothesis, and so on – this is the only context in which Pit Corder could have discussed it, in the early 1970s, with pragmatics still a decade away. But the arrival of pragmatics does not deal with all aspects of the question. The point can be illustrated with reference to the notion of 'comprehension'. The present-day distinction between semantics and pragmatics has been helpful in drawing our attention to two levels of interpretation that are needed to elucidate this notion, but the Global English scenario is drawing our attention to the need for a third, cultural level. A common idiom provides an example. The semantic level: if I say, *it's raining cats and dogs*, the idiom requires the achievement of what we might call *semantic comprehension* if it is to be grasped: 'it is raining heavily'. The pragmatic level: it is a commonplace of British English that one talks often about the weather, so that it would be appropriate to say these words by way of conversation even to strangers, say, at a bus-stop. To know that one may do this is to have achieved *pragmatic comprehension*. Traditionally, that would be enough. But the Global English situation now draws attention to the importance of a level of *cultural comprehension*. I recall a conversation with a friend from Singapore once, who was visiting me in Wales, and when I said 'It's raining cats and dogs' he looked at the rain and said 'You don't know what cats and dogs are like until you've been to Singapore'. Some years later I went, and understood, culturally, what he meant.

The term *understanding* can itself be approached in the same way. If I say 'I understand English', it means I understand the semantic meaning of the words. If somebody says 'I understand what you're saying', it means that although they have understood the semantic meaning, there are some pragmatic problems about acting on it. Recently, for example, in a negotiation between two parties, a financial offer was made by Mr X to Mr Y, to which Mr Y responded with exactly that: 'I understand what you're saying' (also, 'I hear what you're saying'). There was a semantic understanding, but not yet a financial understanding – in the sense of an agreement. And, to illustrate my third level, if someone says – perhaps as a result of something Mr Bush has just said – 'I shall never understand Americans', then a deeper sense of cultural understanding is involved.

Here is a South African political example, taken from the pages of an English language Sunday newspaper (Branford and Branford, 1978/1991): 'It is interesting to recall that some verkrampte Nationalists, who pose now as super Afrikaners, were once bittereinder bloedsappe.' If we replace the unfamiliar words by glosses we get an intelligible sentence: 'It is interesting to recall that some bigoted Nationalists, who pose now as super Afrikaners, were once die-hard members of the United Party'. You now understand the semantics of the sentence, but you do not yet know anything about its pragmatic or cultural sense. At a pragmatic level, just how forceful are such words as *verkrampte* and *bittereinder*? I have no idea if these are emotionally neutral or extremely rude. If I met such a person and called him a *bittereinder bloedsappe*, would he be delighted or punch me on the nose? Can the words be used for both men and women? I have no sense of their pragmatic force. Nor do I have a cultural sense, because I do not know what the United Party was, in its politics then or now. Does it still exist? Whereabouts on the political spectrum is it? How does it relate to the names of other political parties? Here, the encounter with global English does not automatically mean global understanding: rather, it shows us just how much we do not understand.

How would we get to understand the full implications of that sentence? There is only one way: to find out about the South African situation, its history and politics. That means we need to engage in its study, in an encyclopedic (as opposed to a linguistic) sense. A few weeks in South Africa, or routine discussion with South Africans, or regular exploration via the Internet, would soon sharpen our sense of the cultural force behind such sentences. Only then, once we have understood the culture, will we know how to use such sentences as the above and truly appreciate the meaning of the words. So, rather than a grasp of South African English leading to South African cultural understanding, it appears to be the other way round: South African cultural understanding leads to a grasp of (the semantics and pragmatics of) South African English. In actual fact, it is a combination of both directions which we use in teaching and learning: unfamiliar words can alert the learner to the existence of a distinctive situation, and exposure to the situation will help sharpen the sense of the new words. But the basic point is plain: language alone, in the sense of semantics and pragmatics, is not enough. It points you in the direction of global understanding, but leaves you well short of that goal.

Just how short requires that we develop a model of the way in which cultural differences are realized through language. They are not all of the same kind, and they make different demands on the learner – which in the case of global English diversity means all of us. From a pragmatic or cultural perspective, there is no difference, in principle, between the demands being made upon me (as a native speaker of British English) as I encounter South African English, and upon others as second or foreign language learners. I am just as lost as they might be. Indeed, I may be more lost than them, especially if their country was one which had close ties with South Africa. Doubtless educated speakers of Shona and Ndebele in Zimbabwe, for example, have a closer intuitive understanding of South African political language in English than I do; and the point is even stronger if we consider mother-tongue speakers of Xhosa or Zulu within South Africa itself. When it comes to global English and global understanding, we are all ultimately in the same boat – first, second, and foreign language speakers alike. Indeed, foreign learners may have a better cultural intuition about English language use than native speakers.

A model of linguistically mediated cultural difference would have to recognize several types of context, each of which makes a different kind of demand on the English learner. I shall restrict the examples to vocabulary – though the points apply also to other language levels. The model would need, firstly, to make a distinction between (a) language which relates to categories of the real world and (b) language which relates to categories of the imaginary world. In the first domain, it is the world which creates the language; in the second domain, it is the language which creates the world. The English vocabulary of tennis is an example of the first domain: we can experience a game of tennis, and in the course of doing so learn the associated terminology. The English vocabulary of quidditch is an example of the second domain: only by reading about this imaginary game in the Harry Potter books can we have any experience of it. But in both of these examples, we are talking about phenomena which are found throughout the English-speaking world. New Englishes have no impact here: the terminology of tennis or quidditch is the same in England, the USA, South Africa, Singapore, or wherever the games are played.

The problems come to light when we encounter activities which are either (i) found throughout the English-speaking world, but with different vocabulary associated with them in different places; or (ii) found only in certain parts of the English-speaking world, and thus presenting unfamiliar vocabulary to anyone from outside those areas. An example of (i) from the real world is the lexicon of eggs, which took me aback when I first visited the USA (*once over easy, sunny side up*, etc.), as this vocabulary was not at the time routinely used in the UK. I remember being asked 'How do you want your eggs', and answering 'Cooked?'. Another example is the lexicon of weather-forecasting on British vs. American (etc.) television: 'there is a 90% chance of precipitation on Tuesday' vs. 'get your macs on tomorrow, it's going to bucket'. An example of (ii) from the real world is the vocabulary of baseball (opaque in the UK) and cricket (opaque in the USA) – areas, note, where the vocabulary is also used outside of the immediate context of the games (as with UK *He played that with a straight bat* or USA *That was out in left field* meaning 'unexpected'). These are both contemporary examples. There is an additional dimension where the examples refer to previous periods – referring to historical events of the past, famous dead people, old cultural practices, and products that are no longer manufactured.

A similar breakdown is relevant for the imaginary, creative world – of literature, cinema, folklore, advertising, and so on. Here too there are activities which, as above, are either (i) found throughout the English-speaking world, but with different vocabulary associated with them in different places; or (ii) found only in certain parts of the English-speaking world, and thus presenting unfamiliar vocabulary to anyone from outside those areas. In this world, under (i) we find the distinctive language (vocabulary, slogans, catch-phrases) associated with a particular internationally known product. Milk, for example, is doubtless advertised everywhere; but the television slogan *Drink a pinta milk a day* became a catch-phrase in the UK only, and led to the item pinta in British English. The Heineken lager slogan, *Heineken refreshes the parts other beers cannot reach* is another example (Crystal, 1995:389). A non-advertising context would be 'Space – the final frontier', known wherever there is a Trekky, which I am told is everywhere, including the titles of papers at BAAL conferences. Under (ii) we have the vocabulary associated with any local product or project, such as a television series which did not travel outside its country of origin, and which yielded catch phrases known only within that country (such as the exasperated 'I don't believe it!' said by the curmudgeonly Victor Meldrew in the series *One Foot in the Grave*). Here too the distinction between present and past time is relevant, but especially so in the case of literature, where the need to interpret the past local culture of a text is routinely accepted procedure in, for example, work on a Shakespeare play. Once again, of course, the distinction between first, second, and foreign learner does not apply. Mother-tongue readers of Shakespeare, as well as those from other backgrounds, have to be taught explicitly about the features of Elizabethan England reflected in those plays.

There must be tens of thousands of pragmatic or cultural linguistic features, but very few have been collated in reference works, and those which have always display a bias towards British and American English only. The *Longman Dictionary of English Language and Culture* (Summers, 1992) is a brave attempt at opening up the area, but this is a dictionary of the language as a whole into which '15000 encyclopedic and culturally significant words' have been incorporated; it is not a book which focuses on culturally mediated linguistic difference. Thus it includes the names of countries and cities, for example, which are of encyclopedic relevance but not (usually) culturally variable. Russia is Russia in all parts of the English-speaking world. On the other hand, it does contain many examples which are distinctive in their local cultural resonance. There are localities with additional meaning: the political associations of *Whitehall, White House*. There are shops and streets with different associations: the fashionable associations of *Macy's* or *Harrods*; *Oxford Street* in London vs. *Oxford Street* in Sydney, *Soho* in London vs. *Soho* in New York. There are the names of newspapers and magazines: what is the resonance of *The Sun* in the UK? of *The National Enquirer* in the USA? There are differences in the names of institutions and organizations, companies and products, fairy tales and nursery rhymes, radio and television programmes, historical notions, and so on. It is so easy to be misled. I know several Brits who have gone shopping in Oxford Street in Sydney, expecting to find the type of product sold in the onomastically equivalent location in London, only to be faced with a rather different and somewhat embarrassing product-range. I imagine some British travellers in New York would find its Soho something of a disappointment, for the opposite reason.

To provide a detailed example of the sort of language any model of cultural comprehension would have to deal with, I take from the beginning of letter J in the Longman Dictionary the items using the word *jack* which are culturally restricted. (I should add that I do not know just how restricted – how widely known they are in the different territories of the English-speaking world.)

> Quite widely used (but not everywhere) are the nursery rhymes *Jack and Jill* and *Jack Sprat*, the folktale *Jack and the Beanstalk*, and the name for frost, *Jack Frost*.

> UK-restricted is the former UK television programme for children, *Jackanory*; the British girl's magazine, *Jackie*.

> In North America we find the fast-food restaurant chain, *Jack in the Box*, and the North American hare, *jack rabbit*.

> Also UK, though of course known elsewhere, is the English murderer, *Jack the Ripper*; and the name of the flag, *Union Jack*.

This is not a bad start; but a quick look at the same word in the *OED* shows that there are dozens more culturally restricted usages. A small selection includes:

> In North America *jack* can be a lumberjack.

> In the USA it can be a game of cards (*California jack*).

> In Newfoundland it can be a type of schooner.

> In parts of South and South-East Asia it can be a type of breadfruit.

In South Africa it can be a type of bird (*idle jack*).

In Australia it can be a laughing jackass, or a slang word for being bored.

In New Zealand, *to jack up* is to arrange or organize.

In the UK, *I'm all right Jack* is the trademark expression of the self-complacent worker.

As I have said, when a country adopts a language, it adapts it. The interesting question is: just how much adaptation takes place? My examples suggest that there is much more than we might expect, and that it is increasing as time goes by. Moreover, as English comes to establish itself in different parts of the world, the range as well as the depth of differential usage is increasing. And we ain't seen nothing yet, for the creative literatures in most parts of the English-speaking world are in their infancy, and it is in the poems, novels, and plays of the future that we will see much of this vocabulary reflected (as the commonwealth literature already available has shown). My examples, moreover, have been only from vocabulary. When discourse as a whole is included in the equation, a new dimension of adaptation manifests itself, complicated this time by the influence of the languages and cultures with which English is in contact. The issue, for example, of forms of address (should one use first name, title, and so on?) will develop additional complexity as English comes to be influenced by the conventions of the countries in which it is used. A single worldwide naming practice is highly unlikely. We must expect to find many more examples of the kind illustrated by the familiar German practice of using both *Professor* and *Doctor* in front of an academic's name. The same proliferation will emerge in relation to many other domains of behaviour, such as whether one gives a toast after or during a meal (and if so, for how long and on what range of topics?), or the subjects which may or may not be used as phatic communion (weather, health, personal appearance, quality of clothing, the cost of house furnishing, the amount of one's income, etc.). So many things – as the idiom goes – 'don't travel'. Humour doesn't. Irony doesn't. Many television programmes don't. Adverts don't.

All of this gives the lie to the simple-minded notion that English imposes its cultural background on the minds of its learners. Cultural imperialism there certainly is; a capital M in Moscow stands as much for Macdonalds as Metro now; but the above examples reinforce my elsewhere-stated view that there is no correspondingly powerful notion of linguistic imperialism. All the evidence points in the other direction – that as English spreads it finds itself being rapidly adapted to the cultural mindsets of the peoples who have chosen to use it. Culturally neutral varieties of standard English also exist, of course – in relation to science and technology, in particular – but they are not as universal as is commonly thought, and it has been in ELT, it seems to me, where the greatest sense of this development exists.

So here we have yet another example of a community of applied linguists – ELT specialists – which is challenging linguistics to come up with a solution. There are theoretical implications in all of this, but the primary challenge in my view is to develop a descriptive linguistics which is not just stylistically informed and pragmatically aware (as recent reference grammars and dictionaries undoubtedly are, e.g. Biber et al., (1999); Summers (2003)), but one which has a full sociolinguistic dimension, including an explicit and comprehensive framework of cultural distinctiveness.

I leave the last word, almost, to Pit Corder. 'Learning a language', he said (p. 105) is not just a question of learning to produce utterances which are acceptable, they must also be appropriate. Linguistics has a lot to say about the former. So far it has little to say about the latter.' That was in 1973. Thirty years on, we have seen the way frontiers have been pushed forward in dealing with this question, first in semantics then in pragmatics. Pit would, I believe, be very happy to see the progress which has been made in explicating the notion of appropriateness in these two areas. But there seems to be no limit to the frontiers involved in this subject of ours. In the 1980s I wrote a paper in clinical linguistics called 'Sense – the final frontier?', thinking that the final solution to my applied problems in that domain would lie in semantics. A decade later I wrote another one, in which I saw pragmatics as the final frontier. Now I find myself rethinking again, with sociolinguistics. And in another decade, what? A neurolinguistic final frontier, perhaps? The conclusion is inescapable. There are no final frontiers. Applied linguists will continue to BAALdly go where no linguist has been before.

References

Ball, M., Code, C., Rahilly, J. and Hazlett, D. (1994) Non-segmental aspects of disordered speech: developments in transcription. *Clinical Linguistics and Phonetics*, 8, 1:67-83.

Biber, D., Johansson, S., Leech, G., Conrad, S. and Finegan, E. (1999) *Longman Grammar of Spoken and Written English*. Harlow: Pearson Education.

Branford, J. and Branford, W. (1978/1991) *A Dictionary of South African English*. Cape Town: Oxford University Press.

Chomsky, N. (1966) *Linguistic theory*. Paper given to the North East Conference on the Teaching of Foreign Languages.

Corder, P. (1973) *Introducing Applied Linguistics*. Harmondsworth: Penguin.

Crystal, D. (1966) Specification and English tenses. *Journal of Linguistics*.

Crystal, D. (1971) Relative and absolute in intonation analysis, *Journal of the International Phonetics Association*, 1, 17-28.

Crystal, D. (1995) *The Cambridge Encylopedia of the English Language*. Cambridge: Cambridge University Press.

Crystal, D. (2000) *Language Death*. Cambridge: Cambridge University Press.

Crystal, D. (2001) *Language and the Internet*. Cambridge: Cambridge University Press.

Crystal, D. and Quirk, R. (1964) *Systems of Prosodic and Paralinguistic Features in English*. The Hague: Mouton.

Grice, H.P. (1975) Logic and conversation. In P. Cole and J. L. Morgan (eds), *Syntax and Semantics III: Speech Acts*. New York: Academic Press. pp. 41–58.

MacDougall, R.C. (1998) Individuals, cultures and telecommunication technology. In N. Ostler (ed.) *Endangered Languages: What Role for the Specialist?* Bath: Foundation for Endangered Languages. pp. 91-8.

Summers, D. (1992) *Longman Dictionary of English Language and Culture*. Harlow: Longman.

Summers, D. (2003) *Longman Dictionary of Contemporary English*. 4th edition. Harlow: Pearson Education.

3 'Doing engineering' globally: negotiating meaning in a world wide community of practice

Esther Daborn
University of Glasgow
TJE Miller
SPEED Laboratory, University of Glasgow

Abstract

The construction of shared meaning in a world wide community of practice is challenging: meaning can be constrained by variation in language, technical terminology and the mode of delivery. Focusing on documentation of computer software, the paper presents an analysis of how shared meaning is constructed by an engineering laboratory. We identify seven features of grammatical explicitness which the writer uses to construct clear meaning, and to present his information as a 'knower'. We show how he balances this by setting up a relationship with his audience which casts him in the role of 'adviser', and fellow engineer. Finally we outline his procedure for establishing a consistent and clear naming system for ease of use. This gives useful insights into the discourse of Electrical Engineering, and how the author can position himself in the text to establish shared meaning in the specialised discourse of the field.

Introduction

Writing documentation in English for an international audience is not a unique problem. In the course of the spread of English as a global language, the general fields of science and engineering have an important role to play in the internationalisation and standardisation of writing (Crystal, 1997; Graddol, 1997). The gatekeepers are the publishers, journal editors, referees of papers and, in this case, one could argue, writers of computer manuals. Over the last few decades the utilitarian function of science and engineering has meant that the products of scientific research are increasingly 'objects with words' i.e. software and technologies (Martel, 2001). It is therefore important to characterise areas of language use in science, technology and innovation such as the language of work in laboratories, the language of networking, and, for the purposes of this paper, the language of software used in industry, business, education.

The general advice in technical writing manuals is 'avoid jargon and cliches', and 'think of your audience' (Markel, 1994; Hirsch, 2000). How to implement such advice eludes many inexperienced writers. It seems useful to look at expert practice. This paper takes as its data the documentation of software produced by the SPEED laboratory at the University of Glasgow, which is licensed world wide to more than 800 users in over 20 countries. This kind of computer software is widely used in engineering for the design of new products and analysis of their physical behaviour. This is the task of professional engineers who usually work in teams. Such teams commonly include individuals from different countries, and experts from different disciplines such as maths, physics, mechanical, and electrical engineering.

We consider these engineering design professionals to constitute a discourse community, defined as a group of people sharing the same habits of communication (Swales, 1990), and whose norms of practice are created by themselves, as users, in the process of use (Berkenkotter and Huckin, 1995). Thus, there are conventions underpinning shared meanings, values, and the way that knowledge is constructed in a particular discipline so that members of that discourse community can understand signification (Bizzell, 1992). To this we add descriptions of scientific language provided by Halliday and Martin (1993), and insights on the roles of the writer in different genres (Skelton, 1997; McKenna, 1997; Hyland, 1999; MacDonald, 1992; Berkenkotter and Huckin, 1995).

As Halliday (1993) points out, the difficulty of technical writing can come more from the grammar (the relations between the words) than from the vocabulary itself. As professionals, the readers of these materials are already socialised into the abstraction of the terms whereby processes are turned into things, but syntactic ambiguity and semantic discontinuity can present problems, especially for those whose first language is not English.

The SPEED laboratory documentation

Engineering writing can be said to be instrumentalist, and in this case it is primarily procedural discourse. There are five texts in this corpus: the theory text book 'SPEED's Electric motors', three user's manuals (*PC-BDC, PC-SRD,* and *PC-IMD*) and one set of tutorials. These together provide the instructions, explanations, and theoretical background and make up the corpus of 230,000 words discussed in this paper.

There are three particular features of this writing worth pointing out at this juncture. The first is that the SPEED team know their audience, their products and their design needs. They periodically run training courses and spend a great deal of time responding to technical enquiries that arise out of the use of the software. The writing is therefore 'socially situated' (Pogner, 1999) and relatively fluid as 'efforts are constantly being made to improve and upgrade the program' (*PC-BDC* p. 2).

Secondly, it is in the interests of the team to strive for a precise and clear style and consistency in the naming system because, if the technical terms are unambiguous, they gain currency throughout the community of designers, which, from a marketing point of view, gives a competitive advantage. Finally, the primary author of the manuals reports that in a sense he writes for himself, 'to give a precise expression of the facts of the matter as I see them'.

Within this discourse community, the writer in a sense positions himself both as 'knower' and 'adviser' (Wikberg, 1992). As knower, he is presenting procedural discourse, and the users are the receivers or learners. As adviser he demonstrates a distinctive way of including the reader and giving guidance on evaluation, interpretation, and discrimination between one method and another. Following McKenna (1997:192) we can say that, in theoretical terms, the text builds a social construction of reality out of the scientific concepts that provide its intellectual foundation, and, at the same time, it is socially embedded in the relations and shared understandings that exist between producer and user.

This position is characterised linguistically by the selections the writer makes from the lexis and grammar to carry ideational, interpersonal and textual material. The text gives the impression of being very readable, and to present a picture of this, we look at three aspects. The first is evidence from grammar to identify the level of explicitness of meaning provided. Redundancy will also assist readers whose first language is not English (Rutherford, 1987). The second is interpersonal elements to view the relations between producer and user. Finally we look at the issues to be addressed in the construction of technical terms.

Evidence from the grammar

This section presents seven textual features of the author's grammatical choices which contribute to clarity and precise expression of meaning. They strike the reader dipping into any part of the text. We suggest that they characterise the writer as the 'knower' and presenter of information. For some of these features statistical frequencies were obtained using the Wordsmith programme.

1 *Use clear topic sentences*: topic sentences are clear, and often read as definitions. 'The most basic field calculation is the open circuit field produced by the magnet'. (*PC-BDC* p. 4)

2 *Signpost text intention*: this is a typical opening sentence in a section of the theory manual. 'This section explains how the basic size of a machine can be determined, starting from the performance specifications and working within the limits of materials properties and temperature rise.' (*SEM* p. 1.14)

3 *Set out clear logical relations*: clear logical relations are established to maintain semantic continuity. This entails a degree of redundancy, but is a key to understanding explanations. The first example takes the reader step by step through an aspect of theory.

a) '**As** the diameter is increased, **both** the current **and** the flux increase **if** the electric **and** magnetic loadings are kept the same. **Hence** the diameter (or radius) appears squared in any expression for specific output. **On the other hand, if** the length is increased, **only** the flux increases, **not** the current.' (*SEM* p. 1.17)

The next two examples show the typical use of 'because' which has 253 occurrences. Of these, 34 are sentence initial, as illustrated in example (b), which also shows the tendency use pre-posed subordinate clauses discussed in 5 below.

b) '**Because** the Hague–Boules and Rasmussen methods are analytical, they are not well adapted to deal with saturation effects, **but** the method is **nevertheless still** useful, **either** for machines where saturation is not important **or** where simplified allowances can be made for it.'(*SEM* p. 2.16)

c) 'These details continually increase in importance, **partly because** of competitive pressure to improve performance and cost-effectiveness, **but also because** of the need to reduce torque ripple and acoustic noise.' (*SEM* p. 2.16)

These examples all show how the explanation uses material or action clauses. They include objections (but), conditions (where), and alternatives (or), and are fine illustrations of the balance of cause and effect.

4 *Make frequent use of defining relative clauses and comment clauses*: the following examples of defining relative clause and comment clause demonstrate the use of 'which 'in the corpus. It is the most frequent relativizer in academic writing (Biber et al., 1999), and occurs 657 times in the corpus. The sequence of four sentences in example (a) typify the occurrences.

a) 'If there is a filter capacitor on the DC side, overvoltage protection is essential. This can be provided by a fast acting 'crowbar'circuit **which** detects overvoltage and connects a dump resistance across DC terminals. The overvoltage problem can also arise with a PM motor if it is driven into an overspeed condition by the mechanical system **to which** it is connected. In this case there is also a possibility of destroying the freewheel diodes **which** rectify the generated current and feed it to the DC link capacitator.' (*SEM* p. 2.24)

In the 657 occurrences there are 101 examples of 'in which', 53 of 'at which', and nine of 'to which'. There are 44 occurrences of 'which is', and 27 where 'which' follows a comma to introduce a comment clause, as in example (b).

b) 'The finite-element solution includes the effect of the slot-openings, **which is** absent from the analytical solution.' (*SEM* p. 2.16)

These examples provide further evidence of the level of redundancy and consequent clarity of grammatical relations.

5 *Take advantage of the pre-posed subordinate clause to thematise propositions*:

this tactic thematises the conditions under which the message is to be processed, making use of the 'periodic' sentence structure which gives focus to new information placed at the end of the sentence.

a) 'Although the inverter is similar to that required for induction motors, usually with six transistors for a 3-phase system, the control algorithms are simpler and readily implemented in 'smartpower' or special-purpose ICs.' (*SEM* p. 1.11)

b) 'When the classical motors are interfaced to switchmode converters (such as rectifiers, choppers, and inverters) they continue to respond to the average voltage (in the case of DC motors) or the fundamental voltage (in the case of AC motors).' (*SEM* p. 1.12)

c) 'Between the extremes of large and small n, there is a value that gives maximum acceleration for fixed values of Tmp and the separate inertias.' (*SEM* p. 1.19)

These examples of concession, time, and place are to added to those in 3 above, where we saw how 'Because' is often used in this way. It is a strategy which Swales (2002) suggests is used by academics to prescribe the circumstances under which a proposition is to be interpreted. Clarity of information structure of this type assists understanding of complex grammatical metaphor.

6 *Keep nominalisations simple*: the author's approach to nominalisation is to avoid what he calls 'concatenated words' which are notorious in German technical terms such as 'die Einphasenasynchronmotoren'. The nominalisations in the corpus generally have a level of redundancy similar to the following example, where brackets show the dependency relations.

a) 'Beyond a certain number (**of** teeth per pole) the torque gain is 'washed out' by scale effects (**that** diminish (the inductance variation (**on which** the torque depends))).' (*SEM* p. 1.12)

Here the grammatical relations of the process are helped by 'of', 'that', and 'on which'.

7 *Aim for clarity of explanation*: the explanation in this typical example appears to have a classical rhythm and clarity in its structure.

a) 'The methods developed by Rasmussen (1999) and by Zhu et al. (1993) go beyond the Hague–Boules method just described by using a direct scalar potential solution that relies on a harmonic series representation of the magnetisation vector.' (*SEM* p. 2.14)

The propositions are held together with the kinds of grammatical relations one might find in a mathematical equation of the kind '$x+y=z$'

These seven categories of grammatical characteristics demonstrate a sureness and certainty in the logical and grammatical relations of language used that reflects the clarity of thinking of the writer as 'knower'. The text offers a comfortable level of redundancy for a non-native speaker. This is complemented by the writer's relationship with the reader discussed in the next section.

Interpersonal elements

The interpersonal elements reveal authorial presence in a series of features which set out a contract with the reader, and maintain a relationship as adviser and fellow engineer, as seen in the following examples.

1 *Set out the contract with the reader regarding aims and limitations in the introduction of the manual*: both these examples are from the beginning of the manual.

a) 'The PC–BDC program is intended for designing and calculating brushless permanent magnet motor with several extensions' (*PC-BDC* p. 1)

b) Design with PC–BDC is interactive and fast. However, PC–BDC **doesn't** produce optimised designs by itself. The user produces them, using PD–BDC as a calculating tool, **rather like** a specialised spreadsheet program. PC–BDC improves the productivity of **the design engineer**, but it **doesn't** do his/her job' (*PC-BDC* p. 1)

There are several points of interest here. The aim is clearly presented. Then 'the engineer' is specifically included in the audience: a mark of respect. Thirdly the expression of certainty and doubt is unequivocal. Any kind of judgement intensifies or de-intensifies a proposition

(Skelton, 1997). Here we find a positive position which intensifies, and a hedge ' rather like', which, while it de-intensifies, at the same time invites the reader to arrive at a decision for themselves. Lastly, the abbreviations express a relative informality. The author reports that he uses this as a means of giving emphasis or information focus.

2   *Use abbreviations for emphasis*: checking for frequencies of such abbreviations Wordsmith finds 25 occurrences of the 'n't' abbreviation in the data. Other examples are:

a) 'Things we **can't** do with the ipsi G'(*Tutorials*)

b) 'It is best to check the EMF and current waveforms every time **you** run **Static design** or **Dynamic design**. Problems often show up first in waveforms. If the waveforms **aren't** right, the output data certainly **won't** be right. It is often easier to see imperfections in the waveforms than in the numbers in the design sheet.' (*PC-BDC* p. 29)

This second example uses an abbreviation together with the second person pronoun 'you': to reinforce the message and include the reader. The implication is 'we have shared knowledge and I am advising you.'

3   *Address the reader with an imperative*: another obvious device for attracting attention is the use of the imperative. This is a common feature of scientific or mathematical instruction, and in the corpus there are 28 occurrences of 'consider' as exemplified in:

a) '**Consider** a load that requires both short periods of acceleration and long periods at constant speed. Then there is a question, can the two values of n be the same? If so, the utilisation of both aspects of motor capability will be maximised at the same time.' (*SEM* p. 1.20)

(For a discussion of the wider use of 'consider' see Swales et al. (1998).) The second example is less common: a negative imperative, but used together with the inclusive 'you'.

b) '**You** can use fractional values (e.g. Ou1) to get a straight roll off, but **do not** use zero.' (*PC-BDC* p. 29)

There are four other examples of 'Do not', all used in sentence initial position in short sentences. The advice is clear!

4 *Include the reader in the calculation process*: apart from the use of 'you' to involve the reader, as noted above, there are 268 occurrences of 'we'. Again, this is common practice in explanations of calculation, for example:

'We consider this as being converted into mechanical power Tw/p, where w/p=2 pi f is the speed in rad/sec. We can obtain the TRV as … and substituting from equations 1.1, 1.2, and 1.3 we get TRV= … (*SEM* p. 1.15)

More interesting is the inclusive 'we', abbreviated for the purposes of information focus (see point 2) as in 'We'll start this tutorial with a simple survey', and 'What we've covered is the basic operation of the PC-BDC…'

5 *Evaluate on several levels*: these evaluations guide the reader on how to interpret the material, and further position the writer in relation to the reader.

i) *The materials:*

The writer comments on the materials:

a) 'All this data is presented in the **successful format used for many years** in the SPEED lab' (*PC-BDC* p. 1)

b) '**The strongest point** of PC-BDC is its speed and convenience in helping the engineer determine the size, control requirements, and performance, over a wide range of parameters.

But it takes several years to build up a reliable understanding of the overall accuracy of a program such as PC-BDC, **so please** check your results and regard them with a healthy scepticism.

The main weaknesses are probably in the traditional areas of difficulty in motor analysis – calculation of the effects of saturation and effects associated with complex flux paths; high frequency effects; core losses (especially with PWM drives).' (*PC-BDC* p. 2)

Again the reader / engineer is included as reference is made to shared experience of difficulty.

ii) *The theory:*

The writer comments on the theory to underline the importance of a reason:

'**It is for this reason that permanent magnets are so necessary** in small motors.'(*SEM* p. 1.10)

iii) *The results:*

The writer comments on the results, relating them to common knowledge in the specialist community:

a) 'This 'optimum' value can be determined by equating the differential co-efficient da/dn to zero, giving x, **which is a well known result** (*SEM* p. 1.19)

iv) *The calculating process:*

The writer comments on the calculating process:

'Once the flux and its distribution are known, **it is straightforward matter** to calculate the fundamental space harmonic component...' (*SEM* p. 2.13)

These interpersonal features all highlight the complex relationship of the writer with his readers, showing how he is both the knower and the adviser. They are receivers and listeners, but also knowers in their own right with the ability to make reasoned judgements based on professional knowledge and experience. Respect for these positions is evident throughout the corpus.

The construction of the technical terms

The previous sections have shown the strategies the writer uses to present his information clearly and how he sets up a relationship with his readers. This section demonstrates the system of presenting the technical terms, known as 'parameters', that are either the same as, or are derived from, the colloquial, everyday, or vernacular names. The entire set of colloquial names is the *terminology* of the subject-matter, which is 'organised around systems of technical concepts arranged in strict hierarchies of kinds and parts' (Halliday and Martin, 1993:6). In this case, the terminology obviously differs from one language to another, but even within English technical parlance, we find examples of the kind of interlocking definitions and different technical taxonomies that Halliday (1993) identifies as problematic. The terms *torque, moment,* and *couple* have essentially the same meaning, but *torque* is more common in engineering practice (the other two being more common in physics). Within engineering itself we can cite the terms *throw, span,* and *pitch,* which have essentially the same meaning, but, as Figure 1 below illustrates, their particular application shows that there is contextual variation.

The parameter *throw* means the number of slots between the two sides of a coil. The term *pitch* is usually expressed in units of mathematical analysis (degrees or radians). The SPEED team choose the term *span* here because a) it is factory terminology, b) it can be used for the same quantity as *throw,* and c) in the SPEED software it denotes not only the width of the coil, but also the polarity.

In this way a colloquial name for a parameter is established as a starting point, but then the software requires a different version of the name for different contexts in the programme, i.e. it needs a mathematical name for

Figure I Applications of 'throw', 'span' and 'pitch'

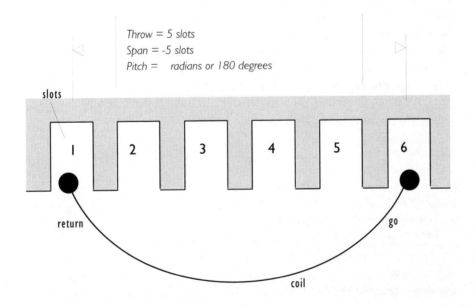

Table I The names			
Name	**Examples**		
Colloquial name	*Slot depth*	*Forward torque*	*Chopping frequency*
Mathematical name	d_{slot}	T_{fwd}	f_c
External name	**dSlot**	**Tfwd**	**fChop**
Internal name	SD	Tf	fC

use in equations, an external name for the glossary of the user's manual, and an internal name to be used in the software source code. This is where it is important to note that the theory underlying the engineering discipline is mathematical in form and function. Table 1 illustrates how mathematics can help in the different contexts.

The table shows how the colloquial name is encoded as a mathematical one. For example, with the parameter '*forward torque*', *torque* is the generic quantity, and *forward* is the specific. For the mathematical symbol the authors can write T_f or T_{fwd} in which the specific case is relegated to a subscript. When it comes to the external name, the software requires a short form and will not allow the use of subscripts or superscripts. The easiest derivative of the mathematical name is **Tf** or **Tfwd**, where the change from upper to lower case distinguishes between the generic and specific part of the name.

This pattern shows how the mathematical theory underpins the system that shapes the names. An additional benefit here is that placing the generic term in first position and the specific term in second is intuitively logical for non-native speakers of English.

Conclusion

The approach to professional communication outlined in this paper shows how the writer positions himself within the discourse community as a knower and an adviser. It shows how the classical concepts of grammatical explicitness and interpersonal relations are translated into the sphere of the highly constrained technical communication required in the documentation of complex engineering software. The grammatical features belong to a writer who had a sound education, is a much practised writer, and who remains interested in how language works. A manual on good writing might well include the seven features presented as evidence from the grammar. There is a level of redundancy which syntactic and semantic clarity, and supports readers whose first language is not English. The style is strengthened by the fact that the writer uses the process of writing to explain the topic clearly to himself.

At the same time his authorial presence is shaped by the writer's respect for the community for whom he is writing. He can set out his aims, outline his limitations, rely on their professional knowledge, and refer to the commonality of the problems they experience using inclusive terms and a degree of informality. In this way the writer establishes a clear relationship with the reader: he leads them through the procedure, but at the same time requires them to take responsibility for making the appropriate choice of method and parameters for their design purposes as professional engineers.

There is equal rigour in the collection of shared meaning for the construction of the technical terms. Selection of a parameter name takes into account that there is variation between languages and within branches of engineering, but commonality in mathematical background. The naming system is structured in a way that is both mathematical and intuitively easy for a non-native speaker to access and use.

This pragmatism is the basis for the writing of successful, usable documentation. There are implications here for technical writers, particularly those who write software documentation. Further examination of the roles the writer creates for himself and the reader would be useful.

References

Berkenkotter, C. and Huckin, T. (1995) *Genre Knowledge in Disciplinary Communication: cognition/culture/power*. New Jersey: Lawrence Erlbaum Associates.

Biber, D., Johansson, S., Leech, G., Conrad, S., Finegan, E. (1999) *Longman Grammar of Spoken and Written English*. UK: Pearson Education Limited.

Bizzell, P. (1992) *Academic Discourse and Critical Consciousness*. Pitsburgh: University of Pittsburgh Press.

Crystal, D. (1997) *English as a Global Language*. Cambridge: Cambridge University Press.

Graddol, D. (1997) *The Future of English?: A guide to forecasting the popularity of the English language in the 21st Century*. London: The British Council.

Halliday, M.A.K. (1993) Some grammatical problems in scientific English. In M.A.K. Halliday and J.R. Martin (eds) *Writing Science: Literacy and Discursive Power*. London: Falmer Press. pp. 69-85.

Hirsch, H.L. (2000) *The Essence of Technical Communication*. New York: IEEE Press.

Hyland, K. (1999) Academic attribution: citation and the construction of disciplinary knowledge. *Applied Linguistics*, 20, 3: 341-367.

Markel, M. (1994) *Writing in the Technical Fields.* New York: IEEE Press.
Martel, A. (2001) When does knowledge have a national language? In U. Ammon (ed.) *The Dominance of English as a Language of Science* New York: Mouton de Gruyter. pp. 27-57.
McKenna, B. (1997) How engineers write: an empirical study of engineering report writing. *Applied Linguistics*, 18, 2:189-211.
MacDonald, S. P. (1992) A method for analysing sentence level differences in disciplinary knowledge. *Written Communication*, 9:533-568.
Pogner, K. H. (1999) Discourse community, culture and interaction: on writing by consulting engineers. In F. Bargiela-Chiappini and C. Nickerson (eds) *Writing Business: genres media and discourses* London: Longman. pp. 101-128.
Pueyo, I.G. and Val, S. (1996) The construction of technicality in the field of plastics: a functional approach towards teaching technical terminology. *English for Specific Purposes*, 15, 4: 251-278.
Rutherford, W.E. (1987) *Second Language Grammar: Learning and teaching.* London: Longman.
Skelton, J. (1997) The representation of truth in academic medical writing. *Applied Linguistics*, 18, 2: 121-140.
Swales, J. (1990) *Genre Analysis.* Cambridge: Cambridge University Press.
Swales, J. (2002) *Is the university a community of practice?* This volume.
Swales, J., Ahmad, U.K., Chang, Y., Chavez, D., Dressen, D., and Seymour, R. (1998) Consider this: the role of imperatives in scholarly writing. *Applied Linguistics*, 19, 1: 97-121.
Wikberg, K. (1992) Diversifying procedural discourse. In *Nordic Research on Text and Discourse.* Norway: NORDTEXT Symposium.

4 Sociolinguistic struggles in outdoor texts in a Creole-speaking community: the significance of 'embedding'

Susan Dray
Lancaster University

Abstract

This paper presents a classification system for outdoor texts in Jamaican, such as billboard posters and graffiti, in order to investigate how social practices influence the writing practices of outdoor texts, and then to consider what these writing practices can tell us about the constructions of literacy within a society. Using theories about language and semiotics from Critical Discourse Analysis, I discuss the dominant model of sociolinguistic variation in Jamaica that shapes attitudes to literacy practices. Different relationships between Creole and English are then identified in the texts. Texts are classified according to the social activity in which they have a role and the nature of this role. I argue that identifying the role as either 'embedded' or 'disembedded' in/from a social activity is key to understanding the complex ways in which the linguistic resources of a community are drawn upon to realise meaning in the text. The relationship between the social activity and the technology used to produce a text is also considered. The influence of these factors on the way in which language varieties are represented in the texts is discussed and two writing practices are identified that construct literacy differently. I conclude that the written language of outdoor texts provides evidence of an ongoing struggle to control the linguistic resources of the community and that in this particular written domain, under certain socially determined conditions, the current model of sociolinguistic variation is not in line with actual writing practices.

Introduction

What can an analysis of the written language of public texts tell us about a society's constructions of literacy? This paper investigates the use of language in written outdoor texts found along the roadside in Jamaica. Such texts include, for example, graffiti, entertainment posters, billboard advertisements and the customised tinted windows of vehicles. The paper contributes to an understanding of the semiotics of these types of written communication, as well as provides useful insights into perceptions of literacy (or more specifically, writing) that can be considered when critiquing current language planning and education policies.[1]

The starting point of this paper is the notion of discourse (written language in this case) in the sense proposed by Fairclough – as a form of social practice, and therefore as socially constitutive. This being the case, outdoor texts, like all discourses, constitute representations of the world, relations between people and social and personal identities (Fairclough, 1992). Discourse, of course, as Kress and van Leeuwen (1996) suggest, can be multi-semiotic. The social semiotic theory of representation developed by Kress and van Leeuwen explores the culture-specific meaning systems inherent in the design of visual images – in the use of colour, materials, line and form as well as the relationship between these images and language. Written language is treated here as a form of visual representation that is imbued with culturally specific meanings beyond its linguistic content.

Taking Kress and van Leeuwen's notion of representation as a 'process' that arises 'out of the cultural, social and psychological history of the sign-maker and [which is] focused by the specific context in which the sign is produced' (1996:6), this paper investigates the 'specific contexts' of the production of outdoor texts, taking into account the production process of texts and the social activity in which they participate. This provides a framework that goes some way to demonstrating and explaining the current struggles over the society's linguistic resources within these texts.

The data that is applied to the classification system consists of a collection of 280 outdoor texts (photographs and field notes) collected throughout Jamaica in 2001 and 2002. This corpus forms part of a larger data set that includes interviews with professional writers as well as members of the Jamaican public. These outdoor texts provide a relevant and available set of data for investigating the writing practices of a society. In other words, they evidence the ways in which people write in their everyday lives, and not just the writing practices of 'professional' or 'trained' writers. All of the texts included in the data contain forms of written language (vocabulary, grammar, spelling, punctuation) that challenge to differing degrees the current sociolinguistic order in Jamaican society.

The sociolinguistic order of the Jamaican 'speech' and 'writing' communities

The broad picture of the sociolinguistic order in Jamaica is as follows: English is the official language of Jamaica. It is the language of education, government and legal institutions. A wealthy elite minority (which includes the dominant social group) primarily[2] speaks Jamaican English. However, the majority of the population (the less wealthy masses) primarily speaks Jamaican Creole, which has no recognised writing conventions. At school, all Jamaicans are expected to read and write in English. This education policy rests on the presupposition, which is supported in practice by the absence of second language teaching provision, that all Jamaicans can speak and understand English. Government documents addressing literacy[3] do not generally mention the language of literacy. Again the assumption is that literacy is (and only can be) achieved in English.

Recent developments in government thinking in Jamaica have led to the following inclusion in the Ministry of Education and Culture's document, *The National Cultural Policy of Jamaica: towards Jamaica the cultural superstate* (February 2003):

> [The Government of Jamaica will seek to] promote a policy and programme that recognises the national language of the society in the formal education system while emphasising the need to learn and use the official language, English, as the language of formal social interaction. (15.7)

This statement clearly articulates how the Jamaican government perceives the appropriateness of English both in the education system and for 'formal interaction'. In spite of the government's apparently progressive stance towards recognising the existence of Creole (which ironically goes unnamed above) within the education system, it is not clear from the above statement if the government is willing to consider its use appropriate in the educational domain. Arguably, the idealised sociolinguistic order of those in power remains unchanged.

In his book, Fairclough (1995) discusses the centrality of 'appropriateness' in models of language variation which implicitly pervade government language education policies. He critiques these models on the basis that they misrepresent sociolinguistic variation and portray 'a political objective as a sociolinguistic reality' (p. 242).

Sociolinguistic order, according to Fairclough (1995), is the dominant perception of the distribution of language varieties within a society. He suggests that this distribution is commonly determined according to notions of 'appropriateness', which are often hegemonic.

Fairclough (1995:248-249) states that one dimension of the hegemony of standard English over other varieties is the 'generating of theories and doctrines of sociolinguistic practice' such as the 'doctrine of correctness'. He notes that such doctrines naturalise hegemonic practices by attributing the constraints which arise from social relations to language itself.

Constraints placed on the uses of Creole and English within Jamaican society manifest themselves in the form of attitudes. That English is 'good', 'correct', 'educated' and 'superior' and Creole is 'bad', 'wrong', 'ignorant' and 'inferior' is accepted as the norm.[4]

Attitudes about language are relevant to the analysis of writing practices because, as Fairclough recognises, they influence each other:

> Practices and attitudes fuel each other. But at the same time there may
> be striking mismatches between what people do and what they think
> they (ought to) do. (1995:249)

So how people write may not necessarily reflect the values they attribute to different written language varieties. An individual may believe that Creole should not or cannot be written, but may write using forms that someone else may consider to be Creole.

These forms may be grammatical or lexical, or they may represent the sounds of a language variety with spelling and punctuation techniques, or they may make use of styles associated with a particular genre of the language variety.

The point is that individuals may each have very different notions of the linguistic boundaries of the varieties that they use when they speak and write. Nevertheless, they all work within a paradigm that recognises two conceptual linguistic categories, or codes. I have called these 'Creole' and 'English', although Jamaicans may not necessarily articulate the paradigm in this way, perceiving the distinction as 'good' and 'bad/broken' English.

This social construct forms the basis for the classification system because the values the society attributes to each of these codes contributes to the meaning and interpretation of the written texts by that same society.

I start from the speech community's own perception that there are two linguistic resources (and grammatical systems), English and Creole/'broken English', which in the context of Jamaica, may be drawn upon in various ways within a text. Writers have at their disposal (unconsciously, perhaps) a series of choices, not only in terms of the grammatical sequences, but also in terms of which code (or code combination) to use. This analysis concentrates on investigating the wording of outdoor texts according to code patterns.

Patterns of use: identifying relationships between Creole and English

In line with Halliday's approach to language as a system for making meanings, I identified English and Creole in the texts according to the following key (Halliday, 1994:xvii):

> 'lexical items' (e.g.verbs, nouns);
>
> 'grammatical items' (e.g. the, if; also includes prepositions);
>
> 'grammatical sequences' (i.e. lexical and grammatical items together).

Because of the close lexical relationship between the two varieties there are many instances where shared items can be attributed to both codes. In these cases, where possible, a decision was made based on the following factors:

> The socio-cultural context of the text and the social practice in which it participated;
>
> The context of the shared item within the text (how it related to preceding and succeeding grammatical and lexical items);
>
> The visual representation of the text (the spelling and punctuation as an indication to the pronunciation);
>
> The stylistic devices/generic styles in the text (their 'membership' in a code).

For example, in Example 2 below, I argue that the text contains more Creole grammatical sequences than English sequences: <JEAN one STOP>[5] (Jean's 'one-stop shop') contains the Creole zero possessive in addition to the Creole lexical item 'one stop'. Possibly the only exclusively English item in the whole text is the plural inflection on the word 'vegetable'. This text also illustrates how Creole and English items do not always belong exclusively to one code. The final phrase illustrates this point:<STRiCLY NO CREDiT> is both a Creole[6] and an English grammatical sequence. I have categorised it as Creole in this text because of the approximation to Creole pronunciation in the representation of 'strictly'.

Where it was possible to distinguish between the codes, texts were categorised according to five relationship types identified between Creole and English[7]:

Relationship 1: Creole lexical and/or grammatical elements items are incorporated in a predominantly English text.

Example 1 (billboard poster; print technology)

<'The #1 deggeh deggeh way to call the U.S.A. is from AT&T.'>

(The one and only way to call the USA is from AT&T.)

A Creole lexical item is 'deggeh–deggeh' (only).

Relationship 2: English lexical and/or grammatical items are incorporated in a predominantly Creole text.

Example 2 (sign; hand technology)

<WELCOME TO
JEAN
one STOP FOR
FRUiTS & VEGETABLES
OF ALL PriCE & SiZE
STRiCLY NO CREDiT>

(Welcome to Jean's 'one-stop shop' for fruit and vegetables of all prices and sizes. Strictly no credit.)

An English grammatical item is the plural inflection on 'vegetable'.

Relationship 3: Creole grammatical sequences are incorporated in a predominantly English text.

Example 3 (sign; print technology)

<THIS MEDIAN IS PROUDLY MAINTAINED BY KFC.
A project of
METROPOLITAN PARKS & MARKETS
Nice Up Your City
Nice Up Yourself >

'Nice up your city…' is a Creole sequence.

These sequences are presented either as: a) representations of speech in the form of idiomatic expressions or proverbs, or are accompanied by images of the speaker, speech bubbles or quotation marks to indicate spoken language or; b) the names of establishments.

Relationship 4: Texts are written entirely in Creole.

Example 4 (wall; hand technology)

<KiNG DANGO MAN RESTAURANT
NUFF RASRECT TO!
THE HON.BOB MARLEY& FAMILY>
(King Dango Man's restaurant. Respect the honourable Bob Marley and
    family)

All the grammatical and lexical items in this text are Creole (although
    some can also be English, e.g. 'restaurant', 'family').

Relationship 5: Creole and English items are combined to produce grammatical sequences that are neither Creole nor English.

Example 5 (signpost; hand technology)

<NO DUMP TO PUT HERE>

In this example, an equivalent Creole command might be 'no dump
    yaso', (no dumping /do not dump here).

Classifying the texts: the effects of discourse as functions of language

Outdoor texts are instances of communicative activity, which contribute to a larger social activity. Although each text is situated in a particular activity in Jamaican life, it draws upon combinations of genres[8], which may be more commonly associated with other social activities. There are several examples in the data: a commercial advertisement (see Example 3) appears to praise a business (KFC) for beautifying a traffic island. This uses language more commonly associated with the promotion of activities undertaken in the voluntary sector. Other commercial texts use the ritualised language of religion to praise God and informal everyday 'spoken' language to express support for the national football team. This same informal 'spoken' language (typical of graffiti) may adopt the style associated with directives, for example, to demand that people refrain from urinating in public spaces and may also appear on the tinted windows of buses and taxis, which sport the latest phrases made popular through the lyrics of the dancehall[9] DJs.

According to Fairclough (1992:64) the effects of discourse are threefold: Discourse constructs social identities, social relationships between people and systems of knowledge and belief. These effects correspond to three functions of language (and systems of meaning), which are present in all discourse (Fairclough, 1992):

Identity: language constitutes social identities.

Relational: language enacts and negotiates social relations between discourse participants.

Ideational: language represents the world.

In addition, Fairclough (2003) distinguishes between two primary types of exchange that occur between discourse participants.

Activity exchange: the focus of the social activity is on people doing things or getting others to do things.

Knowledge exchange: the focus of the social activity is on the exchange of information.

Fairclough discusses exchange types with respect to written texts as well as spoken dialogue. Similarly, Bakhtin (1981) argues that texts are part of an exchange because they are produced in response to a previous text (or utterance) and instigate future responses. He (1986:62) makes the point that even novels are utterances in the same way that private letters and everyday dialogue are. Outdoor texts then can be considered to be part of an exchange (albeit across time) between the writer of the text and the audience.

The outdoor texts are considered here in terms of the functions and exchanges identified above. The *primary* language function and exchange type for each social activity is listed in Table 1. Sometimes the exchange type is explicit in the text. For example, a sign reading <dis a di REAL ROCK Sold here> is explicit about the nature of the exchange being performed. The activity is the buying and selling of Real Rock Beer at a particular outlet. The commercial nature of the social activity determines the primary function of the language of the text, which is to establish a buyer–seller relationship with the text's audience.

Other texts are more opaque. In Example 4, although the exchange type of the social activity is identifiable – an activity exchange of buying and selling food through a specific business outlet (King Dango Man's restaurant) – the primary function of the language of the text is deceptive. The function of the language in the text appears to be identificational. It is presenting the religious identity of the restaurant owner through the religious language of Rastafarianism. This is signalled by the references to 'king' and its Rastafarian equivalent – 'ras', and the reggae star Bob Marley, who was a Rastafarian. Included also in the text is the symbolic Rastafarian image of a crown. This language promotes the restaurant as 'rastafarian' without actually stating that the establishment is such. The effect of this is the implication that the food here will comply with Rastafarian dietary requirements. This is an inference that will automatically be made by readers of the sign who possess the relevant sociocultural (and linguistic) knowledge. The religious language of this text may initially seem peripheral to the primary function of getting people to buy food. It is however instrumental in clarifying to the audience, not merely the religious identity of the restaurant's owner, but also valuable information about the product being offered. This text demonstrates how texts may have primary and secondary functions, which work together in complex ways. In Example 4, the primary function of language is to establish a relationship between the seller and the potential buyer. This is achieved through the secondary function of promoting a Rastafarian identity.

All written acts (like spoken language) will necessarily say something about the identity of the writer. Le Page and Tabouret-Keller (1985:14), for example, claim that people 'reveal both their personal identity and their search for social roles' through their linguistic behaviour. However, the significance of identity as a primary function of the text varies according to the social activity. The primary language functions of the various social activities of the outdoor texts are listed in Table 1. This table is explained in detail in the following sections.

Table 1 Classification of outdoor texts (containing Creole or non-standard forms) according to their role in the social activities of which they are a part

Social activity and Exchange type	Specific function of text as part of social activity	Primary language function(s) and most common code-relationship(s)	
		Embedded texts	Disembedded texts
Buying and selling	Promotion of goods and services	Relational function #1 (grammatical items only) #3 (names only) #4	Relational and identity functions #1 (lexical items) #3 (speech representation only)
Activity exchange	Promotion of events	[no instances]	Ideational function #1 (lexical items only) #3 (speech representation only)
Social control Activity exchange	[not applicable]	Relational function #1 (grammatical items only) #4	Relational and identity functions #3 (speech representation only)
Public information Knowledge exchange	[not applicable]	Identity function #1 (grammatical items only) #4	[no instances]
Social advocacy Knowledge exchange	[not applicable]	Relational and identity functions #4	Ideational functions #1 (lexical items only) #3 (speech representation only)

Key to technologies	Key to code relationships	

	'Hand' production technology	#1 #2	Creole lexical/grammatical items in English text English lexical/grammatical items in Creole text
	'Print' production technology	#3 #4	Creole grammatical sequences in English text Creole only text
	Both technologies	#5 #6	Creole and English items combined to produce sequences that are neither Creole nor English.

Embedded and disembedded communicative activities

The communicative activity of the text may take place independently of the social activity of which it is a part, in which case it is disembedded from the related activity, which occurs at a different time and in a different place. Typical examples of this type of disembedded text are the promotional texts of billboards or the protesting texts of graffiti.

Embedded texts are texts whose communicative activity is embedded in the social activity to which it contributes. It is therefore locally situated within that activity, and is contextualised by that activity. Typical examples of embedded texts are signs on roadside stalls or handcarts naming the product, which is being sold, and is simultaneously on display, and also the placards of public demonstrators who are protesting simultaneously.

The role of the text in the social activity – whether it is part of it (embedded), or independent of it (disembedded) – shapes the language of the text. For example, one aspect of the social activity of buying and selling goods for profit involves making the potential buyers of these goods aware of their existence, through promotional activity. If the promotional activity is embedded in the activity of buying and selling, the language of the text will reflect this: The seller is present, is able to promote the product verbally, and the product is on display. These embedded commercial texts in my data tend to be short and sometimes almost peripheral to the selling which is able to 'promote' itself. Image A below provides an example. The text is minimal – serving only to announce the presence of the goods for sale and is supported with the real product – unprepared and pre-prepared coconuts on display in the background and foreground. In fact, it is common in Jamaica to see such activities being undertaken with no written promotional 'support'

Image A

<COME IN
WE/ARE
OPEN>

<ICE.ColD JELLY>

(Ice cold coconut 'water'
and coconut 'flesh')

whatsoever. Roadside sellers of jelly coconut, roasted peanuts and sugar cane, for example, often promote their goods by announcing their presence verbally.

Texts that are disembedded from the social activity are decontextualised. They cannot assume the same degree of context that is provided by the physical actions occurring simultaneously around embedded texts. For example, texts promoting goods which are being sold elsewhere, in an unspecified place and at a different, unspecified time (such as billboard posters), assume a different role in the activity of buying and selling. These texts alone provide the promotional activity. It is as a result of seeing these that the potential 'buyer' becomes aware of the product and at some point later may make the decision to buy the product. These texts have a lot of work to do if they are to influence people's buying habits over time and space. They have to remain in the audience's memory. One of the ways they do this is by attempting to identify with the audience (Bernstein, 1997). By drawing on combinations of different genres (and visual imagery) in complex and creative ways they attempt to create an identity that is compatible with the identity that the target audience has of itself. For disembedded commercial texts, the identity function of language and the relational function of language are equally significant, since the text establishes the relationship between seller and potential buyer through appealing to a particular type of 'buyer' identity.

Production technology

Another way in which disembedded texts stay in the memory of the audience is by maintaining a high level of visibility, through technologies of mass-production, namely the printing press. This often has consequences on the end product: The text may include sophisticated photographic and digital imagery, and is likely to have undergone proofreading processes, which tend to steer the language of the text towards standard English spelling and punctuation conventions. The life of these texts is short. They tend to be printed onto paper and take the form of either billboard posters (e.g. Image D) or campaign posters. These are either frequently replaced as a strategy to maintain consumer/public interest or left to deteriorate once the promotional/social campaign ends.

Embedded texts, on the other hand, are not mass-produced. They tend to be individually written for a particular context and are hand painted directly onto an appropriately situated surface, such as the side of a handcart, a cool box or a wall. This 'low' technology produces texts that are more permanent than those of disembedded texts.

In the data it is no coincidence that all texts that belong to the same social activity and are embedded in it employ the same type of production technology – hand produced. (This is indicated in Table 1 by dark grey.) Similarly, all disembedded texts belonging to the same social activity employ the same type of production technology: Disembedded texts regulating social behaviour ('social control') and those promoting goods and services use sophisticated print technologies (indicated by light grey in Table 1). Disembedded texts that advocate particular beliefs and opinions are hand-produced. The only social activity that uses both hand and print technologies is the promotion of entertainment events – specifically those of the dancehall culture (indicated in Table 1 by black). This category is the exception. Dancehall posters tend traditionally to be hand written and then printed or photocopied (Image B). Increasingly it is common to see posters make use of computerised graphics and photographs (Image C).

An interesting question is why texts contributing to this particular activity should display such extreme differences in production technology. The answer can be partly found by considering the social activity in which these texts participate – that of 'selling' entertainment events. The 'selling and buying' of these events is different to that of products and services. The nature of the social activity is such that it cannot be embedded in the actual activity of the dancehall performance. The success of the event (unlike a product or a service) can only be 'consumed' once – in a particular place at a particular time. The pre-event (disembedded) promotion is crucial to its

Image B
Poster for a dancehall event
produced with 'hand technology'

Image C
Poster for a dancehall event
produced with 'print technology'

success. The promotional strategy of an entertainment event is also unlike the promotion of goods and services. Texts promoting entertainment events do not appeal primarily to the identity of the target audience, since the dancehall goers already know who they are. What the audience needs to know is who is providing the entertainment. The more sophisticated dancehall posters foreground the performers/soundsystems through the use of photographs and coloured fonts. Elements of the traditional handwritten poster are incorporated, such as the name of the event and the formulaic language in which it is presented. This usually follows the structure of 'X and Y promotions present a night called '...'. The name of the night is significant. It tends to embody values associated with the dancehall culture. These are values that are also taken up in the social commentary of the lyrics of the performers. Performers (and 'sound systems') may promote religious consciousness, social consciousness or what the Jamaican public call 'slackness' ('vulgar' and 'lewd' lyrics), or any combination of these. Potential dancehall goers will decide whether or not to spend their money at a dancehall event, principally on the night's line-up. Testimony to this is the fact that hand produced texts promoting little-known artists also offer prizes (such as cologne and champagne) to entice people to attend. Such competitions are unnecessary for the printed texts promoting the big names. The primary function of the language of these texts is ideational – it promotes a particular view of the world, principally through the title of the event. So sophisticated imagery is not relied upon in these texts in the same way that it may be in other types of promotional text that rely partly on images to project a particular identity, and for which print technology is more suitable.

A further explanation as to why dancehall posters vary in the type of technologies employed (where other social activities consistently employ either hand or print technologies) is that the amount of funding available to the different promoters of dancehall events varies enormously (Stolzoff, 2000).

Application of data to the classification system
Table 1 summarises the application of my data to the classification system described above. The outdoor texts have been grouped principally according to the social activities[10] in which they are participate. These are:

Buying and selling as a profit making activity of which the texts play a promotional role. These texts were typically commercial advertisements.

Regulating social behaviour Typically, the embedded texts were directives that stated what was not allowed in a specific place (e.g. <ONE BLOOD NO PISS YASO> (We are all one. Do not piss here)). The authority of these texts relies on implicit knowledge of the relevance of legal structures to the command being given. This regulation of particular sites was in contrast to the disembedded texts, which tended to state what was allowed or should be done (e.g. <KEEP FATALITIES DOWN. DRIVE RIDE AND WALK GOOD>). The social control to which these texts contributed was more general, and long-term.

Providing public information Typically these texts advised the public or simply served as 'labels', such as street names.

Advocating social identities and actions The embedded texts were typically placards or banners being held during protest marches. The disembedded texts tended to be either graffiti or designed into the tinting on bus and taxi windows.

Table 1 shows a further subdivision of the texts which makes a distinction between texts produced with 'print' technology and 'hand' technology. This is indicated by the different shading: The dark grey tone indicates texts that have been produced with more traditional, hand technologies (in almost all cases, this means hand painted, stencilled or crafted) and the light tone indicates texts produced with more complex mechanical and computer technology (in all cases this involves printing).

The role of language code

Table 1 also lists the most common relationship types between Creole and English in the texts. These code relationships indicate tendencies in the writing strategies in texts belonging to a particular social activity. By considering them in the light of the exchange type, the production technology and the role of the text in the social activity (whether it is embedded or disembedded), a pattern emerges. This pattern is shown in Table 2 below. Two patterns of relationship types are evident in Table 2.

a) Written Creole Texts written entirely in Creole (#4) are produced by hand technologies, never by print. In these texts, whether they are influencing behaviour (activity exchange) or knowledge and beliefs (knowledge exchange), Creole fulfils all the language functions of the text. It serves to establish relationships, identities and world views. Most significantly, it therefore fulfils the primary language function(s) of these texts.

This constructs Creole as a legitimate, or 'appropriate' form of written communication. Whether the primary function of language in these texts is to represent social identities or to negotiate social identities, Creole alone is the medium through which meaning is conveyed. Texts written by hand, in contrast to those that have been printed, are able to flout the society's current perception of 'correct' writing practice and challenge the sociolinguistic order by using Creole not only in a written form, but as a written form that represents a system of meaning that stands independently of English.

b) Written English with Creole 'tokens' Texts produced with print technologies on the other hand do not use Creole exclusively, but rather position Creole within an English text, either as an individual lexical item (#1) or as a phrase associated with spoken language (#3). Most printed outdoor texts in Jamaica

Table 2 Distribution of types of relationship between Creole and English in embedded and disembedded texts according to exchange type and technology

Exchange Type	Embedded texts		Disembedded texts	
	'Print' technology	'Hand' technology	'Print' technology	'Hand' technology
Activity (aims to influence physical behaviour of audience)	[no instances]	#1 (grammatical items) #3 (name 'labels') #4	#1 (lexical items) #3 (speech representation)	Entertainment posters only: these are an exception so have not been included here.
Knowledge (aims to inform or influence the beliefs/opinions of the audience)	[no instances]	#1 (grammatical items) #4	[no instances]	#1 (lexical items) #4

are written entirely in English. These English texts are not part of this analysis, but are mentioned here because they are the 'norm' and therefore any printed text using Creole is likely to do so as a deliberate strategy for accomplishing a particular language function. For example, in the activities of buying and selling and regulating social behaviour, printed texts contrast Creole with English as a means of negotiating a relationship with the audience through the projection of a 'Creole-speaking' identity. This may be a relationship that sets up a 'them and us' class-based distinction within Jamaican society or a collective representation that focuses on Jamaican nationhood and culture. In these texts, Creole is frequently represented as speech and therefore fulfils the identity function whilst English is used to establish the relationships between the text and the audience. Image D exemplifies this relationship.

English fulfils the relational function in this text. It is used to establish the relationship between buyers and sellers by suggesting that milk is for sale: <There's a better way to get Fresh cows milk>. The Creole, in this text at least, sets up this relation, since without the context provided by the young girl's comment (and the image of the cow), the English text makes little sense. This text also provides an example of how the Creole in these types of text is hinted at, rather than representative of genuine speech. '100% fresh cows milk' is advertising language that would not be expected from a young Creole speaking child.

Image D

<Mama I bring home de 100% fresh cows milk!>

(Mother, I've brought home the 100% fresh cow's milk!)

<There's a better way to get fresh cows milk!>

This contrast in the functions for which English and Creole are used constructs Creole as an 'inappropriate' form of written communication. It is presented in a written form but nevertheless as the speech of a particular community. The paradox is that although the text recognises Creole as the language of the community with which it seeks to identify, it uses English to establish relations between participants of the exchange.

These texts are disembedded and therefore not contexualised by the social activity they contribute to. Successful communication of the message and interpretation relies entirely on the text. That printed texts use English to ensure 'successful' communication can be partly explained by the notion of 'regulation' (Sebba, forthcoming). Printed texts are likely to undergo more rigorous proofreading procedures that will ensure that a text conforms to standardised grammatical forms (in this case those of standard English). This would also explain why the use of Creole in these texts appears 'tokenistic'. It represents an approximation to the vernacular speech of a community rather than an accurate representation.

These texts present written Creole as an inappropriate code for written communication. As a medium of written communication it is dependent on a context provided by English, and at the same time is contrasted with English as vernacular speech rather than written language. This writing practice reflects a similar model of language variation to that of the Jamaican government and the dominant sociolinguistics order. In order to legitimise the use of Creole in the text, it is represented as speech, because to do otherwise would be to write 'bad' English.

Conclusion

This paper contributes towards an understanding of the semiotics of outdoor public texts. A classification system is described that accommodates all the various types of outdoor texts that contain vernacular written forms as well as the English of a Creole-speaking society. This system considers the ways in which the 'embeddedness' of texts relates to different production technologies in various social activities. This framework is then used to investigate the functions of Creole and English in the outdoor texts. I show that the two language codes have different distributions and functions and briefly discuss these in terms of their 'legitimacy' as written language in the speech community that produces them.

Through the classification system, the 'struggles' over linguistic resources are illuminated and the extent to which the doctrine (attitude) of 'correct' written language matches the practice of producing written texts for public consumption is examined. I identify two different groups of writers (distinguished by production technology and (dis)embedding of the text in the activity), whose practices (but not necessarily attitudes) represent (but not necessarily evaluate) the 'appropriateness' of written language varieties differently. One group's practices perpetuate the dominant model of sociolinguistic variation by constructing Creole as an exclusively spoken variety and English as the language of literacy. The other group's writing practices represent an approximation to the sociolinguistic realities of the community, by constructing Creole as a legitimate written medium of communication.

Acknowledgements

I thank both my supervisors, Norman Fairclough and Mark Sebba, for their comments and advice on previous drafts.

Notes

1   This is explored further in my doctoral thesis, currently in progress.

2   The language situation in Jamaica has been described by linguists as a continuum, where the speech of an individual can span several consecutive lects falling between two distinct codes: 'standard' Jamaican English and Jamaican Creole. Thus, Jamaican English speech may include Creole elements/phrases and Creole speech may include English items. This 'reality', however, is not recognised in the society's dominant model of language variation which views the varieties as distinct.

3   See for example the Literacy Initiative of the Ministry of Education Youth and Culture

(http://www.moec.gov.jm/literacy_initiative/literacy.htm accessed April 2003). One exception is the explicit mention of English in the Education White Paper (2001) which says that the state pays special attention to its citizens 'being literate in the basic areas of English, Mathematics, the Humanities, Science and a foreign language'. Creole is excluded from the discussion. (http://www.moec.gov.jm/white_paper.htm accessed April 2003).

4   The following comments taken from interviews about writing with members of the Jamaican public exemplify the different qualities [in italics] attributed to Creole (or 'Patois') and English and perceptions of the relationship between them:

'Well I think [the teacher] would try to *correct* the child because I think [ ] you will just try to learn more English because that's what you definitely have to do, I mean, *English is the language*... He can read and write but he will make a lot of *mistakes* if he reads and writes. He's not very very *bright*. You know, like I speak English fluently like this, he will not be able to do this. He will speak half English half Patois in everything he does.'

'OK, for instance, we used the different phrase back and forth like the verb and the noun. We just *jumble, mix it up* you know. That's how this Patois come in. For instance you would never say 'come over here' or, you know, 'this is this, take this over there' you know that? We would say 'tek dis over dere-so', so we start off with the English but just *broken up*. So sometimes you know English is – pronounce the verb and the noun and the things *proper*. We doesn't you know... I find a lot of times if I'm writing, you know, you write-sometimes you write to how you think. Right? Because a lot of times I'll be writing a line, a letter or something, and there goes! You *messed up* ( ) So I find at times you know, you get caught up by *mixing up* sentences you know and you have to think carefully.'

5   The text within the angle brackets < > denotes the same orthographic representation as the original text. Translations are given in rounded brackets ( ) where necessary.

6   It could be argued that since adverbs do not usually have a suffix in Jamaican Creole, 'strictly' should therefore be defined as English on a grammatical basis. However, the use of 'strictly' is common in spoken Creole (my observation) and I therefore argue that it has become lexicalised.

7   The English that I speak (British English) and the English that Jamaicans speak (Jamaican English) can at times be strikingly different. I have endeavoured here to consider the differences between Creole and English in terms of the English spoken in Jamaica and I am indebted to David Morrison for his help in clarifying any uncertainties I had in interpretation. Any errors or oversights are my own.

8   I use the term genre to refer to a *typical* way that a society has for talking about and carrying out a particular activity (its language use). Bakhtin defines genres as 'typical forms of utterances' (1986:63). *Actual* utterances (or events) draw on these typical forms to produce spoken or written texts that may be more or less recognisable as belonging to the genres of the society. Actual texts do not *belong in* a genre, but rather 'they *draw upon* the socially available resource of genres in potentially quite complex and creative ways' (Fairclough, 2003:51).

9   Dancehall culture in Jamaica is a significant part of everyday life. The artists (DJs and singers) perform live and compete with one another on stage for the admiration of the crowd. Their 'weapons' are their lyrics, which must provide relevant social commentary as well as demonstrate considerable improvisational skills with rhythm and rhyme (see

Devonish, 1996 and Stolzoff, 2000).

10 This table is not exhaustive. I do not want to suggest that these are the only activities undertaken by public texts in Jamaica, since other texts that are written entirely in standard English have not been considered, and may be part of other social activities.

References

Bakhtin, M. (1981) *The Dialogic Imagination*. Austin: University of Texas Press.
Bakhtin, M. (1986) *Speech Genres and other late essays*. Austin: University of Texas Press.
Bernstein, D. (1997) *Advertising Outdoors: Watch this space!* London: Phaidon Press Limited.
Devonish, H. (1996) Kom groun Jamiekan daans haal liriks: memba se a plie wi a plie / Contextualising Jamaican 'Dance Hall' music: Jamaican Language at play in a speech event. *English World-Wide*, 17, 2: 213-237.
Fairclough, N. (1992) *Discourse and Social Change*. Cambridge: Polity Press.
Fairclough, N. (1995) *Critical Discourse Analysis: The critical study of language*. London: Longman.
Fairclough, N. (2003) *Analysing discourse and text: Textual analysis for social research*.
Halliday, M.A.K. (1994) *An Introduction to Functional Grammar*. 2nd edition. London: Edward Arnold.
Kress, G. and van Leeuwen, T. (1996) *Reading Images: The grammar of visual design*. London: Routledge.
Le Page, R. and Tabouret-Keller, A. (1985) *Acts of Identity*. Cambridge: Cambridge University Press.
Sebba, M. (forthcoming) *Spelling rebellion*. To appear in J. Androutsopoulos and A. Georgakopoulou (eds) *Discourse Constructions of Youth Identities*. Amsterdam: Benjamins.
Stolzoff, N. (2000) *Wake the town and tell the people: Dancehall culture in Jamaica*. Durham and London: Duke University Press.

5 Computer-mediated interaction: using discourse maps to represent multi-party, multi-topic asynchronous discussions

Sandra Harrison

Coventry University

Abstract

This paper illustrates the use of discourse maps as a research tool to represent patterns of interaction in email discussions. Developed from an idea by Black et al. (1983), the discourse map can represent visually the complex interaction of an email discussion list, showing patterns of speaker activity, the distribution of turns across parallel topics, and the spread of contributions over time. This method of representation facilitates the identification of significant features in the discourse, such as consecutive turns by the same participant, multiple topics within a single message, and topics which fail to generate a response. Discourse maps also facilitate comparison of patterns of interaction in different discussion groups. Data samples taken from different discussions can be seen to differ in several respects, such as the number of topics that fail to get a response, and the level of participation in individual topics. This technique has been developed in order to represent email discussions, but it can also usefully be applied to other forms of discussion in different media for the purpose of comparison. This paper uses discourse maps to compare different email discussions, and also to illustrate the different interaction patterns of a sample of newspaper letters and a radio discussion.

Introduction

The discourse map was developed as a research tool to address the problem of handling data in the complex multi-party multi-topic context of email discussions. The project for which the discourse map was initially developed was an investigation of the discourse structure of email discussions (Harrison, 2002).

An examination of email discussions reveals an apparent contradiction. Initially, the observer receives an impression of 'anarchy' (Crystal, 2001:34), with many participants making uninterruptible, and often simultaneous, contributions to parallel topics. However, a reading of the email discussion data shows that these discussions are not really chaotic. For most of the time participants carry out recognisable discussions, interacting in ways that resemble other forms of verbal interaction: they know which discussions they are contributing to, and what has gone before. It was likely, therefore, that an investigation would reveal patterns of interaction, in the way that Sacks et al.'s (1974) work on turn taking in spoken conversation revealed patterns in a form of discourse that was at the time itself thought to be chaotic (see e.g. Sinclair and Coulthard, 1975:4).

Previous research

Few studies have addressed the structure of computer-mediated communication (CMC) in any depth, although many have commented on its differences from casual conversation. In one of the earliest papers on CMC, Black et al. (1983) compare the interactions of two groups of students – one group using face-to-face communication and the other group using an electronic messaging system for teacher-led discussion. They devise a 'discourse map' to illustrate the patterns of topics and speakers, and to enable comparison across electronic and face to face discussions (the map of their CMC interaction is reproduced in 'The need for maps' section, below). They are interested in the lack of sequentiality in email discussions, and their maps provide an illustration of this as compared to the sequentiality of face to face discussions.

In the time since Black et al.'s paper was written, we have become accustomed to the multi-party multi-topic environments of CMC. Subsequent research has paid some attention to the structure of interaction in such environments: see for example Murray (1985) working on a computer messaging system, Wilkins (1991) on computer conferencing, and Cherny (1995) on the interaction of a MUD (Multi-User Domain). A useful survey of research on 'cross-turn coherence' in CMC is found in Herring (1999). Herring states that CMC is 'interactionally incoherent' but nevertheless attractive to users because 'a persistent textual record of the conversation renders the interaction cognitively manageable' (1999:2). She identifies two 'obstacles to interaction management': 'lack of simultaneous *feedback*' and 'disrupted turn *adjacency*' (1999:3, italics in the original). Herring believes that one reason for the popularity of CMC is the 'intensity' experienced when participants are involved in several interactions at once (1999:17). She provides diagrams which show how messages are related to each other in small samples from an IRC (Internet Relay Chat) sample and from an email discussion. The diagram of the email discussion, with a sample of only 16 messages, eight participants and three topics, is already complex, and could not easily be extended for use with a much larger data sample.

This complexity of email discussion data is a major challenge to the researcher. Multi-party spoken discussions have widely been thought to be difficult to analyse, with the result that, although multi-party data has been used in Conversation Analysis from the beginning (see for example talk from group therapy sessions analysed in the lectures from Fall 1965 in Sacks 1995 Vol 1:36ff), most of the studies that use the Discourse Analysis framework of the Birmingham tradition focus on two-party interaction. The early work of Sinclair and Coulthard (1975) addresses classroom discourse, but their data do not include group interaction and indeed they state that their framework would not handle 'discussion groups' (1975:6). Instead, they focus on exchanges between teacher and pupil where the teacher remains constant but the pupils change, and despite this change in pupils the effect is that of a series of short two-party sequences. Subsequent workers in this tradition also focus on two-party interaction. For example Stenström's (1994) data samples are mostly two-party or very small group interaction. She does include one example of a discussion among eight committee members, but recognises that this interaction could not easily be described in terms of her framework of analysis (1994:187).

Coulthard himself states that his own framework gives problems when applied to multi-party discussions:

> It is quite striking that whereas we were able to produce a detailed and quite compelling analysis of doctor/patient interaction at exchange rank, broadcast discussions proved pretty intractable, we were left with quite large chunks of speech for which we could produce no analysis at all. (Coulthard, 1981:26)

However, email discussions are not only multi-party, but also multi-topic, and participants readily contribute to more than one discussion in parallel. Moreover, one of the challenges of the current study was to identify a method of comparing patterns of interaction across different email discussion samples. The discourse map was developed as a tool to assist in addressing this problem.

Data and method

The project for which these maps were developed took its primary data samples from email discussion lists, as described below. To provide a comparison, a small corpus of spoken (radio) and written (newspaper) discussions was also collected. Debates about the written and spoken features found in email often compare the email with casual conversation or with written text, without indicating why casual conversation should be chosen (rather than any other form of spoken discourse) or which form of written language is being considered. This study aimed to make a more meaningful comparison by taking sources of spoken and written data which have a similar purpose to the email data. By selecting data where the type of participants, the power relationships and the purpose of the interaction are broadly similar, any differences we can identify are likely to arise from the differences in media.

Therefore all of the data for the current investigation are taken from discussions: the email data from email discussion lists, the spoken data from radio discussions (recorded from Radio 4, from *Women's Hour*, *Saturday Review*, *Thinking Allowed*, and *A Good Read*), and the written data from letters to newspapers (the *Guardian* and the *Independent*). The spoken and written data in the current study thus have several features in common with the email data: voluntary participants, a discussion on a theme, a non-participating audience, and the opportunity to plan the discourse, while the audience and participants in all three media share an interest in following or participating in themed discussions. In all of these discussions, the role of the researcher is a similar one, having the same access to the context as potential participants on the email list or newspaper letters, and the same as the rest of the remote audience in the radio discussion, with the further advantage that these data can be observed and collected without any influence on the data by the researcher.

The email discussion samples are naturally occurring data from UK-based email discussion lists collected from the publicly available Mailbase site archives at http://www.mailbase.ac.uk/lists (now available from http://www.jiscmail.ac.uk). Samples of 60 messages were chosen because it was found that this was sufficient to allow at least one (and normally more than one) entire discussion to start, develop, and reach completion in each sample. There are 360 email messages in total, 60 messages from each of six email discussion lists:

Writing development in higher education	1 March 1998 – 25 March 1998
Business ethics	2 July 1998 – 2 November 1998
Feminist theology	7 September 1999 – 18 September 1999
Humour research	2 July 1999 – 3 October 1999
Probation Practice	7 September 1999 – 27 October 1999
Dyslexia	25 September 1999 – 11 October 1999

The email data were chosen as follows:

> Some email lists are used predominantly for announcements (job announcements, conference announcements, etc.) while others are used for a mixture of purposes including discussions on relevant topics. Since the object of this research was to investigate discussions, lists which were used only for announcements were excluded.

> Since the intention was to investigate multi-party discussions, the samples had to include a discussion which involved at least three participants.

> Samples must include at least one complete discussion.

The Mailbase (now JISCmail) archive allows searching of lists by the initial letter of the list. A letter was chosen and the lists beginning with that letter were searched until a sample was found which met the above criteria. When a suitable sample was found, searching continued, but using a different letter. This helped to ensure that the samples covered a range of topics (if searching continued on the same letter, say B, one might have had, for example, six lists all relating to some aspect of business). When a suitable sample meeting the above criteria was identified, 60 consecutive messages were collected.

All the lists in the study are unmoderated, i.e. messages are sent directly to all members of the list without being read, filtered or edited by anyone.

In the current data there are between 16 and 29 active participants in the 60-message samples. Moreover, the topics are progressing simultaneously:

between 10 and 23 topics in each sample. In general, participants specify the topic to which they are contributing in the subject line of each email message, and for the purposes of this study a broad definition of topic has been used which corresponds as far as possible with the participants' own assignments. In these samples is was normal for each message to deal with only one broad topic, and for participants to assign a meaningful subject line to their messages. Each message was checked to ensure that the content corresponded to that indicated by the subject line, and on the comparatively rare occasions when a message did address more than one subject, it was assigned to both of these topics. Frequently, the same subject line is retained for the whole of a thread, although some variation is found. If more than one subject line was used within the same thread, these were assigned to the same topic. This approach does not capture subtle changes in topic, but does provide a high level category within which such changes could be further explored. This practice is in line with that of Black et al. (1983), who assigned the three topics on their map to coincide with the three questions asked by the teacher.

The need for maps

In spoken data the interaction is predominantly linear, usually there is only one topic under discussion at a time (unless the conversation splits into factions with different participants in the different parts), and the turns are relatively short, with the result that the pattern of participation is apparent from the transcript. However, this is not the case for email discussions, where a message may not be related to those which immediately precede or follow it. Moreover, the individual turns in email discussions are long compared to conversation (in the six email data samples the mean turn length, excluding header information and quotations, ranged from 97 to 332 words with the shortest message being two words, and the longest 3724; in the five radio discussion samples, the mean turn length ranged from 24 to 67, with the shortest message being one word and the longest 297). When reading an individual message from the email discussions it is difficult to maintain an awareness of the whole context. The writers use various techniques to link their messages to preceding ones from the same topic (see Harrison, 2002), but this does not provide the whole picture, as other topics are also underway, often involving some of the same participants. In addition, the researcher can choose to read all messages chronologically, in which case one might lose a sense of how much activity is taking place on a given thread, or one might choose to sort the messages into threads and read each thread separately, in which case a sense of the overall activity could be lost. A further alternative is to sort the messages by speaker, which would facilitate an investigation into participant activity, but lose the continuity of individual discussion threads. A basic tool available to the reader is the list of messages in the email inbox, or in the archive catalogue. These can be sorted by date, by topic, or by sender — all useful, but nevertheless limited in that each of these options gives only a partial view of the interaction.

The maps of our email data were developed from the initial idea by Black et al. (1983) who displayed a short sequence of speakers and topics by a discourse map (Figure 1) in order to illustrate the patterns of topics and speakers, and to enable comparison across electronic and face to face discussions.

This discourse map shows an asynchronous networked classroom discussion, which was initiated by a teacher who introduced a topic (heading P) and then asked three questions (headings 1-3) within one message. The teacher's questions, although all related to the broad theme of ethnography, are quite separate and could have been treated as three separate essay questions. This particular form of initiation by the teacher led to the response

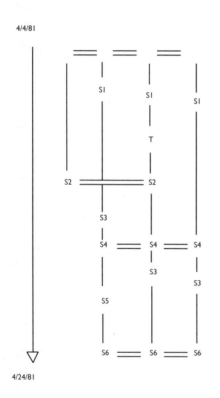

Figure 1 Discourse map from Black et al. (1983:65)

pattern shown in the discourse map, where a response was likely to address more than one part of the initial message and hence to relate to more than one topic. This asynchronous discussion seems to have constraints which have arisen from the classroom situation: in the map that Black et al. provide, only the teacher initiates a topic, and the students confine their responses to one or more parts of the teacher's message.

The kind of multiple topic initiation used by this teacher is unusual in our email discussion data, where in general a topic initiation message will initiate only one topic, and participants usually send separate messages with differentiated subject lines to respond to separate topics. Spinuzzi (1994) comments that participants often send separate messages (even rapidly following each other) when they want to communicate about different topics and this is indeed the case in the data for the current study. The basic principles used in Black et al.'s map are, however, equally useful for a situation in which each message addresses only one topic, and a situation in which an individual message addresses more than one topic.

Mapping in other formats has been used elsewhere to fulfil specific functions in relation to discourse, for example Roberts and Sarangi (2002) use maps in order to present to a medical audience the empathetic and retractive features of medical students' interactions with 'patients' during simulated consultations in order to show what makes such communication effective. In the current study, our maps are not used in order to communicate with an audience from a different specialism, or to address effectiveness in communication, but to produce an accessible overview of a complex interaction for the purposes of contextualisation, pattern identification, and cross-sample comparison. Thus the purpose of our own maps is similar to those of Black et al., although we are using them to illuminate much larger and more complex data samples. Tufte's work on 'envisioning information' shows that well-designed maps and charts can reveal the 'detail and complexity' of their subjects without 'confusion and clutter' (Tufte, 1990:53), handling a wealth of information in a manner that can be readily assimilated by the user. If we isolate and analyse one thread from the discussion, or instead of maps use the limited lists of messages from the email inbox or archive catalogue, we find that these do not give us all of the information we need to make comparisons.

If the visual task is contrast, comparison, and choice – as so often it is – then the more relevant information within the eyespan, the better...Micro/macro designs enforce both local and global comparisons and, at the same time, avoid the disruption of context switching. All told, exactly what is needed for reasoning about information. (Tufte, 1990:50)

The discourse maps in the current study were developed to represent the whole interaction from an email discussion sample in a way that facilitates comparison and the identification of patterns in the interaction. The function of these maps is to:

1   Provide an overview of the whole interaction within a sample.
2   Give the context for any selected message.
3   Chart the data using selected categories (date, topic, sender), and make these categories accessible.
4   Help the researcher to identify patterns in the interaction.
5   Facilitate comparison between different samples.

Email discussion example: Feminist Theology
A discourse map which displays all 60 messages of one sample, from the Feminist Theology list, is shown in Table 1. This map takes the form of a table in which topics are represented by the columns, and turns by the rows. The turns are displayed chronologically, with the first turn at the top of the table, and these are numbered sequentially (FT1, FT2, FT3, etc.). Topics are numbered sequentially in the order that they first occurred in the sample (T1, T2, T3, etc.). The participants in each data set were numbered sequentially in the order that they first contributed to the list (S1, S2, S3, etc.), and the table shows which contributions were made by each participant. The dates are listed on the left.

The map gives us a profile of the interaction. In the sample, Feminist Theology has 26 active participants and 10 topics. The sample covers a period of 12 days in September 1999. The messages from this list give the reader a strong sense of community, revealed both by the friendly tone of the messages (as shown, for example, in the widespread use of phatic tokens, see Cheepen and Monaghan, 1990), by the helpful, supportive responses to issues raised, and by the level of participation in the topics. The participants show

Message	Date	Topic									
		T1	T2	T3	T4	T5	T6	T7	T8	T9	T10
FT1	7 Sep 99	S1									
FT2	8 Sep 99	S2									
FT3	8 Sep 99	S1									
FT4	8 Sep 99	S2									
FT5	9 Sep 99		S3								
FT6	9 Sep 99	S4									
FT7	9 Sep 99	S1									
FT8	9 Sep 99		S5								
FT9	9 Sep 99	S6									
FT10	9 Sep 99			S7							
FT11	9 Sep 99			S4							
FT12	10 Sep 99	S1									
FT13	10 Sep 99	S1									
FT14	10 Sep 99				S8						
FT15	10 Sep 99					S9					
FT16	10 Sep 99		S10								
FT17	11 Sep 99		S3								
FT18	11 Sep 99	S2									
FT19	11 Sep 99	S1									
FT20	11 Sep 99	S11									
FT21	11 Sep 99						S12				
FT22	11 Sep 99	S5									
FT23	12 Sep 99	S1									
FT24	12 Sep 99							S13			
FT25	12 Sep 99				S10						
FT26	12 Sep 99							S5			
FT27	12 Sep 99				S5						
FT28	12 Sep 99										
FT29	12 Sep 99							S13			
FT30	12 Sep 99	S11						S14			
FT31	12 Sep 99							S11			
FT32	12 Sep 99						S6				
FT33	13 Sep 99	S2									
FT34	13 Sep 99							S13			
FT35	13 Sep 99				S9						
FT36	13 Sep 99				S15						
FT37	13 Sep 99	S16									
FT38	13 Sep 99							S17			
FT39	13 Sep 99							S18			
FT40	14 Sep 99							S11			
FT41	14 Sep 99							S13			
FT42	14 Sep 99		S8		S8						
FT43	14 Sep 99				S19						
FT44	14 Sep 99						S20				
FT45	14 Sep 99							S20			
FT46	15 Sep 99		S13								
FT47	15 Sep 99							S21			
FT48	15 Sep 99				S21						
FT49	15 Sep 99					S22					
FT50	16 Sep 99								S23		
FT51	16 Sep 99							S13			
FT52	16 Sep 99					S9					
FT53	17 Sep 99				S13						
FT54	17 Sep 99									S24	
FT55	17 Sep 99	S2									
FT56	17 Sep 99					S22					
FT57	17 Sep 99					S22					
FT58	17 Sep 99					S9					
FT59	18 Sep 99										S25
FT60	18 Sep 99									S26	

Table 1 Discourse map of the Feminist Theology data

considerable interest in the topics generated in this sample, and respond readily to the topics under discussion: all of the topic initiating messages receive a reply within the sample period except FT59, although the map shows that some topics generated more interest than others e.g. T1, T7.

One interesting feature here is found in FT42 where one participant contributes to two topics, T2 and T4, within the same message. Combining of topics within a single message is unusual in the data. It does not occur at all in three of the six samples under investigation. Another feature here is that some participants take two consecutive turns, e.g. S11 has two turns on different topics in messages FT30 and FT31, S20 in messages FT44 and FT45, and S21 in turns FT47 and FT48. These three pairs can readily be explained by the convention of only one topic per message. However, there are two other pairs: S1 has two turns on the same topic in messages FT12 and FT13, and S22 has two turns on the same topic in FT56 and FT57. We might wish to investigate such pairs further (for example, we find that FT12 and FT13 are addressed by name to two different previous contributors on this thread).

The map suggests that Feminist Theology is a successful discussion list: several topics are under discussion in the twelve days covered by the sample, and these topics normally receive a response. An examination of the data supports this conclusion in that the tone of the list is friendly and the content seems to be considered appropriate. The map of the Business Ethics list, overleaf, reveals a sharp contrast.

Email discussion example: Business Ethics

The sample from Business Ethics has fewer active participants (16 in total) than the Feminist Theology sample. It has more than twice as many topics (23 in total), and it takes place over a much more extended time period (four months). In this whole period, only one topic, T4, involves more than one participant. T4 has a total of 36 messages. T16 has two messages, both by the same participant (a conference announcement and a correction to the conference information), and T18 also has two messages (both sent by the same speaker and containing exactly the same text — presumably a duplicate was sent in error). All of the remaining topics have only one message each. The main topic, T4, is highly active for eight days, and receives one further message six days later. But apart from this burst of activity the list is very quiet, and the 60 messages of this sample cover the greatest time span of the

Message	Date	Topic T1	T2	T3	T4	T5	T6	T7	T8	T9	T10
BE1	2 Jul 98	S1									
BE2	9 Jul 98		S2								
BE3	10 Jul 98			S3							
BE4	10 Jul 98				S4						
BE5	10 Jul 98				S5						
BE6	11 Jul 98				S6						
BE7	13 Jul 98				S5						
BE8	13 Jul 98				S7						
BE9	13 Jul 98				S6						
BE10	13 Jul 99					S6					
BE11	13 Jul 98				S5						
BE12	13 Jul 98				S5						
BE13	13 Jul 98				S6						
BE14	14 Jul 98				S5						
BE15	15 Jul 98						S2				
BE16	15 Jul 98				S8						
BE17	15 Jul 98				S5						
BE18	15 Jul 98				S7						
BE19	15 Jul 98				S5						
BE20	15 Jul 98				S6						
BE21	16 Jul 98				S9						
BE22	16 Jul 98				S5						
BE23	16 Jul 98				S5						
BE24	16 Jul 98				S9						
BE25	16 Jul 98				S9						
BE26	16 Jul 98				S5						
BE27	16 Jul 98				S8						
BE28	16 Jul 98				S7						
BE29	16 Jul 98				S7						
BE30	16 Jul 98				S7						
BE31	16 Jul 98				S5						
BE32	16 Jul 98				S5						
BE33	16 Jul 98				S7						
BE34	16 Jul 98				S5						
BE35	16 Jul 98				S6						
BE36	16 Jul 98				S5						
BE37	16 Jul 98				S7						
BE38	16 Jul 98				S7						
BE39	16 Jul 98							S10			
BE40	17 Jul 98				S5						
BE41	17 Jul 98				S5						
BE42	23 Jul 98								S2		
BE43	23 Jul 98			S2							
BE44	23 Jul 98									S2	
BE45	27 Jul 98										S11
BE46	30 Jul 98										
BE47	31 Jul 98										
BE48	13 Aug 98										
BE49	1 Sep 98										
BE50	1 Sep 98										
BE51	14 Sep 98										
BE52	14 Sep 98										
BE53	18 Sep 98										
BE54	16 Oct 98										
BE55	16 Oct 98										
BE56	20 Oct 98										
BE57	23 Oct 98										
BE58	24 Oct 98										
BE59	29 Oct 98										
BE60	2 Nov 98										

Table 2 Discourse map of the Business Ethics data

Topic

T11	T12	T13	T14	T15	T16	T17	T18	T19	T20	T21	T22	T23
S11	S2	S12	S13	S6								
					S14 S14	S11	S15 S15					
								S16	S13	S6	S15	S5

Table 2 Discourse map of the Business Ethics data continued

samples in the data. This profile of participation suggests a less satisfactory discussion list than Feminist Theology, and this suggestion is confirmed by the content of T4 which was a hostile exchange primarily between S5 on the one hand and S6 and S7 on the other.

We might be led to wonder about BE43, the final message of topic T4, arriving as it does so long after the action on this topic seems to be over. An examination of the data reveals that the penultimate message, BE41, is most unusual, in that it is a deliberate, and successful, attempt by S5 to close the topic. After this, no-one attempts to revive the hostilities, and there is no further response for six days, when suddenly the list owner sends message BE43 asking participants to avoid such personal communications, and to keep to the stated purpose of the list. So although from a reading of the content of the messages, it looks as though the list owner ended the thread, in fact the dates show that S5 had effectively ended it in BE41.

As with Feminist Theology, the Business Ethics map shows consecutive turns by the same participant. These consecutive turns can be used to make contributions on different topics, for example, BE42, BE43 and BE44, all by S2, contributing to topics T8, T4 and T9 respectively. Consecutive turns on the same topic by the one participant, S5, are found on four occasions within Topic T4. An examination of the data here reveals that for much of this topic S5 is conducting two simultaneous and parallel series of exchanges, with S6 and S7. Some of the messages from S6 and S7 explicitly refer to each other, and S5 sometimes refers to S6 in a message to S7, and vice versa. Nevertheless, S5 consistently writes separate messages to these two participants.

A comparison between the Feminist Theology and the Business Ethics maps show clear differences in the patterns of interaction, but the detail of these maps might suggest further avenues of investigation. For example, in Business Ethics topic T4, the topic initiator, S4, never contributes again, on this or any other topic, whereas topic initiators in Feminist Theology often return to the discussion (see especially T1 and T7 where the topic initiators are frequent contributors).

Usefulness of the email discourse maps
Discourse maps such as the above are a very useful tool for representing email discussions. They provide a visual representation of complex asynchronous multi-party parallel discussions, showing the pattern of

contributions to each topic, the patterns of contributions from each participant, and distribution of turns over time. They enable the researcher to locate specified features such as consecutive turns by the same participant, multiple topics within a single message, and topics which fail to generate a response, and they also facilitate the identification of unpredicted patterns through 'unmotivated inquiry' (Sacks et al., 1974:699). Discourse maps also facilitate comparison of the patterns of interaction on different lists.

Of course, the discourse maps cannot replace a thorough examination of the data, but they can support it: even while reading an individual message, a map can be used alongside this reading to give the researcher a summary of the context for that message.

What these maps do not provide, and what we might hope for in the absence of sequentiality, is an indication of how messages within a thread relate to each other. For example, in Feminist Theology topic T7, the first three messages are directly and sequentially related to each other, but the fourth message, FT29 relates to the first message in this thread, without reference to any of the intervening messages. In principle, it would be possible to include this information on the maps, perhaps by linking messages with coloured lines, but in practice this would make the maps cluttered and difficult to use, so instead it was decided to use a separate flow charting system to illustrate the relationship between messages for the same thread (see Harrison, 2002).

Comparisons across media

The discourse map can also be used to display the profile of interaction of other types of discourse. Discourse maps can be used to compare the patterns of interaction in the newspaper and radio discussion data with the patterns found in the email data.

Newspaper letters example: Independent A discourse map of the first 60 letters in the *Independent* newspaper letter data is provided in Table 3.

The map shows that there are 60 participants in this part of the sample, and 38 topics (using a broad definition of topic) over a time period of four days (a further 14 letters were published on 28 October, the last day shown on this map). There are some topics which have only one contribution, and others which elicit several letters, sometimes all published on the same day, and sometimes in batches appearing at intervals. (Clearly, if contributions are

Message	Date	Topic																			
		T1	T2	T3	T4	T5	T6	T7	T8	T9	T10	T11	T12	T13	T14	T15	T16	T17	T18	T19	T20
IND1	25 Oct 98	S1																			
IND2	25 Oct 98		S2																		
IND3	25 Oct 98	S3																			
IND4	25 Oct 98	S4																			
IND5	25 Oct 98			S5																	
IND6	25 Oct 98			S6																	
IND7	25 Oct 98				S7																
IND8	25 Oct 98					S8															
IND9	25 Oct 98					S9															
IND10	25 Oct 99					S10															
IND11	25 Oct 98					S11															
IND12	25 Oct 98					S12															
IND13	25 Oct 98						S13														
IND14	25 Oct 98						S14														
IND15	25 Oct 98							S15													
IND16	25 Oct 98								S16												
IND17	25 Oct 98								S17												
IND18	25 Oct 98									S18											
IND19	25 Oct 98										S19										
IND20	25 Oct 98											S20									
IND21	25 Oct 98													S21							
IND22	25 Oct 98														S22						
IND23	26 Oct 98															S23					
IND24	26 Oct 98																S24				
IND25	26 Oct 98	S25																			
IND26	26 Oct 98																	S26			
IND27	26 Oct 98																		S27		
IND28	26 Oct 98																			S28	
IND29	26 Oct 98																				S29
IND30	26 Oct 98																				
IND31	26 Oct 98																				
IND32	26 Oct 98																				
IND33	26 Oct 98																				
IND34	26 Oct 98				S34																
IND35	26 Oct 98																				
IND36	26 Oct 98																				
IND37	26 Oct 98																				
IND38	26 Oct 98																				
IND39	27 Oct 98																				
IND40	27 Oct 98																				
IND41	27 Oct 98																				
IND42	27 Oct 98																				
IND43	27 Oct 98																				
IND44	27 Oct 98																				
IND45	27 Oct 98																				
IND46	27 Oct 98																		S46		
IND47	27 Oct 98																				
IND48	27 Oct 98												S48								
IND49	27 Oct 98												S49								
IND50	27 Oct 98					S50															
IND51	27 Oct 98																				
IND52	27 Oct 98																				
IND53	27 Oct 98																				
IND54	27 Oct 98																				
IND55	27 Oct 98					S55															
IND56	27 Oct 98																				
IND57	27 Oct 98														S57						
IND58	27 Oct 98	S58																			
IND59	28 Oct 98																				
IND60	28 Oct 98	S60																			

Table 3 Discourse map of 60 letters from the Independent data

Topic

T21	T22	T23	T24	T25	T26	T27	T28	T29	T30	T31	T32	T33	T34	T35	T36	T37	T38
S30																	
	S31																
		S32															
			S33														
				S35													
					S36												
						S37											
							S38										
								S39 S40									
								S41									
									S42 S43								
			S44							S45							
											S47						
												S51					
													S52				
														S53			
															S54		
																S56	
																	S59

Table 3 Discourse map of 60 letters from the Independent data continued

published on the same day unlike the email messages they cannot respond to each other but may all be responding to the same published article.)The Independent map shows that letters on several different topics are published each day. Sometimes more than one letter is published on the same topic on a single day (in this sample, up to three letters on the same topic on a given day). After this initial publication, some topics are not taken up again, but others are returned to – some (like T1) being taken up on several subsequent days. There are no occurrences of consecutive letters from the same participant, indeed participants are rarely allowed a second contribution (one participant, S20, does in fact make a second contribution in letter 99 of the sample).

This map reveals some similarities with the email data: multiple participants take part in multiple simultaneous topics over an extended time span – indeed there are many more different topics per day than in the email data. However, the participants are not genuinely interacting with each other because each participant normally has only one turn, and even when a participant responds to a previous letter this response does not address the previous writer directly: newspaper letters are neither locally managed nor 'interactionally managed' (Sacks et al., 1974:725) by the participants themselves. Because of this lack of interaction, there is less information to be revealed by newspaper discourse maps, but the Independent map does show the development of topics over time, and also assembles the features of the discourse in a form suitable for comparison with the email data.

Radio discussion example: Second weddings It is possible to create discourse maps for the radio data, but these show a very different profile. Because the topics in these radio discussions take place in real time they are, unlike the email and newspaper discussions, basically linear, and each sample consists of one topic (using a broad definition of topic comparable to the definition used for topic in the email and newspaper data). In addition there are far fewer participants: the majority of multi-party discussions on radio have a total of three participants (host plus two others), while a few have four (host plus three others) – perhaps because the need to make the participants identifiable to the distant audience results in a constraint on the number of participants. Moreover, the discussions occur synchronously, and are complete within a few minutes. What the discourse maps do show, however, is the distribution of turns among the three or four speakers. In particular, we can see the

Turn	Second Weddings
SEC 1	S1
SEC 2	S2
SEC 3	S1
SEC 4	S3
SEC 5	S2
SEC 6	S3
SEC 7	S1
SEC 8	S3
SEC 9	S2
SEC 10	S3
SEC 11	S2
SEC 12	S3
SEC 13	S2
SEC 14	S3
SEC 15	S2
SEC 16	S3
SEC 17	S2
SEC 18	S3
SEC 19	S2
SEC 20	S3
SEC 21	S2
SEC 22	S3
SEC 23	S2
SEC 24	S1
SEC 25	S2
SEC 26	S3
SEC 27	S2
SEC 28	S3
SEC 29	S2
SEC 30	S1
SEC 31	S3
SEC 32	S1
SEC 33	S3
SEC 34	S2
SEC 35	S3
SEC 36	S2
SEC 37	S3
SEC 38	S2
SEC 39	S3
SEC 40	S2
SEC 41	S1
SEC 42	S3
SEC 43	S2
SEC 44	S1
SEC 45	S3
SEC 46	S2
SEC 47	S1
SEC 48	S2
SEC 49	S1
SEC 50	S3
SEC 51	S1
SEC 52	S3
SEC 53	S2
SEC 54	S1
SEC 55	S3
SEC 56	S1
SEC 57	S3
SEC 58	S1
SEC 59	S3
SEC 60	S2
SEC 61	S3
SEC 62	S1
SEC 63	S3
SEC 64	S1

Figure 5
Discourse map of the
Second Weddings data,
broadcast on
Women's Hour, Radio 4,
10 November 1999

participation patterns of the host, S1. In the radio map that follows, the host's turns have been highlighted in bold.

Normally the host begins by giving an introduction to the topic. At the end of this introduction, the host brings in the first participant. The host then brings each of the remaining participants into the discussion in turn. This pattern can be seen in the Second Weddings map (figure 5). There are three participants, the host and two guests. The host (S1) brings in the first guest participant (S2), then takes another turn to bring in the remaining participant (S3). As the discussion proceeds the guest participants interact between themselves, and the host has lower profile at this point. The map shows sequences of exchanges between S2 and S3, with little intervention by the host, who does, however, participate occasionally in order to steer the discussion. Finally the host resumes control and takes the last turn of the discussion to draw it to a close.

Although the radio discourse map provides a summary of the interaction, there is less information to display than on the email and newspaper maps because the radio sample has only one topic and only three participants. As with the newspaper map, the main purpose of the radio map is to display the features of the discussion in a standard format in order to illustrate some of the ways in which the radio discussion differs from email discussions.

Conclusion

When used to chart email discussions, discourse maps serve a useful function in that they offer a visual summary of the whole interaction of an email discussion sample that is not available as succinctly in any other way. They enable researchers to visualise the whole of the interaction in a discussion sample, to assimilate many factors involved in a complex interaction, to locate individual messages in the context of the sample, and to identify patterns, both predicted and unpredicted, of activity within that interaction. Such patterns could form the basis of further investigation, for example:

Into participants who contribute frequently across different topics (gender/power issues);

Into messages which do not receive a response (to identify factors that might prospect responses);

Into messages which encompass more than one topic (to investigate whether this is a feature of the discussion group concerned, or whether the topics are in some way related).

Moreover, the consistent charting of selected features for a whole data sample facilitates comparison across samples. The maps can be used to compare samples from different discussion lists, or to compare samples taken at different times from a single list, or even to compare email discussions with discussions in other media. The discourse map is therefore a useful tool with which to begin the investigation of the complex interactions found within email discussions.

References

Black, S. D., Levin, J. A., Mehan, H. and Quinn, C. N. (1983) Real and non-real time interaction: Unraveling multiple threads of discourse. *Discourse Processes*, 6: 59-75.

Cheepen, C. and Monaghan, J. (1990) *Spoken English: A Practical Guide*. London: Pinter publishers.

Cherny, L. (1995) *The MUD Register: conversational modes of action in a text-based virtual reality*. PhD thesis, Stanford University, available from http://www.research.att.com/~cherny/chap1.ps, (accessed 10 July 1998).

Coulthard, M. (1981) Section 2 Developing the Description, in Chapter 1 Developing a Description of Spoken Discourse. In M. Coulthard and M. Montgomery (eds) *Studies in Discourse Analysis*. London: Routledge and Kegan Paul. pp. 13-31.

Crystal, D. (2001) *Language and the Internet*. Cambridge: Cambridge University Press.

Harrison, S. (2002) *The Discourse Structure of Email Discussions*. PhD thesis, University of Central England.

Herring, S. (1999) Interactional coherence in CMC. *Journal of Computer-Mediated Communication*, 4, No 4, http://www.ascusc.org/jcmc/vol4/issue4/herring.html (accessed 18 December 2001).

Murray, D. (1985) Composition as Conversation: The Computer Terminal as Medium of Communication. In L. Odell and D. Goswami (eds) *Writing in Nonacademic Settings*. New York: Guilford Press. pp. 203-227.

Roberts, C. and Sarangi, S. (2002) Mapping and assessing medical students' interactional involvement styles with patients'. In K. Spelman Miller and P. Thompson (eds) *Unity and Diversity in Language Use*. London: Continuum. pp. 99-124.

Sacks, H. (1995) *Lectures on conversation Volumes I and II*, edited by Jefferson, G. Oxford: Blackwell.

Sacks, H., Schegloff, E. and Jefferson, G. (1974) A Simplest Systematics for the Organization of Turn-Taking for Conversation. *Language*, 50: 696-735.

Sinclair, J. and Coulthard, M. (1975) *Towards an Analysis of Discourse*. Oxford: Oxford University Press.

Spinuzzi, C. (1994) A Different Kind of Forum: Rethinking Rhetorical Strategies for Electronic Text Media. *IEEE Transactions on Professional Communication*, 37: 213-217.

Stenström, A-B. (1994) *An Introduction to Spoken Interaction*. London: Longman.

Tufte, E. (1990) *Envisioning Information*. Cheshire, Connecticut: Graphics Press.

6 'Now I didn't mean to break his teeth': applying topic management to problems of power asymmetry and voluntary confessions

Georgina Heydon
Aarhus University, Denmark

Abstract

This paper presents the findings of an investigation into the discursive features of police-suspect interviews and the production of a voluntary confession by suspects. The analysis draws upon the notion of a 'police preferred' version of events, which is produced as an alternative to the suspect's version of events. The analysis is concerned primarily with the discursive practices that police officers use in their attempts to construct their version of events in such a way that it is 'oriented to' by the suspect. The interview data are analysed in relation to interactional resources such as topic management tools and formulations in order to demonstrate the impact of asymmetrical speaker roles on the 'voluntariness' of the suspect's confession. By taking a Conversation Analysis approach, this paper also demonstrates that CA can be usefully employed in the analysis and description of power in institutional discourse.

Introduction

The confession of a suspect obtained in a police evidentiary interview comprises the key piece of evidence in most criminal cases under the adversarial legal system. It is crucial to the successful prosecution of a defendant that the confession is voluntary and not a product of threats or physical violence and that any written confession is a true and accurate record of the suspect's words during the interview. In many jurisdictions, the introduction of tape-recorded police interviews has eliminated some of the more obvious problems associated with ensuring that all these criteria are met. Despite these advances, the police interview process remains problematic for a number of reasons, especially as it is not always clear when pressure is being brought to bear on the suspect to conform to a police version of events due to the subtlety of power play in discourse.

This paper finds that the interactional resources available to participants in police interviews are allocated in such a way as to endow the primary interviewing officer with an 'interactional authority' over the other participants, and especially over the suspect. In ordinary conversation, changes in topic can be achieved in a number of ways (Jefferson, 1984, 1988), however, an institutional setting which preallocates turn-types according to speaker roles will impose restrictions on the introduction or maintenance of topics by participants (Frankel, 1990; Greatbatch, 1988). If, as discussed above, the elicitation of a voluntary confession is the overriding institutional concern of the interview (Heydon, 2002:79), then it is important to recognise that such constraints on the availability of topic management tools will necessarily restrict participants' access to the floor in order to provide new information voluntarily. Therefore, it is important that we have an understanding of the way that topic maintenance and shift is achieved in the interviews and this will form the focus of the following section.

In order to further explore the use of an 'interactional authority' by police interviewers, the analysis of topic management tools will be considered in light of the construction of a 'police version of events'. The construction of differing versions of events is the focus of research undertaken by Auburn, Drake, and Willig, 1995. Crucial to their study of accusations of violence in police evidentiary interviews is the finding that the police officer's primary objective in an interview is to gain a confession from the suspect 'and implicit in this purpose is the presumption that the suspect is guilty of the crime' (Auburn et al., 1995:355). Their study examines the negotiation of the narrative by the participants and the way in which one particular version of events is favoured by the police participants, known as the 'preferred version', a label that reflects 'its status as a version which facilitates the functioning of the criminal justice system in disposing of suspects' (p. 357). That is, it is the version through which legal considerations are addressed (e.g. establishing that the crime occurred and there was criminal intention on behalf of the suspect) and the guilt of the suspect is constructed as an underlying assumption (p. 356). Auburn et al., 1995 find that in the preferred version, the suspect is attributed responsibility for acts of violence through the use of footing (Goffman, 1981), by constructing the event as distinctively and noticeably violent, and by constructing the suspect as a person with a history of perpetrating violence. Importantly, the researchers note that the articulation of the preferred version through the course of the interview is a project that is achieved jointly insofar as 'displaying and agreeing on the preferred version requires a mutual adherence to a background assumption of intersubjectivity' (p. 357). Thus the preferred version must be negotiated by the participants to maintain the 'basic assumption of social life' that any viewpoint is substitutable for any other (Billig, 1991:170). Viewpoints that are non-substitutable must be accounted for in some way, which is part of the process of establishing the precedence of the preferred version.

The interactional resource commonly used by police officers in this process is a 'formulation', which is a term coined by CA researchers to describe utterances that summarise, gloss or develop the gist of the recipient's earlier contributions (Heritage, 1985; Heritage and Watson, 1979). Importantly, notes that formulations have a 'controlling' function and provide 'a way of leading participants into accepting one's own version of what has transpired, and so limiting their options for future contributions' (p. 136). Formulations will be first considered as part of the analysis of topic management which follows, before being discussed specifically as a tool in the construction of a 'guilty suspect' by police interviewers.

Topic shift by police interview participants

A feature which differentiates the interactions produced in police institutional interviews from those produced in ordinary conversation is the availability of certain discursive resources to police interviewers when shifting from a current topic to a new topic. In particular, the following turn construction is described by Harvey Sacks as a general feature of the topical organisation in conversation:

> movement from topic to topic, not by a topic-close followed by a topic beginning, but by a stepwise move, which involves linking up whatever is being introduced to what has just been talked about, such that, as far as anybody knows, a new topic has not been started, though we're far from wherever we began. (Sacks, Lecture 5, spring 1972, pp.

15-16, cited in Jefferson, 1984.)

However, analysis of the police interview data reveal that for the professional participant, the police interviewer, this 'general feature of the topical organisation in conversation' observed by Sacks does not apply. By way of demonstration, Extract 1 below from an interview between a female constable, pio1, and a male suspect, SPT1, contains examples of both stepwise and 'disjunctive' topic shifts (Jefferson, 1984). The suspect is describing his thoughts and actions on the day he received a threatening phone call which warned him to stay away from his ex-partner, 'Betty'.

Extract 1

87	pio1:	so <u>wad</u>cha do then
88	SPT1:	(0.5) w'l (1.1) <u>made</u> meself another cup of <u>coffee</u>
89		and I just <u>thought</u> about it
90		and I said what's going <u>on</u>
		((11 lines omitted – SPT1 describes relationship with Betty))
102		and we get on <u>all right</u> just as <u>friends</u>
1031		like we bump into each other in the <u>street</u>
04		(0.5) //<u>best</u> of* <u>friends</u>
105	pio1:	thi-* this <u>phone</u> call happened at ten-thirty in the morning
106	SPT1:	(0.4) bout <u>ten</u> ten-thirty in the morning
107	pio1:	right so what you <u>thought</u> about it all day long
108	SPT1:	SPT1:and I thought about it <u>all</u> day long
109	pio1:	(0.3) yep <u>then</u> //what happened*
110	SPT1:	I* <u>come</u> to Middletown

We can see that SPT1 uses a series of stepwise transitions to shift from the topic initiated by pio1 in line 87/pio1: *so wadcha do then* to the topic of his relationship with Betty. Just as SPT1 reaches the description of his friendship with Betty, pio1 takes up the transition relevance place (TRP, Sacks, Schegloff, and Jefferson, 1974) at the end of line 103 and initiates a disjunctive topic shift, requesting confirmation that 105/pio1: *thi-* this phone call happened at ten-thirty in the morning* . Although SPT1 had not intended to finish his turn at the TRP at the end of line 103 and his next utterance occurs in overlap with pio1's false start *thi-*, SPT1 does not attempt to hold the floor beyond the end of his utterance in line 104/SPT1: (0.5) *//best of**

friends and instead passes the floor to pio1 so that she can restart her request for confirmation in line 105, which she has produced as a formulation (Heritage, 1985; Heritage and Watson, 1979).

As the formulation is a first pair part, SPT1 offers a second pair part response in line 106/SPT1: *(0.4) bout ten ten-thirty in the morning* , but he does not attempt to hold the floor and continue his narrative. Instead, he passes the floor back to pio1 who uses a formulation-confirmation pair in lines 107-108 to summarise SPT1's narrative turn prior to re-initiating the topic of *then //what happened★* . However, the topic actually indicated by the formulation in line 107/pio1: *right so what you thought about it all day long* , is not the same topic as the final utterances of SPT1's prior narrative turn, which concerned his friendship with Betty. In fact, the topic pio1 has initiated is more closely related to the one which appears near the beginning of SPT1's narrative turn, in line 89/SPT1: *and I just thought about it* , and the subsequent utterances which develop the theme of his good relationship with Betty are effectively ignored by pio1's formulation.

Thus the version of the narrative which is 'ratified' by the participants is based only on the earlier, police initiated topic of what SPT1 'did next' – 87/pio1: *so wadcha do then* – and not on the topics introduced by SPT1 in stepwise transitions, which concern his efforts to act responsibly and maintain a friendship with Betty. These latter observations are important to SPT1's version because they support his assertion that the threatening phone call he received warning him not to approach Betty was both unprovoked and upsetting, and that his subsequent actions were as a result of his distress at what he saw as a unwarranted attempt to curtail his friendship with his ex-partner.

The extract above demonstrates that pio1 is able to employ her access to a wider range of topic management tools in order to present a summary of SPT1's narrative without including information supporting his version of events. In fact, throughout this interview, pio1 systematically and consistently fails to take up the topics which SPT1 initiates by stepwise transitions to provide background information supporting his version. One further example illustrating this finding is given in Extract 2 below where the participants are discussing the injuries suffered by 'Ian', who was assaulted by SPT1 on the day of the threatening phone call.

Extract 2

281 pio1: yeah (0.2) so the two (0.2) lacerations on your hand are
282   actually from his mouth
282   are they
283 SPT1: that's //right   *
284 pio1: from* his teeth
285 SPT1: yep   now I didn't mean to break his teeth
286   I didn't know I did that
287   (0.8) I'm sorry I did that
288   but I didn't know I was doing it
289 pio1: well you've hit him on the-
290   (.) with your right ha:nd
291   to almost the right side of his face
292   (0.9) pretty much at the front
293   at the right side   //and* you've
294 SPT1: right   *
295 pio1: smashed his front tooth out completely
296 SPT1: (0.6) right   //°I didn't know th-°*
297 pio1: was it <u>bleeding</u>* there an then

Here we see that in lines 285-288 SPT1 uses stepwise transitions to initiate topics that support his version that the damage to Ian's teeth was unintentional and regrettable. These topics are not taken up by pio1 who instead, in lines 289-293 and line 295 presents a version which describes SPT1's actions using terms of violence such as *hit* and *smashed* without any recognition or response to SPT1's claims about the accidental nature of the injuries he caused. In the following line 296 SPT1 makes one further attempt to reintroduce his topic of 'accidental injury' °I *didn't know th-*°*, though this is softly spoken and overlaps with pio1's next turn 297/pio1: *was it bleeding* there an then . Once again, the topic management tools available to pio1 permit her to initiate topics which promote the police version of events while ignoring topics initiated by SPT1 in support of his version of events.

Extract 3 is from an interview between a male senior constable, pio2, and a male suspect, SPT2, who is to be charged with an assault on his girlfriend,

'Leila'. As in the previous examples, pio2 initiates topics about blame and responsibility, but ignores SPT2's initiations about remorse and his attempts to seek professional help, and down-plays the possible provocation of the assault.

Extract 3

276	pio2:	(0.6) um (.) was there any reason why you had to e::rm
		(.) <u>treat</u> 'a this way at all
277	SPT2:	(1.2) it was a <u>combination</u> of things (.) y' know
278		I (0.4) didn't like the <u>fact</u> that (0.4) y' know-
279		(0.6) here <u>I</u> am goin' out with a girl
280		and she (0.6) jumps into <u>bed</u> with (0.2) one of my so-called <u>mates</u>
281	pio2:	(0.4) OK well regardless of that may have been the <u>case</u>
282	SPT2:	auh-
283	pio2:	um (0.6) not to say whether that the case or <u>not</u>
284		but regardless of that <u>might've</u> been the case
285		(0.4) do you agree that that ah (.) <u>warranted</u> your actions
286		(0.4) by <u>draggin'</u>'er out by the arm
287		(.) <u>pullin'</u>'er by the hair
288		(0.8) // <u>forcibly</u>★ removing'er from the <u>house</u>
289	SPT2:	nuo-★ (1.0) nup

Towards the end of this interview, and following a discussion of SPT2's possible use of force against his girlfriend, SPT2 is asked by pio2 if there was *any reason why you had to e::rm   (.) treat 'a this way at all* . The use of the extreme case formulation (Pomerantz, 1986) in phrases like *any reason...at all* implies that reasons for this sort of behaviour are unlikely to exist, however SPT2 is able to supply a fairly straightforward explanation – Leila's apparent infidelity – which, while it does not excuse his behaviour, certainly provides a reason for it. It is interesting, therefore, that pio2's next turn functions to deny the relevance of SPT2's contribution by overtly excluding his explanation from the set of things which might warrant SPT2's actions 281/pio2: (0.4) *OK well regardless of that may have been the case* . SPT2 then produces a response marker – 282/SPT2: *auh-* – which is hearable on the recording as a preface to an objection to pio2's prior utterance. Pio2 immediately qualifies his prior turn, making it explicit that he is not questioning the veracity of SPT2's explanation, only its relevance as a reason for his behaviour – 283/pio2: *um   (0.6) not to say whether that the case or not* . The sequence is continued from line 290 in Extract 4 below. Having discarded SPT2's version of 'reasons why he assaulted Leila', pio2 then formulates his version that *there was   (0.6) absolutely no reason*   for SPT2's behaviour and presents it for confirmation by SPT2.

Extract 4

```
290  pio2:   (2.0) so there was    (0.6) absolutely no reason
291          (.) why you should have treated 'er in that manner
292  SPT2:   (1.0) nup
```

We have seen that in this sequence, pio2 elicits one version from SPT2, where SPT2 gives a reason for his actions, and then uses his role as interviewer to overtly set aside SPT2's version – *regardless of that may have been the case* – and replace it with his own version in which there can be found *absolutely no reason*   for SPT2's actions.

In the cases we have examined so far, it seems clear that the police officers are able to utilise the topic management resources available to them as interviewers in order to construct their own version of events. They are greatly assisted in this activity by the restricted topic management tools available to the suspects and in particular, by the fact that the tools that are available to suspects (i.e. stepwise topic transitions and second pair parts) minimise the obligation on police interviewers to respond to topics initiated by suspects. Thus, a police interviewer is able to ignore topic initiations that contribute to the suspect's version of events. A suspect, on the other hand, is often in a position of having to respond to police topic initiations because they are produced as first pair parts, such as formulations or requests for confirmation, which obligate the recipient to produce a topically relevant response. As a result, the police version of events can be not only constructed, but favoured as the agreed-to version. The examples in Extract 3 and Extract 4 involving SPT2's reasons for assaulting his girlfriend demonstrated the extent to which a police interviewer can dismiss the suspect's contributions in favour of the police version and then present the police version as a formulation of everything that has been said on the topic. In the case mentioned, this resulted in the agreement by the suspect with a police version that did not represent the suspect's original version of events at all. In the next section, we will draw on these observations and consider the discursive practices of police interviewers in the negotiation of two competing versions of events.

Formulating the guilty suspect

We have seen in the prior analyses that the police versions being constructed by pio1 and pio2 differ in certain recognisable respects from the suspect versions. For instance, in both interviews, the police interviewers omit sections of the suspects' versions. In Extract 1 and Extract 2, pio1 produces a summary of SPT1's prior turn that does not include SPT1's description of his friendship with Betty, his ex-de facto partner. By including this information in his version, SPT1 had provided the listener with a possible reason for his behaviour. SPT1 conveys the closeness of his friendship with Betty and this can then be drawn upon to explain why he is so upset by the threatening phone call and why he feels compelled to respond to the call with violence. Conversely, by excluding this information in her version of events, pio1 diminishes the impact of the threatening phone call on SPT1's state of mind, facilitating the interpretation of SPT1's assault of Ian as unmitigated and irrational.

Similarly, in Extract 3 and Extract 4, we saw that when pio2 constructs his version of 'reasons for the assault', he overtly excludes SPT2's explanation that his girlfriend *jumps into bed with (0.2) one of my   so-called mates* . Instead, pio2 presents a version where there was *absolutely no reason* for SPT2's actions. Again, the information omitted by the police interviewer when summarising the suspect's utterances is contextual information that serves to explain the suspect's behaviour.

This approach by the police interviewers in these two interviews can be compared with the findings of Swedish researchers that 'written police reports of interviews with suspects ... emphasised the actions of the suspects which pointed to their guilt compared with the original version offered by the suspect which contained much contextual material designed to explain and excuse the offence' (cited in Auburn et al., 1995 355-6).

In addition to constructing a police version of events which omits contextual information provided by the suspect, the police interviewers also use formulations to include aspects of the narrative which were not mentioned by the suspect. These types of interactions are present in some interviews examined where actions are mentioned by the police interviewers that are specifically not undertaken by the suspects.

One of the most contested aspects of the first interview is the allegation of criminal damage to the door of the shop where the incident took place. In the latter part of the interview, there is a lengthy discussion about the manner in which SPT1 closed the door as he left the shop, following the assault. When describing his actions the first time, SPT1 says that he closed the door hard as he left and the glass in the door cracked. As his jacket had caught in the door, he re-opened the door to free the jacket and then closed it, at which point the glass shattered and fell to the ground. Rather than present for analysis the entire description and subsequent discussion, as it runs to over 80 lines, it is sufficient to note SPT1's choice of words to describe the events. SPT1 says 408/SPT1: *as I closed the door I admit I closed it a little bit too ha:rd* to describe the initial closing of the door, which he claims was the moment that the glass cracked. He then describes the second part of the incident as 419-421/SPT1: *and closed it again that's when the whole sho- (0.2) the whole glass just shattered* . The following extract (Extract 5) picks up the interview at the point where SPT1 has completed this description and pio1 begins her response to his account.

Extract 5

```
422  pio1:   so you pretty much slammed it the first time
423  SPT1:   yeah
424  pio1:   (0.3) very hard
425          and it's (0.3) cracked all the gra- all the glass
426  SPT1:   yeah that's //right*
427  pio1:   you've* reopened it
428          to get your //jacket* out
429  SPT1:   ja-* yeah
430  pio1:   and you've slammed it shut again
431          causing all the glass to shatter to the ground
432  SPT1:   that's right
```

433 pio1: uh you <u>saw</u> the glass shatter to the ground
434 SPT1: (0.4) I just kept <u>walking</u>
435   (0.2) I just got in the <u>car</u>
436   and <u>Rob</u> (0.6) me <u>friend</u> said what the hell's going <u>on</u>
437   (0.4) whadcha <u>do</u>
438 pio1: (1.2) so you didn't bother <u>saying</u> anything to them
439   that the <u>glass</u> was <u>broken</u>   or

It is important to recognise that pio1 is intending to charge SPT1 with criminal damage, which means that SPT1 is believed by the police to have intentionally caused the damage to the door. In the segment presented above, we can see that pio1 embarks on a process moving the shared understanding of the incident from one represented by SPT1's description (e.g. as *I closed the door I admit I closed it a little bit too ha:rd   … and closed it again*) to one represented by pio1's formulation (e.g. *so you pretty much slammed it the first time   … and you've slammed it shut again*). It is interesting that pio1 prefaces the term *slammed* with the phrase *pretty much* which links her version to SPT1's version by 'roughly' equating one with the other. The device *so*, common to formulations (Heritage and Watson, 1979), explicitly displays her construction as a restating of SPT1's utterances, rather than a separate version of events.

Apart from the term *slammed* introduced by pio1 in lines 422 and 430, several other elements are added to the formulation of events in her turns of which perhaps the most critical is her introduction of causality. Whereas SPT1 has said only that he closed the door *and* the glass broke, pio1 describes this so that SPT1's action is formulated as 431/pio1: *causing all the glass to shatter to the ground* . She follows this in her next turn with the formulation 433/pio1: *uh you saw the glass shatter to the ground* .

By altering the verb used from *closed* to *slammed* in both instances of the action taking place, she increases the degree of violence in SPT1's actions. Combined with her assertion of causality between these actions and breaking of the glass, this makes for a much stronger case of intentionality as regards the damage.

This demonstrates the power of formulations as a tool in the construction of a police version of events. Formulations are commonly used to provide a 'summary' of prior talk for the purposes of clarification and necessarily contain different words and phrases from the original as a demonstration of comprehension by the producer of the formulation (Heritage and Watson, 1979). In the cases being discussed in this section, formulations are used to create the illusion that the police version is really only a summary of the suspect's version with some changes that may be required for clarification by the police interviewer. However, the changes that are made to the suspect version systematically introduce terms of violence and intentionality that were not present in the original utterances. In Extract 5 above, pio1's subsequent turn in lines 436 and 437 alters SPT1's description of returning to the car after the door broke to a description of a failure on the part of SPT1 to inform the 'others' (Betty and Ian) of the damage and she is thus able to associate with SPT1's actions an allegation of deliberate negligence – that SPT1 *didn't bother saying anything to them* . In a broader sense, pio1 is taking an approach to the negotiations at this point that is based around the association of violent or antisocial acts with the suspect's version of events. Her shift from the verb *close* to *slam* gives SPT1's actions a violence that his version does not contain and this enables her to introduce causality more plausibly in the following turn. By recasting SPT1's action of leaving the shop as an act of negligence, she is further able to support a version of events where SPT1 has wilfully and knowingly engaged in a destructive activity.

Incidentally, the fact that SPT1 offers agreement tokens to pio1's assertions does not adequately represent the suspect's response to these assertions. He later reiterates his original version of *closing* the door, and, although he eventually concedes that he did *slam* the door the first time, he continues to defend the view that the damage was accidental.

In the previous section, Extract 3 was found to demonstrate an overt alteration of the suspect's version where the reason given by SPT2 for the assault on his girlfriend was dismissed by pio2 and replaced with the police version that there was *absolutely no reason* for the assault. We have already seen that, in interactional terms, pio2 was able to achieve these changes through his access to topic management tools unavailable to SPT2, specifically, pio2's access to topic initiation devices which strongly obligate SPT2 to respond to the topic in favour of any topic SPT2 may raise himself. However, it is also pertinent that in order to dismiss SPT2's reason, pio2 employs a construction which juxtaposes SPT2's reason – *she   (0.6) jumps into bed with (0.2) one of my   so-called mates* – with formulations of SPT2's actions and asks if the reason, already weakened through utterances such as *regardless of that might've been the case* in line 284, warranted these actions.

As we saw in the previous analysis of the first interview, it is clear that in this interview pio2 strengthens the supposition of unwarranted actions by introducing terms of violence as formulations of the suspect's prior turns. In lines 286-288, pio2 formulates SPT2's actions by using the verb phrases *draggin' 'er out by the hair, pullin' by the arm and forcibly removing 'er from the house*. In each case, the word that most emphasises the violence of the actions is stressed. This is particularly apparent in line 288 where the word *forcibly* is given greater stress than the main verb in the utterance, *removing*. By using these three utterances to formulate SPT2's actions, pio2 does, of course, edit out many other descriptions of the events offered by SPT2 during the interview. For instance, SPT2 describes 132/SPT2: *yellin and screamin at 'er* , 161/SPT2: *arguin an' pushin' n' pullin'* and 219/SPT2: *sitting on the ground wif her after she (0.2) fell o:ver* , but none of these actions are included in pio2's formulation. It is noticeable that the first two examples from SPT2's version of events do contain terms of violence but they imply either non-physical violence – *yellin, screamin* and *arguin* – or interactional, two-sided actions – *arguin, pushin n' pullin*. These descriptions do not support the version pio2 is constructing of a level of violence perpetrated by SPT2 that is out of all proportion to the reason which SPT2 has supplied. The case pio2 builds is apparently very convincing and SPT2 takes up the TRP at the end of line 287, before pio2 has even finished his formulation, in order to indicate that his reason did not warrant these acts of violence. It is this acceptance of pio2's version by SPT2 that ultimately weakens SPT2's reason for the assault to the extent that pio2 is able to formulate SPT2's reason as *absolutely no reason* despite the contradiction inherent in this claim.

Finally, a segment from a third interview (Extract 6) demonstrates that the question-answer pairs that dominate this particular interview do not appear to lend themselves as easily to the task of creating a police version of events.

Extract 6

221 pio3: (0.8) all right (.) and <u>who</u> hung up[1] in the back shed
222 SPT3: <u>I</u> did
223 pio3: (0.6) <u>how</u> did you do that
224 SPT3: (0.6) tied em up with a <u>rope</u>
225 pio3: (0.4) and <u>why</u> did you do that

226 SPT3: (0.9) so that wouldn't <u>go</u> everywhere
227 pio3: (0.6) so they <u>wouldn't</u>
228 SPT3: <u>go</u> everywhere
229 pio3: (0.4) oh <u>right</u>   (0.6) I'll <u>put</u> it to you that you <u>put</u> em
there to <u>dry</u> out
230   (0.8) for <u>later</u> use
231 SPT3: (1.1) no (0.2) just (0.2) to (0.4) get out of the <u>way</u>
232 pio3: right   (2.3) OK and then <u>explain</u> to me what <u>happened</u>

Pio3 is attempting to establish the reason why SPT3 tied the marijuana plants together and then hung them in a shed. Specifically, pio3 is proposing that SPT3 hung the plants in the shed with the intention of allowing them to cure, thus providing him with consumable material at some later stage. This interpretation of SPT3's actions would have the double implication of firstly casting SPT3's actions as suspicious and having criminal intent and secondly casting SPT3 himself as a heavy drug user, potentially in possession of a large quantity of cured marijuana. However, SPT3's version has already minimised these interpretations as he has responded to pio3's questions about his actions by claiming that he only hung them up and tied them together to be a tidy shed user, as he explains in line 226/SPT3: (0.9) *so that wouldn't go everywhere* . By the time pio3 comes to formulate SPT3's version, SPT3 has already had the opportunity, by responding to the three prior content questions, to strengthen his version and to preemptively weaken pio3's formulation that SPT3 *put em there to dry out* *(0.8) for later use* . Furthermore, pio3 prefaces this utterance with the phrase *I'll put it to you that* which does not have the effect of 'naturalising' the process of formulation in the way that pio1 and pio2 were able to do. We saw that in the extracts from the other interviews, the police interviewers used utterances that implied that their construction of a police version was merely a re-stating of the suspect's version. This effect was achieved primarily through the use of formulation first pair parts to summarise the interviewee's prior talk. However, pio3 produces his utterance in lines 229-230 more transparently as a police version by using the police institutional construction *I'll put it to you that*. It appears to be less interactionally problematic for SPT3 to reject pio3's proposal and reiterate his own position (231/SPT3: *(1.1) no (0.2) just (0.2) to (0.4) get out of the way*) than it was for SPT1 or SPT2 to counter the claims made by pio1 and pio2 respectively.

It would appear that a more transparently institutional approach to the construction of the police version of events enables the suspect to have greater access to the interactional tools required to reject this version and maintain his own version of events. Nonetheless, pio3's proposed version has in common with the examples from the other interviews the purpose of presenting the suspect's actions as having criminal intent and of characterising the suspect himself as antisocial and violent.

Conclusion

It is perhaps not so very surprising that an analysis of the topic management tools in police interview data reveals that topic shift is predominantly initiated by the interviewing officers and that police participants have available to them a wider range of resources through which topic shift may be achieved. For instance, it was found that whereas a suspect may only initiate topic shift using a 'stepwise transition' which minimises the impact of the topic shift on the interaction, a primary interviewing officer may initiate new topics disjunctively and even interruptively. Furthermore, topic initiation resources accessible to suspects were found to be less likely to obligate the recipients to respond to the topic.

Nonetheless, the observation, however mundane, that topic management resources are asymmetrically allocated does in fact provide a powerful analytic tool with which to investigate the negotiation of two competing versions of events in a police interview. Analysis of the topic management tools used by suspects and police demonstrates that, at the level of turn-taking, suspects are in a vastly disadvantageous position when trying to support their version of events.

The use of formulations by police officers to further support their version of events is another tool that is asymmetrically distributed amongst the participants. Formulations are only available as first pair parts and are therefore inaccessible to suspects under normal interview conditions. It is particularly interesting that police interviewers make use of formulations to introduce terms of violence and uncooperative behaviour to the narrative. That is, the turn-taking structure permits an opportunity for police officers to make moral judgements of the suspect's actions. The imposition of moral frameworks by police interviewers is the subject of another part of this research project, however it is sufficient to note here that such behaviour is clearly inappropriate in a forum intended only for information gathering.

It is important to remember that the institutional purpose of interviewing a suspect is to record his or her version of events and that this will form part of the evidence in any subsequent court case. The purpose of the interview is not to persuade the suspect to accept a police version of events and such interviews, in which the suspect is unable to present his or her version of events, may not be accepted as evidence in Court. Clearly, this will seriously undermine the position of the police prosecution. In other words, the more that police interviewers rely on the institutionally-endowed topic management tools at their disposal to compete with a suspect's version of events, the more likely they are to jeopardise the integrity of the evidence and their case.

Appendix

Transcription conventions. The conventions used in the transcription of data for this study are adapted from those outlined in Levinson, 1983.

Symbol	Description
pio1, pio2 etc.	primary interviewing officer in Interview 1, in Interview 2 etc.
SPT1, SPT2 etc.	Suspect (interviewee) in Interview 1, in Interview 2 etc.
//	overlapping speech commences
*	overlapping speech ends
(0.6)	silence measured in seconds
(.)	micro-pause of less than 0.2 seconds
°word°	softer than surrounding speech
<u>word</u>	syllables having greater stress than surrounding sounds
–	high rise intonation
	low rise intonation
	level intonation
	falling intonation
::	the sound is lengthened by one syllable for each colon
–	truncated word

Note

1 This is a speech error. The target utterance is 'who hung it up' and refers to bundles of marijuana plants being strung up in a shed.

References

Auburn, T., Drake, S., and Willig, C. (1995) 'You punched him, didn't you?': Versions of Violence in accusatory interviews. *Discourse and Society*, 6,3: 353-386.

Billig, M. (1991) *Ideology and Opinions: Studies in Rhetorical Psychology*. London: Sage.

Fairclough, N. (1989) *Language and Power*. Harlow: Longman Group.

Frankel, R. (1990) Talking in interviews: a dispreference for patient-initiated questions in physician-patient encounters. In G. Psathas (ed.) *Interaction Competence*. Washington DC: University Press of America. pp. 231-262.

Goffman, E. (1981) *Forms of Talk*. Philadelphia: University of Pennsylvania Press.

Greatbatch, D. (1988) A turn-taking system for British news interviews. *Language in Society*, 17: 401-430.

Heritage, J. (1985) Analyzing news interviews: aspects of the production of talk for an overhearing audience. In T. A. V. Dijk (ed.) *Handbook of Discourse Analysis*. London: Academic Press. Vol. 3, pp. 95-117.

Heritage, J., and Watson, D. R. (1979) Formulations as conversational objects. In G. Psathas (ed.) *Everyday Language: Studies in Ethnomethodology*. New York: Irvington Publishers. pp. 123-162.

Heydon, G. (2002) *'Do you agree that she would have been frightened?': An investigation of discursive practices in police-suspect interviews*. Unpublished PhD, Monash University: Melbourne.

Jefferson, G. (1984) On stepwise transition from talk about a trouble to inappropriately next-positioned matters. In J. M. Atkinson and J. Heritage (eds) *Structures of Social Action: Studies in Conversation Analysis*. Cambridge: Cambridge University Press. pp. 191-222.

Jefferson, G. (1988) On the sequential organization of troubles-talk in ordinary conversation. *Social Problems*, 35,4: 418-441.

Levinson, S. C. (1983) *Pragmatics*. Cambridge: Cambridge University Press.

Pomerantz, A. M. (1986) Extreme Case formulations: A way of legitimizing claims. *Human Studies*, 9: 219-229.

Sacks, H., Schegloff, E., and Jefferson, G. (1974) A simplest systematics for the organisation of turn-taking for conversation. *Language*, 50, 4: 696-735.

7 Using CHILDES tools for researching second language acquisition

Emma Marsden, Florence Myles,
Sarah Rule and Rosamond Mithcell
University of Southampton

Abstract

The second language acquisition research community needs datasets of oral production in order to study linguistic development. The use of digital technologies, as already seen in other areas (ranging from L1 acquisition research to corpora building) has the potential to improve the collection, analysis and sharing of such data. Attempts to develop uniquely Second Language Acquisition specific tools have been abandoned. This paper evaluates some of the CHILDES (Child Language Data Exchange System) tools (MacWhinney 2002, http://childes.psy.cmu.edu/), originally developed for first language acquisition research, in the context of a project investigating linguistic development of French as a second language« The research project 'Linguistic Development in Classroom Learners of French' was directed by Florence Myles, and funded by the Economic and Social Research Council (Award No. R000223421). Further details can be found at http://www.regard.ac.uk. The CHILDES tools are part of an active and well-funded international community of language researchers, and consequently keep pace with relevant technological developments (e.g. digitised sound and video files, XML compatible formats). Although considerable time was required to become sufficiently familiar with the tools, and some project-specific modifications were necessary in order to benefit from the recently-developed computerised French morphosyntactic analysis tools (e.g. changes to the lexicon, and developments in the use of syntactic and other types of coding), we argue that the CHILDES package can offer the SLA community flexible and efficient means of data preparation, analysis and sharing. Our experience suggests that training in and use of the tools could significantly enhance current practice.

Introduction

One of the major challenges facing communities of second language acquisition researchers is a growing need for powerful analysis tools that can handle large data sets, particularly oral production data. However, working with such data presents several challenges: representing speech in written form, devising coding that is helpful both for specific hypothesis-testing and for exploratory investigations, collecting sufficient data to withstand rigorous statistical tests and analysing these large datasets efficiently and reliably.

The development of digital technologies is transforming the methods available to applied linguistics. To date however, these technologies have had their main impact in fields such as lexicography, pedagogic grammar, and discourse analysis (see e.g. Thomas and Short, eds 1996; Stubbs, 1996; Hunston and Francis, 1998; http://www.cobuild.collins.co.uk/). In first language acquisition research, the internationally known Child Language Data Exchange System (CHILDES) has developed robust systems for the management and analysis of language data (MacWhinney, 2002 http://childes.psy.cmu.edu/; Sokolov and Snow, 1994) and has been used by researchers from a range of different theoretical approaches e.g. functional, generative, conversation analysis and phonological perspectives. For clinical purposes, computerised phonological and grammatical analyses have been compared with manual procedures, and shown to be quicker and equally or more accurate (e.g. Long, 2001; Long and Channell, 2001). However, as yet the impact of such developments on SLA studies remains relatively small (Rutherford and Thomas, 2001).

This paper describes and evaluates some of the CHILDES tools in terms of their usefulness for a morphosyntactic study of linguistic development of French, which was the main focus of this project (see below). The discussion here is mainly based on our experience of using the CHILDES tools for an analysis of the early expression of negation in French (e.g. Rule and Marsden, 2002). The investigation was largely from a Universal Grammar perspective, exploring the initial state of learners' systems: the status of functional categories and the relationship between morphology and syntax. By searching directly in the codes produced by a morphosyntactic parser (one of the CHILDES tools) we were able to analyse the use of negative particles and their linguistic contexts (e.g. before and/or after inflected and/or uninflected verbs) and the use of subject clitics in inflected or uninflected clauses. The tools enabled both a top-down analysis, comparing what is known about first language development with second language development, and an exploratory bottom-up analysis, revealing patterns of language use that are particular to interlanguage.

It is suggested here that in their current off-the-shelf form, the CHILDES procedures require some SLA- and project-specific refinement. However, it is argued that with adequate support and training, the SLA research community could draw significant benefit from this package, which has potential to help several important research agendas.

The project and its needs

First, a brief summary of the project will highlight the need for well-developed coding and analysis tools for a range of SLA research agendas, and gives the broad objectives against which the tools have been evaluated.

The 'Linguistic Development in Learners of French' project had the following general aims:

> to document linguistic progression among classroom learners of French in Years 9, 10 and 11, extending an existing corpus of oral French interlanguage data for younger learners ('Progression in Foreign Language Learning': Mitchell and Dickson, 1997);[1]

> to analyse the development of a number of morphosyntactic structures in spoken learner French, including sentence structure, verbal morphology, gender, interrogation, negation, embedding, pronominal reference etc.;

> to analyse the creative construction process, from the Initial State and beyond, and its interaction with formulaic language among instructed learners.

The sample consisted of three groups of 20 learners in each of Years 9, 10, 11 in an English secondary school. Each learner undertook four oral tasks with an adult interlocutor (see Appendix 1). The project collected approximately 50 hours of spoken French and, together with data from the previous project, the Southampton dataset now constitutes a corpus of some 250 hours.

Efficient means of carrying out detailed linguistic analyses on such data, given the nature of the research questions and the size of the sample, are crucial. The dataset from the 'Progression in Foreign Language Learning' project, mentioned above, comprises analogue audio recordings and their transcriptions in plain text files appropriate for use with concordancing tools such as Wordsmith. The resulting publications, however, (see for example, Myles, Mitchell, and Hooper, 1999) have so far drawn on relatively small subsets of data from the corpus, partly due to the fact that the tools available did not facilitate rapid analyses of the complete dataset.

This illustrates an issue that has been increasingly discussed in second language acquisition studies: theoretical claims have proliferated while the scale of empirical research to test these claims has often remained quite small. There have been calls (e.g. Ellis, 1999) for a change of scale when documenting linguistic development amongst learners and when testing rival explanations for observed developmental phenomena.

Attempts were made in the 1990s to develop software dedicated to the analysis of L2 oral data. However the resulting packages COALA (Pienemann, 1992) and COMOLA (Jagtman and Bongaerts, 1994) are both now inactive. Extensible Markup Language (XML) is becoming increasingly popular for tagging and sharing many types of data (http://www.ucc.ie/xml), and some SLA researchers have adopted it (e.g. for tagging written French interlanguage in Granger, 2002). Learning and adapting the XML procedures is beyond the limits of most SLA projects and Oshita 2000 demonstrated the time-intensiveness of developing the necessary computer program. We therefore investigated whether an 'off-the-shelf' language-specific package could meet our requirements: CHILDES (MacWhinney, 2000 and 2002), as strongly recommended to SLA researchers in Rutherford and Thomas 2001.[2]

A brief introduction to CHILDES

The CHILDES[3] set of tools was originally conceived for first language acquisition data, but it has also been used, in a limited way, by second language researchers (Malvern and Richards, 2002; Housen, 2002; Paradis, Le Corre, and Genesee, 1998). CHILDES tools have been used in well over 1300 published studies ranging from L1 acquisition to computational linguistics, language disorders, narrative structures, literacy development, phonological analyses and adult sociolinguistics (MacWhinney, 2002).

Besides the features of specific interest to language researchers discussed in the following sections, CHILDES has several important advantages. First, the tools are constantly up-dated by a well-funded team of programmers, there is an active community of users, the system promotes data-sharing and all the tools can be downloaded free of charge from the Internet.

CHILDES consists of three integrated components:

> The large and diversified database (Talkbank) consists primarily of child speech recordings and transcriptions, but also includes some language disorder data and bilingual data. It is a condition of using CHILDES tools that our data will become part of the Talkbank database. There are currently just five SLA datasets available in Talkbank.

> CHAT (Codes for the Human Analysis of Transcripts) are the transcription procedures, which have been developed to be compatible with the analysis programmes.

> CLAN (Computerized Language Analysis) consists of about 40 core computer commands for carrying out searches and counts, along with a range of 'switches' that can be used to customise each command. This is a powerful and flexible software package that can carry out rapid and detailed analyses and is designed to recognise the tagging conventions of CHAT.

Recording the data Although digital sound files are not required in order to use the CHILDES tools, the TALKBANK database has now been entirely digitised[4]. This clearly facilitates complete data-sharing. The advantages of digital data also have important consequences for realising the potential of linguistic data. Digital recording machines themselves are quieter and less intrusive, the quality and durability of the sound is much better, negotiating through files is significantly more efficient than working with audiocassettes and the timing of pauses can be more easily done. Digital sound files can be 'linked' to the transcript, enabling simultaneous access to the written and spoken forms, compensating, to some extent, for the inevitable shortcomings of written representation of speech, and giving other researchers the opportunity to code the spoken data. Waveforms of the digital file can also be displayed and linked precisely with the transcription in 'Sonic Mode'.

Transcribing from digital sound files Although the 'VoiceWalker' facility is available in CLAN for transcribing digital files, we found that Soundscriber (http://www.lsa.umich.edu/eli/micase/soundscriber.html) offers more flexibility for moving around the sound file whilst transcribing. The keyboard is used to play, pause, auto-rewind, fast-forward or 'walk' through the sound file (e.g. every five second segment is repeated x times). This freeware completely replaces traditional transcribing machines.

CHAT transcribing and coding procedures

Headers Every file has a set of 'headers' so that the computer can process relevant details from each file. Anything that the researchers feel could potentially influence the findings (e.g. elicitation task, date, transcriber etc.) can be recorded in these headings. A 'readme' file must accompany each dataset giving a brief description of the project and sample, and information to other researchers regarding the transcription and coding decisions taken (for example, in the current study, overlapping and precise phonological codes were not documented).

Main line The data is transcribed on to a main line as a set of standard language word forms. Each utterance is transcribed on to a separate line and starts with * followed by the speaker code; this line shows what was actually said, in contrast with lines starting with a % sign which contain linguistic tags. The CHAT manual (MacWhinney, 2000) contains codes (see Appendix 2 for a small selection) that have been developed by various contributors addressing a wide variety of linguistic research agendas, including, for example, codes for Conversation Analysis, the analysis of written data, sign language, and for phonetic, prosodic, morphological and syntactic features of speech. It is now possible to enter Unicode IPA in CLAN using the recently developed SILIPA Unicode font (see http://childes.psy.cmu.edu/html/wintools.html). CHAT also allows new codes to be used to address project-specific questions.

A programme called CHECK can ensure your file meets minimum requirements to be recognised by CLAN (for example by indicating where the human transcriber has not followed basic procedures, such as starting each main line with *)[5].

Tiers for coding In addition to the main line, there can be multiple 'dependent tiers' that provide ancillary information. These tiers are preceded by a % sign to indicate they are strings of tags. Researchers can decide how many dependent tiers are appropriate for their own purposes. Our data has a *%err* tier (error) and a *%mor* tier (morphosyntax), though researchers using our data in the future are free to add other coding tiers depending on their interests[6].

%err tier The %err line has a well-developed system of codes to be entered manually onto a tier beneath the main line. Although the name 'error tier' is perhaps a remnant of the Error Analysis perspective still popular when the CHILDES tools were first conceived at the beginning of the 1980s, as Rutherford and Thomas 2001 point out (pp. 204–5), such coding is simply a way of labelling interlanguage and does not necessitate adherence to 'error analysis' perspectives, especially given the flexibility of the CLAN programmes. The *%err* tier is used by some SLA researchers but had several disadvantages for us e.g. it would have been a particularly arduous task given the interlanguage of beginners, resulting in cluttered coding. More importantly, unless *all* non-target-like features are coded, project-specific error tiers can restrict the questions one can ask of the data. In contrast, using a MOR tier combined with some tagging of the main line, both described later, does not constrain future interrogation of the data to the same extent.

One feature of the error tier was retained in our project. A word that was clear from the context but would probably have been unintelligible in isolation was, when this did not affect our objectives, transcribed as target-like so that it was recognised by the automatic parser. For example, *bouée* (rubber ring) (given to the learners as a written prompt) was frequently mispronounced, but *'bouée'* was written on the main line and what was actually said was recorded on the error tier. This illustrates that even with a highly systematized transcription procedure, project-specific aims still influence methodological decisions.

%mor tier The *%mor* tier encodes syntactic categories and morphological inflections, indicating tense, aspect, person, number and gender features. It is possible to generate a morphosyntactic description of the main line semi-automatically by using two CLAN tools, MOR and POST. Versions of MOR have been produced for a range of languages (10 at present[7]); the parser for French was developed by Christophe Parisse in 2001[8]. For the programme to parse data from a particular corpus correctly, some time must be spent adding to the lexicon in the programme to ensure it recognises all the words in the corpus (though one of the CLAN programmes helpfully extracts all 'unrecognised' forms). The parsing done initially by the MOR programme gives a variety of possible morphosyntactic analyses of words on

the main line. The initial product of MOR, much of which is redundant, must then be 'disambiguated', which is mainly done by POST. This programme checks for permissible morphosyntactic combinations and eliminates discordant/unwanted analyses. For example, an initial analysis using MOR might tag the item '*le*' both as an object pronoun and also as a determiner. A second analysis using POST works out from the linguistic context which category was intended and eliminates the redundant tags. The researcher then has to do the final disambiguating semi-manually, for around 5% of the data, by deciding which parsing options need to be rejected and which accepted, for example, whether '*aiment*' should be parsed as a third person plural indicative or subjunctive. During this disambiguation, researchers can write their own morphosyntactic codes if none of those offered are suitable. Extracts from a transcription of learner French that has been through the processes described above is given here (only one item required manual disambiguation in this extract):[9]

```
*21L:     la famille est arrivée dans le lac.
%mor:     det|la&FEM&SING n|famille&_FEM
          v:aux|être&PRES&3SV v:pp|arriver&_FEM&_SING
          prep|dans det|le&MASC&SING n|lac&_MASC.

*21L:     euh c' est grand+mère.
%mor:     co|euh pro|ce/ces&SING v:exist|être&PRES&3SV
          n|grand+mère&_FEM.

*21L:     euh deux enfants c' est à la pêche .
%mor:     co|euh num|deux n|enfant-_PL pro|ce/ces&SING
          v:exist|être&PRES&3SV prep|à det|la&FEM&SING
          n|pêche&_FEM .
```

However, the automatic parsing provided by the procedures described above was not always to our satisfaction. For example, *au* was coded as a preposition only, without any recognition of the masculine article within it, which would clearly affect our 'gender' research question. Such 'blips' were easily remedied however, by changing entries in the lexicon files of the programmes e.g. the original coding for *au* (prep|au) was changed to prep:det|au&_MASC&_PL. It is clear that the French MOR and POST programmes have not yet fully eradicated the need for manual revision.

Other CLAN commands

CLAN can carry out lexical, morphosyntactic, discourse and phonological analyses, amongst others, depending on how the data has been coded. CLAN programmes such as FREQ, KWAL and COMBO facilitate analyses of the frequency and linguistic context of interlanguage features. FREQPOS does a frequency analysis by sentence position and MLU calculates the mean length of utterance. In addition, the results of one analysis can be 'piped' through another analysis, allowing multiple analyses.

Analyses can be carried out on specific tiers by customising the commands. For example, COMBO searches can search for specific words, word sequences or combinations of lexical items and morphosyntactical and/or 'error' codes. The COMBO command given here was one used for Rule and Marsden (2002) for the analysis of the expression of negation:

combo +t%mor 10N.mor.pst +s'*ne^*pres"

where:

combo	specifies the command to search for strings of items
+t	specifies the tier
%mor	the command is to be carried out on the %mor tier
14N	participant ID, in our project giving information about learner and task
.mor.pst	extension given to file after it has undergone MOR and POST programmes
+s	the 'switch' to say look for a string
"	a metacharacter to mark the start of the string
*	any character (on the MOR tier there can be some other symbols / characters between 'det' and the following word's code)
ne	we are looking for the word 'ne'
^	followed by
pres	we are looking for the syntactic code 'pres' (which has been given by MOR to all verbs inflected in the present)
"	marks the end of the string

Project-specific issues and flexibility of the tools

The CHAT and CLAN tools are reasonably flexible, and can accommodate project-specific concerns. This is illustrated with four issues arising from the current study.

Phonetic versus orthographic transcription French has differences between its phonetic and orthographic systems (for example, regular present tense er verbs have five orthographic but just three phonetic realisations). Thus, transcribing /e/ verb endings (written *aller, allé, allez*) can be problematic in the absence of an auxiliary or pronoun (furthermore, learners may have had no intention to distinguish between the functions). A *%pho* tier is available for an entirely phonetic transcript but this would have been diversionary from our research objectives. We therefore opted for an orthographic transcription, a decision which may have drawbacks from phonological perspectives of language development, but which has the clear advantage that our data could be parsed automatically (the MOR and POST programmes only recognise standard orthography). Some phonetic symbols were used for certain neologisms relevant to our agenda e.g. the use of over-regularisation such as fair/e/, prend/e/. These forms were then given specific syntactic categories in the CLAN programmes.

Representing interlanguage forms English learners of L2 French often use phonologically indistinguishable forms of the definite and indefinite articles, lying between '*le*' and '*la*' and between '*un*' and '*une*'. Similarly for '*a*' / '*est*' and '*je*' / '*j'ai*'. CHAT suggests @*n* can be used to code such morphological 'neologisms', which can be added to the lexicon and interpreted by the computer as the researcher decides in order to track their use. For example we instructed MOR to code such items as follows (neologisms underlined):

    *21L: le@n famille
    %mor: neo:def:det|le@n n|famille&_FEM
    *21L: un@n grand+mère
    %mor: neo:indef:det|un@n n|grand+mère&_FEM

Tracking the function of learner forms Related to the previous issue was the need to record the function of the learners' interlanguage. Although it is acknowledged that the notion of '% occurrence in obligatory context' as an indication of acquisition is not without controversy (Pienemann, 1998), this measure was necessary both to calculate progression towards target-like production and a functional analysis of learners' forms. For example, the emerging grammars under study include many apparently uninflected verb forms which, in isolation, lack indication of tense, person etc. e.g. *je jouer*★ is used where the context stipulates that one or other of the standard forms *je joue, il joue, j'ai joué, je vais jouer, tu joues?* might have been expected. By tagging the interlanguage form with a code indicating the 'underdeveloped' feature (e.g. by coding non-target non-finite forms with @p for present contexts, @f for future contexts and @c for past contexts), we can begin to trace their use automatically. Such tagging can result in the following MOR coding:

| 32P: | samedi dernier | je | nager@c |

%mor: n|samedi adj|dernier&masc_sing pro:subj|je&1S v:inf:past|nager.

This makes automatic retrieval of relevant 'target forms' and their corresponding interlanguage possible, without searching the data for (a possibly infinite number of) contextual clues, and has removed the need for a complete error tier.

Syntactic roles in code-switching Our data has a significant amount of both utterance-internal and –external code-switching. CHILDES tools have been used for the study of bi-lingual data (e.g. Sebba http://talkbank.org/data/LIDES/) though we could not locate studies where the morphosyntactic role of both languages has been tracked. Tags for the main line were therefore devised to represent the syntactic categories we were interested in tracking: @d, after L1 nouns, @v after L1 verbs and @a after L1 adjectives. These codes were then written into the MOR programme to produce the following coding:

★21L: pour   le   skirt@d

%mor: prep|pour det|le&MASC&SING n:eng|skirt

It was then possible, for example, to search for combinations of masculine determiners followed by English nouns.

Concluding Remarks: Is it worth it?

Both Rutherford and Thomas (2001) and MacWhinney (personal communication, 23 May 2002) lament the paucity of SLA studies using CHILDES tools to date (although see the optimistic claims to the contrary by Eubank and Earley, 1992). Rutherford and Thomas (pp. 200-201) point out that significant portions of the SLA work claimed to have been done with CHILDES tools have simply not materialised in Talkbank[10]. This is supported by anecdotal evidence collected during our study, which also indicates that CHAT transcription procedures are frequently followed and word searching and concordancing facilities in CLAN are indeed used, but other CLAN programmes are not fully exploited. Our experience suggests that one reason may be that the investment of time to learn and adapt the tools for SLA- and project-specific purposes is, as yet, considerable. This project required approximately 750 hours to get 50 hours of near-beginner speech into CHAT format with sufficient coding to answer our (extensive) research questions, and to gain sufficient knowledge of the necessary CLAN programmes.

These time demands were mainly due to our initial lack of expertise in the tools. A formal comparison of efficiency and accuracy, all other things being equal, such as in Long (2001) and Long and Channell (2001), would be a valuable exercise. A preliminary comparison of this nature did emerge from this project. Computerised searches on the MOR tier of about 10 hours of data for Rule and Marsden (2002) took under two hours. However, these searches did not account for the expression of negation in 17% of the obligatory contexts[11]. For Rule, Marsden and Myles (2002) a manual search on the main line of the data took longer (approximately 12 hours) but found these 'missing' contexts and the results for several categories were slightly more accurate.

However, the two different searches did not result in different conclusions to the research questions. Furthermore, although the manual analysis of the main line could clearly have been done without investing in CHILDES expertise (e.g. by using in-house transcription procedures), our data is now ready to be interrogated with different questions and, as such, is more useful to the community.

It is stressed that the time intensiveness of our experience with the CHILDES tools was heavily influenced by the fact that CHAT and CLAN are not yet embedded in common practice. We suggest that the use of such packages needs to be a long-term endeavour, shared by a community of researchers. For example, we could not find any SLA researchers using the French MOR and POST programmes and it was these tools, recently-developed for first language acquisition studies, that required the most attention. However, the expertise gained in this project has already directly influenced several other projects. Clearly, any comparison of manual versus automatic morphosyntactic analyses needs to consider such benefits to the community, as well as the longer-term advantages of having coded data banks which can be automatically interrogated with readily available language-specific tools.

In fact, many of the issues discussed in this paper illustrate general problems with the transcription and coding of French interlanguage, which require attention regardless of the analysis package chosen. For example, the inherent tension between keeping the main line as user-friendly and yet as authentic as possible, is further aggravated by complex grapheme/phoneme relationships in French and by the audible impact of the high priority given to written forms in UK school foreign language classrooms. Nevertheless, we found the CHILDES tools were sufficiently flexible to allow us to make appropriate decisions. Overall, we believe that these are powerful tools, capable of both top-down and bottom-up analyses, which will enable SLA researchers to test hypotheses on large datasets and to remain flexible in terms of the frames of reference used, whether this is the target language or some other hypothesis of interlanguage development.

Appendix 1 Elicitation tasks

Picture Story: In this task, learners had to tell a story on the basis of a series of pictures. The purpose of this task is to elicit a narrative that enabled us to study sentence structure, verbal morphology, pronominal reference, gender and embedding, as well as narrative discourse features.

Interrogative elicitation task: This task is an information gap activity in which the learners had to find out from the researcher missing information regarding the appearance, location and actions of people on a picture.

One-to-one interview with photos: a directed conversation in which the learner had to ask questions related to a set of photos and also respond to questions. This task was intended to elicit all the structures investigated, with a particular focus on past tense and future verbal morphology, as well as interactive discourse features.

Negative elicitation task: The learner had to describe a famous person by saying what they do and don't do, and the researcher guessed the mystery person.

Appendix 2 Selection of CHAT symbols

xxx	unintelligible speech, not a word
()	non completion of a word
xx	unintelligible speech, treated as a word
0word	word omitted
[?]	best guess
+	compound word
[*]	error on main line
=	'target' on error tier
[//	repeated material
+/. +,	interrupted single utterance
[%eng:]	L1 material excluded from analyses
#	pause

Notes

1   The research project 'Progression in Foreign Language Learning' was directed by Rosamond Mitchell and Peter Dickson and funded by the Economic and Social Research Council (Award no R000234754). For further details of this project see http://www.regard.ac.uk. The data is currently being converted to CHILDES format in an ongoing project directed by Rosamond Mitchell and Florence Myles (ESRC Award no R000220070).

2   In any case, the benefits of XML are now available to users of CHILDES tools as an XML converter has been developed (MacWhinney, info-childes discussion forum 23 October 2002). The database is now available in XML format see http://xml.talkbank.org.

3   For a useful introduction to CHILDES see MacWhinney (1999) and http://childes.psy.cmu.edu/.

4   The CHILDES research group offer free digitisation of data that will be offered to TALKBANK. For this project the digital recordings were stored as wav files. This is necessary in order to use Soundscriber software, described later, and it is also becoming the standard format adopted by those using CHILDES tools.

5   Some CLAN commands can be used with transcriptions that are not in strict CHAT format by simply typing +y next to the normal command so the program would consider each line as one tier. +y1 would consider utterances as delimited by full stops, question marks, and exclamation marks.

6   One CLAN command can take out all codes and tiers, leaving a 'friendly' transcript, useful for eyeballing and presentations.

7   Cantonese, Danish, Dutch, English, French, German, Hungarian, Italian, Japanese and Spanish.

8   Christophe Parisse's advice during the project is gratefully acknowledged, as is Brian MacWhinney's.

9   The extract is from a Year 10 pupil, after about 280 hours of learning French (four years of lessons, two hours per week), doing the picture-story narration task.

10 Though the ESF data is now available from Talkbank.

11 This was due to the fact that, whilst constructing the computer searches, we could not predict the wide variety of interlanguage forms being used to express negation. In addition, a small number of strings in the MOR tier were (inexplicably) undetected by the COMBO commands.

References

Ellis, N. (1999) Cognitive approaches to SLA. *Annual Review of Applied Linguistics*, 19: 22-42.

Eubank, L. and Earley, K. (1992): Access to L2 data: the CHILDES archive. *Studies in Second Language Acquisition*, 14: 451-2.

Granger, S. (1998) (ed.) *Learner English on Computer*. London: Addison Wesley Longman.

Granger, S. (2002) *Les français des apprenants.* Paper presented at AFLS conference, Les Français du Corpus at the University of West England, 16 Feb 2002.

Housen, A. (2002) A corpus-based study of the L2-acquisition of the English verb system. In S. Granger, J. Hung and S. Petch-Tyson (eds) *Computer Learner Corpora, Second Language Acquisition and Foreign Language Learning.* Amsterdam: John Benjamins. pp. 77-116.

Hunston, S. and Francis, G. (1998) Verbs Observed: A Corpus-Driven Pedagogic Grammar. *Applied Linguistics*, 19, 1: 45-72.

Jagtman, M. and Bongaerts, T. (1994) Report – COMOLA: a computer system for the analysis of interlanguage data, *Second Language Research*, 10,1: 49-83.

Long, S. (2001), 'About Time: A Comparison of Computerized and Manual Procedures for Gramatical and Phonological Analysis'. *Clinical Linguistics and Phonetics*, 15, 5: 399-426.

Long, S. and Channell, R. (2001) 'Accuracy of four language analysis procedures performed automatically'. *American Journal of Speech-Language Pathology.* 10, 2: 180-8.

MacWhinney, B. (1999) The CHILDES System. In *Handbook of Child Language Acquisition.* Academic Press. pp. 457-494.

MacWhinney, B. (2000) *The CHILDES project: tools for analyzing talk. Volume 1: Transcription format and programs. Volume 2: The database.* 3rd ed. New Jersey: Lawrence Erlbaum.

MacWhinney, B. (2002) http://cnts.uia.ac.be/childes/

Malvern, D. and Richards, B. (2002) Investigating accommodation in language proficiency interviews using a new measure of lexical diversity. *Language Testing*, 19, 1: 85-104.

Mitchell, R. and Dickson, P. (1997) Progression in Foreign Language Learning, *Centre for Language in Education Occasional Paper* No.45. University of Southampton.

Myles, F., Mitchell, R., and Hooper, J. (1999) Interrogative chunks in French L2: A basis for creative construction? *Studies in Second Language Acquisition*, 21: 49-80.

Oshita, H. (2000) What is happened may not be what appears to be happening: a corpus study of 'passive' unaccusatives in L2 English. *Second Language Research*, 16: 293-324.

Paradis, J., Le Corre, M., and Genesee, F. (1998) The emergence of tense and agreement in child L2 French. *Second Language Research*, 14, 3: 227-57.

Pienemann, M. (1992) COALA-A Computational System for Interlanguage Analysis. *Second Language Research*, 8, 1: 59-92

Rule, S. and Marsden, E. (2002) *Expression of negation in French L2 classroom learners*. Paper presented at the BAAL / CUP seminar 'Linguistic Development of French' at the University of Southampton, July 2002.

Rule, S., Marsden, E. and Myles, F. (2002) *The acquisition of negatives in the French L2 classroom*. Paper presented at Eurosla, Basel, Switzerland, September 2002.

Rutherford, W. and Thomas, M. (2001) The Child Language Data Exchange System in research on second language acquisition. *Second Language Research*, 17, 2: 195-212.

Sokolov, J. and Snow, C. (1994) (eds) *Handbook of Research in Language Development using CHILDES*. New Jersey: Lawrence Erlbaum.

Stubbs, M. (1996) *Text and Corpus Analysis*. Oxford: Blackwell.

Thomas, J. and Short, M. (1996) (eds) *Using Corpora for Language Research*. London: Longman.

8 Rationales for foreign language education in the 21st century[1]

Rosamond Mitchell

University of Southampton

Abstract

This paper reviews a range of traditional rationales which have underpinned foreign language education in mainstream schooling. The recent influence of these different rationales in FL education within the UK context is examined, together with what is known about their relative effectiveness in motivating language learners. It is argued that UK discourses have been dominated disproportionately by instrumental rationales, which are less than appropriate against a 'global English' background, and have largely failed with UK learners. The potential value of alternative rationales for UK FL education is reassessed, especially in light of 21st century educational preoccupations with globalisation, citizenship and values education.

Introduction

The year 2002 was a significant one for foreign language education in England. After a 20 year trend to raise the profile of modern foreign languages (MFLs) in education, and increase in both the proportion of learners studying languages and the length of time for which they are studied, a significant policy shift took place. The Green Paper published for consultation in Spring 2002 by the Department for Education and Skills (DfES) proposed cutting back the five-year compulsory MFLs element within the National Curriculum, by making language study optional from age 14 rather than from age 16 (DfES, 2002). This was a major setback for those who have argued for 'languages for all', not least the members of the Nuffield Languages Inquiry (NLI, 2000) for example, who have argued for compulsory language study to age 18, at least for university entrants.

This paper reviews some of the reasons for the apparent failure of language specialists to convince the broader society about the desirability of 'languages for all'. In particular, it examines and critiques the rationales which have been advanced in support of FL study in an English–L1 setting. This critique is partly a priori, examining the coherence, consistency and relevance of the rationales proposed and the extent to which they are actually implemented. Where possible it also draws on empirical evidence about the actual impact of these rationales and related programmes. The paper then makes some alternative proposals to secure the future of FL education in the unique circumstances of English–L1 societies in an age of global English.

General rationales for FL education

Given the current world role of English, what underlying rationales survive for the continuance of FL education in English-dominant societies? Why is it not sufficient to accept an accidental communication advantage, and let others do the language learning? And more particularly: What is the rationale which has supported the development of a 'languages for all' philosophy in English education, over the last 30 or so years, and do the arguments advanced have continuing currency for the 21st century?

Looking historically at the development of languages as an academic/school curriculum subject, a range of rationales for FL education can be distinguished, which have been valued at different times and places:

1   Languages as vehicles of 'high' culture, philosophy, literature etc. (mimicking the 19th century role of the classics in middle class education);

2   Languages as intellectual/ cognitive discipline, developing 'language awareness' (in alliance with mother tongue teaching), and/or developing 'learning strategies' (for effective later learning of whatever other languages may be needed);

3   Languages as tools of practical communication, for instrumental and vocational purposes (from leisure and tourist travel, to international

business, administration, diplomacy, higher study);

4   Languages as a means for personal self-development, self-expression, creativity, and identity formation;

5   Languages as tools for exploring alternative contemporary cultures, developing intercultural communication and international understanding;

6   Languages as tools for political projects such as European integration.

(More extended discussion of these rationales and exemplification can be found in Mitchell, 2002a.)

At different times a selection of these rationales have been offered more or less explicitly for FL education in English-speaking contexts. In UK debates, it has always been recognised that a certain number of language specialists would be needed for instrumental reasons such as trade or diplomacy (Rationale no. 3). Additionally, since the late 19th century languages had taken their place in the curriculum of the grammar school elite, grounded in Rationale no. 1 (and perhaps no. 2: see e.g. Clark, 1988; Howatt, 1984 for historical accounts). However, the concept of 'languages for all' first really came on the agenda in England in the 1960s and 1970s, partly as a byproduct of wider school reform. (See Hawkins, ed. 1996 for detailed accounts of this period and subsequent developments.) The comprehensivisation movement sought to extend much of the grammar school curriculum to a wider public, and language educators were confronted with a 'democratisation' challenge, to which they rose with considerable enthusiasm. (In the 1960s it must be noted, Rationale no. 6 was also operative, as these events coincided with prolonged UK efforts to join the European Community.)

A strong advocate of the 'languages for all' movement, Eric Hawkins of the University of York, produced the major theoretical work underpinning these developments (1981). In his writings however, Hawkins did not advance an instrumental 'skills' rationale as the most central reason for the promotion of FL education in a British context. Committed to a postwar vision of education as key to individual liberation and the achievement of wider democracy, he was in no doubt about the rationale which applied most centrally for FL education:

The educational value of foreign language learning is precisely that it can offer the pupil an experience different from that of the mother tongue and so contribute to an understanding of the polyglot world, and emancipate the learner from parochialism. (Hawkins, 1981: 32).

This clear expression of what is here called Rationale no. 5 is complemented elsewhere in Hawkins' writings by sustained advocacy of Rationale no. 2 (an interdisciplinary strategy which would link FL and mother tongue education, developing comparative and analytic perspectives on the nature of language, or 'language awareness' as it came to be called).

However despite these ambitious rationales, the first 1970s phase of 'languages for all' extending FL education to the full range of pupils in the comprehensive school was somewhat problematic (see the frank account given in Hawkins, 1981: Chapter 1, and e.g. the school inspectors' report which identified a range of adaptation problems: HMI, 1983). A first solution was found in the 'Graded Objectives' movement (see Page, 1996), a grassroots collection of some dozens of local schemes based in local education authorities (LEAs) which introduced defined FL syllabuses, graded tests and certificates to boost learners' sense of achievement. In their most developed form, these schemes connected with the new international movement for communicative language teaching, and with the Europe-wide Council of Europe project promoting functional syllabuses and a range of student centred pedagogies (e.g. Clark, 1988, whose Lothian project was perhaps the most striking example in UK FLs curriculum development of a commitment to a progressivist rationale of type no. 4). Other local schemes however found security in a reduced syllabus, and the rote learning of fixed dialogues, reflecting an instrumental rationale of tourist communication.

Out of this mixed scene there emerged in 1988 the new unified national examination for learners aged 16-plus, the General Certificate of Secondary Education (GCSE). This examination replaced the former Ordinary Level of the General Certificate of Education (GCE O Level) which targeted grammar schools and the more 'academic' learners, and the former Certificate of Secondary Education (CSE), which targeted secondary modern pupils. The GCSE examination has subsequently dominated the MFLs curriculum in the middle years of comprehensive secondary education. While different examination boards reflected more or less ambitious and creative interpretations of the FL curriculum at GCSE level, there was a strong strand of 'relevance'/instrumentality across all programmes, some cultural content but little serious sign of cultural analysis or critique, and a general neglect of the 'language awareness' agenda.

Rationales underpinning the National Curriculum for Modern Foreign Languages

With the 1990s came the great centralising shift in UK curriculum planning, with the introduction of a National Curriculum for all subjects, including MFLs. Structurally this reflected a great advance for the 'languages for all' movement, because for the first time a foreign language was to be a required 'foundation' subject for all five years of compulsory secondary education (ages 11-16). With hindsight however this curriculum had to be written at an awkward moment, while the FL teaching profession was still adjusting its expectations and skills to teaching the entire age cohort, after a bumpy start in the 1970s, and relatively limited time using the Graded Objectives approach. There was controversy over the standard which could reasonably be aimed for and the targets which could reasonably be set, as is apparent from comparison of early draft versions of the National Curriculum for MFLs with the final version (NCMFLWP, 1990; DES/WO, 1990, 1991).

The first official National Curriculum for MFLs (DES/WO, 1991) did not provide its own rationale statement, but instead quoted one deriving from the original Working Party document (1990). This eight point list covers the full range of possible rationales identified above:

> To develop the ability to use the language effectively for purposes of practical communication;

> To form a sound base of the skills, language and attitudes required for further study, work and leisure;

> To offer insights into the culture and civilisation of the countries where the language is spoken;

> To develop an awareness of the nature of language and language learning;

> To provide enjoyment and intellectual stimulation;

> To encourage positive attitudes to FL learning and to speakers of

foreign languages and a sympathetic approach to other cultures and civilisations;

To promote learning skills of more general application (e.g. analysis, memorising, drawing of inferences);

To develop pupils' understanding of themselves and their own culture.

(DES/WO, 1991)

However the Attainment Targets set out for measuring learners' progress, christened 'Listening', 'Speaking', 'Reading' and 'Writing', related only to the first item on this list. So, as with many of the Graded Objectives schemes, it seemed that the only component of FL education which would be valued in summative assessment, and for which teachers would be held more and more closely accountable, was an instrumental one ('practical communication').

The second version of the National Curriculum for MFLs (DfE/WO, 1995) rather curiously omitted to include any rationale for FL study at all. The latest version (1999) has reinstated a rationale in the following terms:

> Through the study of a foreign language, pupils understand and appreciate different countries, cultures, people and communities – and as they do so, begin to think of themselves as citizens of the world as well as of the UK. Pupils also learn about the basic structures of language. They explore the similarities and differences between the foreign language they are learning and English or another language, and learn how language can be manipulated and applied in different ways. Their listening, reading and memory skills improve, and their speaking and writing become more accurate. The development of these skills, together with pupils' knowledge and understanding of the structure of language, lay the foundations for future study of other languages. (DfEE/QCA, 1999).

This version refers clearly to 'international citizen' and 'language awareness' Rationales, as well as to 'learning how to learn', and preparing to be a more efficient language learner in the future. Elsewhere in the 1999 document there is reference to the contribution of FL study to pupils' spiritual moral, social and cultural development (a 'personal development' rationale?), and to the contribution of FLs to key skills and thinking skills. However, the all-important Attainment Targets are little changed, retaining their continuing focus on 'practical communication' alone. The overall assessment principles presented on the National Curriculum website (http://www.nc.uk.net) reflect this focus:

> During Key Stage 3 [age 11-14] pupils begin to understand, speak, read and write at least one modern foreign language. They become familiar with the sounds, written form and grammar of the language, and use this knowledge with increasing confidence and competence to express themselves in role plays, conversations and writing. They improve their understanding of the language by listening to people talking about different subjects and by reading a range of texts. They also increase their cultural awareness by communicating with people who speak the language and by using materials from countries and communities where the language is spoken.

> During Key Stage 4 [age 14-16] pupils begin to use a modern foreign language more independently, drawing on a firmer grasp of grammar and a wider and more complex range of expression. They adapt their use of the language according to context, purpose and audience. They learn to understand a more extensive range of unfamiliar language by reading and listening to a variety of materials from countries and communities where the language is spoken. They also increase their cultural awareness through more direct contact with people who live in those countries and communities.

While the final sentences in these two paragraphs reflect concerns with cultural awareness, these are not reflected in the actual assessment procedures, which focus exclusively on the skills of listening, speaking, reading and writing. The practical effect, once assessment 'backwash' is taken into account, is that classroom procedures generally focus on the development of practical language skills. Thus, MFLs education as currently implemented in schools seems to be driven primarily by a quite narrowly instrumental rationale. (See e.g. Mitchell and Martin, 1997 for an observational study of classroom practices centring on 'delivery' of National Curriculum requirements at Key Stage 3.)

The impact of 'languages for all' on participation and student learning

What has been the impact of more inclusive MFLs education policies on participation and achievement among school age learners? In 1977, just one child in 10 in England and Wales achieved a GCE O Level pass or CSE Grade 1 in a foreign language (HMI, 1977, cited in Hawkins, 1981: 17). By 2001, according to current DfES statistics, one child in four achieved a GCSE pass at Grade C or above, in a foreign language. Table 1 shows broad trends in examination entries over the last 30 years, with language entries keeping pace comfortably with a general expansion in entries.

Table 2 provides a closer look at the last six years, and shows basically a steady state for the largest languages, with a large drop in German for 2002, but a continuing slight rise for Spanish and for Welsh L2.

Overall therefore it seems that considerable progress was made during the 1990s, in bringing more students than ever before at least to the level of GCSE. However, Table 2 shows that the 'peak' GCSE entries for most languages occurred sometime in the mid 1990s, contrary to expectations that the National Curriculum commitment should be driving a continuous increase in numbers. Moreover the statistics for languages at GCE A level,

Table 1 Selected GCE, CSE and GCSE exam entries, 1965-95

Subject	1965 GCE and CSE	1975 GCE and CSE	1985 GCE and CSE	1995 GCSE
English	390,175	865,065	185,809	648,987
French	171,996	265,440	310,983	350,027
German	33,723	62,383	74,471	129,386
Spanish	10,011	16,375	17,769	40,762
Other FLs	10,118	17,136	12,665	27,049
All FLs	225,848	361,334	415,888	547,224
Total subject entries	2,400,996	4,946,761	6,297,781	5,431,625

Source: Hawkins (ed.) 1997

Table 2 GCSE entries 1996-2002, six popular languages (peak years underlined)

Year	French	German	Spanish	Welsh L2	Urdu	Italian
1996	353,570	136,433	43,754	7,859	7,328	5,763
1997	337,993	135,466	44,703	7,438	7,222	6,011
1998	341,169	135,717	48,364	8,132	6,779	5,681
1999	335,816	135,158	47,969	7,877	6,348	5,313
2000	341,011	133,662	49,981	9,166	6,723	5,625
2001	347,007	135,133	54,236	11,623	6,423	5,506
2002	338,468	126,216	57,983	11,719	?	?

Sources: CILT 2002, www.tes.co.uk

which reflect the study choices of students aged 18+ once they are free to follow an all-optional programme, cast a much more clearly negative light on the impact of languages for all.

Table 3 shows recent trends in A level entries in the most popular languages, which reflect significant declines, with French dropping by 50 per cent since its peak year, and German by 30 per cent. Among the 'smaller' languages, only Spanish and Chinese seem stable at this level.

Similar trends are apparent in Scotland, where numbers taking languages in the Higher examination (taken at age 17+) have fallen significantly in the last 25 years both absolutely and proportionally (see McPake et al., 1999).

Student motivation for language learning and attitudes towards current FL education programmes

So what has gone wrong with 'languages for all'? In this section we consider the attitudes of UK classroom learners, towards current FL programmes. Learner attitudes have been quite well studied in the United Kingdom (e.g. Lee et al., 1998; McPake et al., 1999; Chambers, 1999). In general, Year 7 learners [aged 11–12] begin their FL study with a positive disposition to a new subject. However motivation declines over the next couple of years

Table 3 A level entries 1990-2002, six popular languages (peak years underlined)

Year	French	German	Spanish	Chinese	Italian	Urdu
1990	27,245	9,476	3,832	?	722	503
1991	30,794	10,583	4,230	?	846	581
1992	<u>31,261</u>	10,338	4,720	?	876	726
1993	29,862	<u>10,857</u>	4,850	?	840	761
1994	28,942	10,832	4,740	?	802	808
1995	27,563	10,634	4,837	?	913	895
1996	27,728	10,810	5,331	1,179	<u>1,021</u>	1,080
1997	26,488	10,708	5,748	1,093	1,017	<u>1,184</u>
1998	23,625	10,189	5,649	1,235	922	675
1999	21,072	9,551	<u>5,782</u>	1,285	858	637
2000	18,228	8,694	5,636	1,359	908	742
2001	17,939	8,466	5,530	<u>1,375</u>	869	485
2002	15,614	7,013	5,572	?	?	?

Source: CILT 2001, 2002, www.tes.co.uk.

(Chambers, 1999), and the subject is commonly rated relatively unfavourably compared with others (Chambers, 1999: Rawlinson, 2001). Learners have internalised a weak instrumental rationale for FL learning, so that FLs are seen as somehow connected with eventual jobs and employment chances, probably unrealistically so (Lee et al., 1998). However, UK learners see themselves as less likely to travel and/or have international contacts than their peers in mainland Europe (Chambers, 1999). Upper secondary students comment that curriculum content during the compulsory phase is narrow, and too centred on mundane everyday life (McPake et al., 1999). At all levels students express lack of confidence about their own attainment.

It may be argued that lessons for beginners must focus on practical communicative skills, before more varied content can be addressed at a level challenging enough to sustain the interest of sophisticated adolescents. This is debatable, but even if true, it puts a premium on programme designers and teachers to ensure that students progress through those elementary stages as rapidly as possible, while starting enthusiasm is still in place. Worryingly however, the 'invisible' London children interviewed by Lee and others also were not able to articulate ways in which their FL skills were developing or to perceive any increasing linguistic challenge in the programme they were following (Lee et al., 1998). All they had noted was a rotation of topics (hobbies, travel and transport, shopping…).

These surveys suggest that the present skills-focussed National Curriculum for MFLs with its relatively lightweight content is not proving successful in capturing and holding the interests of young people. In itself, this is not a uniquely British problem. Surveys in other countries also show that young people engaged in the process of learning English as a foreign language may find aspects of their school language programmes boring and demotivating. (See e.g. Chambers, 1999 on young EFL learners in Germany, or Park, 2002 on EFL learners in Korea.) However in these EFL settings, the students' dissatisfaction with the actuality of day to day classroom experiences is countered by their awareness of strong instrumental (and to some degree cultural) reasons for pressing on with FL study. FL education programmes in English-dominant society cannot benefit from this type of strategic contextual support, or the social consensus among parents, employers etc. which reinforces it. UK learners can switch off and drop out in ways that learners of EFL cannot, without obvious immediate penalties in terms of their life chances. Other education systems may therefore get away with less than ideal curricula, poor quality pedagogy, and over powerful assessment backwash, without losing their market. In an English speaking environment, every aspect of provision has to be excellent if the interest and achievement of the general population is to be maximised, and also if enough young people are to be enthused for the advanced study of languages, and to become specialist linguists of the future.

Very good advice is available for language teachers on how to maximise the positive motivation of classroom learners (e.g. Dorynei, 2001a, 2001b). Classroom action research drawing on some of Dornyei's ideas has proved successful in improving learner motivation, at least in the short term (Ashley, 2001; Rawlinson, 2001). However, to maximise student motivation and achievement in the longer term, while retaining a commitment to 'languages for all', it is argued below that more fundamental curriculum change is needed.

Directions for a new National Curriculum for MFLs

Vocationalism for all? It has been argued in earlier sections in this paper, that since the inception of the National Curriculum, there has been an ongoing failure to articulate a clear and focussed educational rationale for 'languages for all', in a society where global English is dominant, and to ensure that this connects both with the content of the MFLs curriculum and with our pedagogic practices and students' day to day learning experience. The rationale which has been articulated is over-general, not to say vague, and is not actually reflected in MFLs course books, Attainment Targets, GCSE syllabuses, or teaching and assessment practices. Instead these have drifted to an implicitly instrumental, skills-training programme, linked to supposedly 'relevant' content (the 'Programmes of Study') which might prepare learners appropriately for a tourist trip to Europe but which in practice offers little cognitive, aesthetic or social challenge to English speaking young people, as seen in the foregoing section.

It has been argued seriously by some, not least the members of the Nuffield Inquiry into the state of language learning in the UK, that this instrumental rationale for languages should be embraced and argued for much more consistently in UK education (NLI, 2000). This would logically imply curriculum content which moved beyond an agenda which targets the leisure-and-tourism needs of the individual language learner, to become more explicitly vocational (e.g. equipping the learner for work in the tourism industry, rather than for tourist consumption). In an age of global English, however, this appears a high risk and perhaps double-edged educational strategy. If the prime reason for language learning is a vocational one, then if language specialists fail to convince the wider society that languages are very regularly needed for trade, business etc. etc., little remains of the 'languages for all' argument, and language learning reverts to meeting the needs of a specialist minority.

The educational alternative: intercultural understanding and personal development
It is argued here that even in a world of global English, there is a continuing educational rationale for foreign language learning for all. However it is not

primarily an instrumental rationale – it is accepted that the number of UK citizens who will need high levels of FL knowledge for work and study in the near future will be a specialist minority.

The primary rationale remains that articulated by Hawkins 20 years ago, and re-stated recently by e.g. the Scottish Ministerial Action Group on Languages (2000) – a humanistic rationale, a combination of numbers 4 and 5 on the list presented in Section 2, which argues that language learning is a key to better understanding of ourselves and others in an increasingly globalised and integrated world. Intercultural understanding has to be two-way, and language learning is a central process in developing this understanding. Thus, the experience of learning the first foreign language has to be sufficiently sustained to give a genuine experience of what it means to control a different language system, and to try to express personal meanings through that system. To fulfil rationales 4 and 5 together, learners do need a) to learn something of language X, and experience what it means to use it for intercultural communication purposes, b) to acquire some substantive knowledge of culture X, and reflect on similarities and differences with the 'home' culture; and c) through these specific experiences in relation to language X, to develop a more generalised and explicit understanding about processes of both language learning and intercultural development.

The prime content: culture/citizenship/values/globalisation Our decisions about why we are teaching languages should guide closely what content we choose to talk about in language lessons, as well as the teaching methods that we use. The current agenda of leisure and tourism is hard to justify in educational terms, and by itself offers little cognitive or social challenge. The logic of adopting an 'intercultural' rationale for FL learning leads to subject content which is geared towards developing some substantive 'insider' understanding of one or more non-British cultures, and more generally, learning how to relate to cultural variation as it evolves in an increasingly integrated and globalising world. Some MFL educators have argued this perspective consistently and have developed procedures for 'ethnographic' cultural studies which are highly apposite (e.g. Morgan and Cain, 2000). There is an obvious synergy with the new subject of 'Citizenship', recently bolted on to the National Curriculum in recognition of historic neglect within the evolution of the NC of a range of issues to do with values, identity and social responsibility. Figure 1 shows some of the core content proposed for

'Citizenship'; an MFLs curriculum focused on the development of intercultural understanding could map closely onto this list and provide a distinctive perspective on its central themes.

Pedagogy, language learning and assessment issues[2]

All the foregoing has clear implications for a revised approach to language pedagogy, which cannot be argued in detail here, but implies all/most of the following:

1 Put 'learning how to learn', and the creation of reflective and autonomous learners who are in control of their own developing language system, at the heart of MFLs classroom activity (see e.g. Grenfell and Harris, 1999; Harris, 2001; Garrett and James, 2000);

2 Reinstate creativity, imagination and risk-taking in the MFLs classroom, e.g. through literature, media, drama, ICT (see e.g. Harris et al., 2000);

3 Promote a stronger cognitive challenge for MFLs learners, through a task based approach to learning and teaching, where the target language is used to explore substantive curriculum themes (e.g. citizenship and cultural themes);

4 Develop an explicit grammar spine for the FL curriculum, in line with research evidence on 'naturalistic' learner progression/ routes of learning, plus an inclusive and accessible pedagogy which promotes grammar control (see e.g. Mitchell, 2000);

5 Renovate the teaching of MFLs reading and writing, and the development of pupils' knowledge about language, through systematic links with the National Literacy Strategy;

6 Promote direct links and experiences of the target FL culture and its people, not only through traditional visits, school exchanges, FLA and pen pal schemes, but now also through exploration and integration of FL Internet resources, email, text messaging and videoconferencing (see e.g. Hood, 2000).

To support these redefined aims and learning and teaching processes, change will be needed to the measurement and reporting of learners' success.

Figure 1 Overview of National Curriculum: 'Citizenship'

---

1 Knowledge and understanding about becoming informed citizens

Pupils should be taught about:

a) the legal and human rights and responsibilities underpinning society, basic aspects of the criminal justice system, and how both relate to young people

b) the diversity of national, regional, religious and ethnic identities in the United Kingdom and the need for mutual respect and understanding

c) central and local government, the public services they offer and how they are financed, and the opportunities to contribute

d) the key characteristics of parliamentary and other forms of government

e) the electoral system and the importance of voting

f) the work of community-based, national and international voluntary groups

g) the importance of resolving conflict fairly

h) the significance of the media in society

i) the world as a global community, and the political, economic, environmental and social implications of this, and the role of the European Union, the Commonwealth and the United Nations.

2 Developing skills of enquiry and communication

Pupils should be taught to:

a) think about topical political, spiritual, moral, social and cultural issues, problems and events by analysing information and its sources, including ICT-based sources

b) justify orally and in writing a personal opinion about such issues, problems or events

c) contribute to group and exploratory class discussions, and take part in debates.

3 Developing skills of participation and responsible action

Pupils should be taught to:

a) use their imagination to consider other people's experiences and be able to think about, express and explain views that are not their own

b) negotiate, decide and take part responsibly in both school and community-based activities

c) reflect on the process of participating.

Related initiatives in the area of assessment could include commitments to:

1   Re-balance MFLs assessment, so that accuracy ceases to dominate the assessment of language skills, and ambition, risk-taking and complexity are appropriately rewarded;

2   Include assessment of wider aspects of the MFLs curriculum, e.g. content knowledge, strategic ability etc., as well as language skill;

3   Link up MFLs assessment with European standards and models (Council of Europe, 2001).

Conclusion

Alongside the Green paper proposals, a range of other initiatives is already being undertaken with the object of renewing and strengthening foreign language education. This includes the promotion of specialist Language Colleges, increased support for foreign language provision in primary schools, and now the piloting of a new Key Stage 3 Strategy for Modern Foreign Languages, modelled on the National Literacy Strategy (DfEE, 1998). After 10 years of centralisation, these initiatives are welcome, and Language Colleges in particular are a zone where alternative models of FL education will hopefully have space and resources to develop. But before we can sort out what to do, far less discover 'what works', we need to clarify why we are doing it, and achieve some social consensus around a renewed rationale for FL education. In this activity, applied linguists surely must play a key role.

Notes

1   This paper was presented at BAAL Annual Meeting 2002, as part of the colloquium 'New Directions for a National Curriculum in Modern Foreign Languages?' Versions of the ideas advanced in this paper have been presented previously in Mitchell 2002a, b.

2   These ideas draw on discussions at a symposium organised at BERA 2001 titled Towards Research Strategy for Teaching and Learning in Modern Foreign Languages.

References

Ashley, S. (2001) *Raising Achievement and Motivation at Key Stage 3 in Modern Foreign Languages, Particularly that of Boys*. Level 1 Report, Best Practice Research Scholarship scheme.

Centre for Information on Language Teaching and Research (2001) *CILT Direct 2001 Languages Yearbook*. London: CILT.

Centre for Information on Language Teaching and Research (2002) *CILT Direct 2002*

Languages Yearbook. London: CILT.

Chambers, G. (1999) *Motivating Language Learners*. Clevedon, Avon: Multilingual Matters.

Clark, J. L. (1988) *Curriculum Renewal in School Foreign Language Learning*. Oxford: Oxford University Press.

Council of Europe (2001) *Common European Framework of Reference for Languages: Learning, teaching, assessment*. Cambridge: Cambridge University Press.

Department of Education and Science/ Welsh Office (1990) *Modern Foreign Languages for Ages 11 to 16: Proposals of the Secretary of State for Education and Science and the Secretary of State for Wales*. London: HMSO.

Department of Education and Science/ Welsh Office (1991) *Modern Foreign Languages in the National Curriculum*. London: HMSO.

Department for Education/ Welsh Office (1995) *Modern Foreign Languages in the National Curriculum*. London: HMSO.

Department for Education and Employment (1998) *The National Literacy Strategy*. London: DfEE.

Department for Education and Employment/Qualifications and Curriculum Authority (1999) *Modern Foreign Languages: The National Curriculum for England*. London: The Stationery Office. (Also available at http:www.nc.uk.net).

Department for Education and Skills (2002) *14-19: Extending Opportunities, Raising Standards*. http://www.dfes.gov.uk/consultations/

Dornyei, Z. (2001a) *Teaching and Researching Motivation*. Harlow: Longman.

Dornyei, Z. (2001b) *Motivational Strategies in the Language Classroom*. Cambridge: Cambridge University Press.

Garrett, P. and James, C. (2000) Language awareness. In M. Byram (ed.) Routledge *Encyclopedia of Language Teaching and Learning*. London: Routledge. pp. 330-3.

Grenfell, M. and Harris, V. (1999) *Modern Languages and Learning Strategies: In theory and practice*. London: Routledge.

Harris, V. (2001) *Helping Learners Learn: Exploring strategy instruction in language classrooms across Europe*. Graz: European Centre for Modern Languages.

Harris, V., Burch, J., Jones, B., and Darcy, J. (2000) *Something to Say? Promoting spontaneous classroom talk*. London: Centre for Information on Language Teaching and Research.

Hawkins, E. (1981) *Modern Languages in The Curriculum*. Cambridge: Cambridge University Press.

Hawkins, E. (1996) (ed.) *Thirty Years of Language Teaching*. London: CILT.

Howatt, A. P. R. (1984) *A History of English Language Teaching*. Oxford: Oxford University Press.

Lee, J. et al. (1998) *The Invisible Child*. London: CILT.

McPake, J. et al. (1999) *Foreign Languages in the Upper Secondary School: A study of the causes of decline*. SCRE Research Report No 91. Edinburgh: Scottish Council for Research in Education.

Ministerial Action Group on Languages (2000) *Citizens of a Multilingual World: Key issues*. Scottish Executive.

Mitchell, R. (2000) Applied linguistics and evidence-based classroom practice: The case of foreign language grammar pedagogy. *Applied Linguistics*, 21, 3: 281-303.

Mitchell, R. (2002a) *Learners, values and FL education in the 21st century*. Plenary paper delivered at the Korean Association of English Teachers international Conference, Busan, July 2002.

Mitchell, R. (2002b) Foreign language education in an age of global English. *Centre for Language in Education Occasional Paper 57*. Southampton: University of Southampton.

Mitchell, R. and Martin, C. (1997) Rote learning, creativity and understanding in the foreign language classroom. *Language Teaching Research*, 1, 1: 1-27.

Morgan, C. and Cain, A. (2000) *Foreign Language and Culture Learning from a Dialogic Perspective.* Clevedon: Multilingual Matters.

National Curriculum Modern Foreign Languages Working Group (1990) Initial Advice. London: DES/WO.

Nuffield Languages Inquiry (2000) *Languages: The next generation.* London: The Nuffield Foundation.

Page, B. (1996) Graded Objectives in ML (GOML). In E. Hawkins (ed.) *Thirty Years of Language Teaching.* London: CILT. pp. 99-105.

Park, J.K. (2002) *Seventh graders' perceptions of learning English in elementary schools.* Paper delivered at the Korean Association of English Teachers International Conference, Busan, July 2002.

Rawlinson, V. (2001) *Boys, MFL and Motivation.* Level 3 Report, Best Practice Research Scholarship scheme.

9 Applied linguistics applied

Celia Roberts

King's College London

Abstract

This paper will look at issues of practical relevance for the applied linguist. It will look, in a reflexive way, at some of the theoretical, methodological, practical and (re)presentational concerns that we have in applying insights to real world problems. The majority of such applications relate to education, but I will focus on discourse studies which are concerned with health and with the relationship that applied linguists have with health professionals, who come from rather different epistemological traditions. I shall argue that we have a long way to travel if we are to be convincing and have an influence on a range of different institutions. If applied linguistics research is to be practically relevant and to have some kind of intervention status, then the design and implementation of the research needs to be negotiated from the start with those who may be affected by it. And since with discourse-based research the insights are in the analytic writing rather than in results which can be implemented, how applied linguists and health professionals can present and write together is also an issue. Applied linguistics is a social linguistics but it is a social linguistics which is put to practical use. It is not easy to work out what difference our research has made to those outside our world, but at least we should be asking ourselves the question and contemplating the conditions which might produce a satisfying answer for both the professional groups we work with and ourselves.

Introduction: focus on the applied in Applied Linguistics in a reflexive way

As the title implies, there is something about the applied in Applied Linguistics (AL) that concerns me. I do not intend to spend much time on the 'What is AL?' debate. This has been part of on-going discussions at AILA congresses and BAAL meetings over the last 20 or even 30 years and the subject of several journal editions (Brumfit, 1991; Mauranen and Sajavaara, 1997; Rampton, 1997). There is a reasonable consensus that AL is about 'real world' problems:

> The theoretical and empirical investigation of real-world problems in
> which language is a central issue. (Brumfit, 1991:46)

and, perhaps with somewhat less enthusiasm, that this means more than
applying language and discourse to real world settings. Other fields, and
Conversation Analysis (CA) is a good example, explicitly reject practical
relevance and see 'applied' as meaning application to different settings only.
For example, Perakyla (1995) states that CA is not primarily motivated to
solve professionals' problems. We can, of course, argue about the degree to
which AL should relate to real world problems. There is a rough continuum
from the most indirect and hypothetical to the most direct and actual: AL
should:

> Address (in the sense of apply oneself to) social problems;
> Be practically relevant;
> Contribute to solving social problems;
> Directly solve them.

And I would not want to be prescriptive about where, on the continuum,
individuals might place themselves. But it seems to me that we cannot really
do any of them, particularly the last two, without forging long-term
relationships across professional boundaries.

In this paper, I want to do three things. The first is to make a call to arms,
bringing practical relevance and problem solving to the centre of our work.
The second is to consider how, in particular, qualitative AL research can
contribute to solving real world problems in institutional settings e.g. medical
settings. And, finally, be more reflexive about how we do this so that we can
understand better both what our contribution could or should be and the
nature of our own discourses within our specialist paradigms.

I want to illustrate how AL knowledge is the product of both our
engagement with practical real world problems and our reflexive
understanding of this engagement.

The 14 responses to an email to BAAL members sent out in the summer
of 2002 suggests that AL continues to address real world problems, although I
do not know how far the responses I had are representative or not. The
following is a summary of them to which I have added some of the applied
AL work in medical settings:

Language policy applications: recommendations to improve post 16 uptake of foreign languages in Scotland; revisiting Navaho bilingual education programmes; changes to Zambian language policy in primary schools; European language policy book aimed at the general public; bilingual/bicultural programmes for the Nicaraguan Caribbean Coast.

Workplace communication: collaborating with human resource managers to produce a communications evaluation model; production of Railspeak for Eurotunnel train drivers and signalmen.

Work with professionals (other than medicine): revising the language of police procedures.

Work in health settings: practitioners and patients using care maps and care calendars developed by researchers; doctor-patient videos published by medical press; assessment of the adequacy of the Occupational English test for work seekers in the health services.

If the word 'Applied' is part of the definition of our particular profession and this engages us in addressing social problems, then part of being an Applied linguist is to reflect on how we do this and build these reflections into our professional, and as far as we can, our institutional lives. What I am talking about is more than reflection. It is a reflexive account; that is reflections that are turned back on ourselves – to a self-understanding which itself produces change in us and our work. In trying to understand ourselves as applied linguists working collaboratively with other professionals, we raise questions about how we constitute ourselves within a set of norms and values and new ways of knowing.

In recent papers on discourse research and practice, researchers have been variously described as:

'The researcher as part of a practitioner collectivity';
'Discourse practitioners as part of a community of inter-professional practice';
'Consultant researchers';
'Interventionist researchers';
and AL 'within a collaborative action-orientated research paradigm.'

These are all rather unwieldy descriptions – but the idea of community, collectivity and collaborators all send out the same message about discourse workers and professional workers negotiating and producing together. And it is on this sense of a community of applied linguists and professionals, as part of a more general call to arms, that I want to concentrate here. This sense of community has been widely experienced but little documented in a reflexive way.

So I am challenging the argument that research comes first and then, later, we can see how practitioners might be able to use it. I would argue with the idea that practical outcomes can only be derived from some pure knowledge – as if the real world did not come rampaging in to research based knowledge. The 'research then application' sequence also leaves practitioners as mere consumers of research – in Jacob Mey's disturbing metaphor (1987) – the researcher as poet handing out knowledge to the peasant.

In the rest of this paper I want to:

First, look in more detail at how qualitative research in institutional contexts can act on social problems – the possibilities and limitations.

Then use the notions of the new work order (NWO) as a tool for being reflexive about our work as action-orientated researchers. NWO is not only something which changes the model of discourses that we have used in workplace research , but also describes rather well the new roles, positions and identities which we take on when we contribute to addressing real world problems. And I will illustrate this with a case study of involvement with the Royal College of General Practitioners over six years.

Finally, comment on some practices which might corral institutions into directly addressing real world problems and reflecting on their own practices as a result.

Possibilities and limitations in addressing social problems

I want to suggest that most applied researchers are more likely to have an impact by trying to change practice with practitioners rather than through grand attempts at engineering policy change. There are researchers who have influenced policy, but qualitative research has particular insights, grounded in the everyday reality that practitioners live by, which makes it appealing to practitioners.

The sociologist Michael Bloor (1997), in a paper on how qualitative researchers can address social problems, argues that the post-modern melt-down of Truth and Authority as absolutes has undermined the researchers' capacity to intervene and make changes. But although Bloor acknowledges that social scientists cannot engineer policy, in the grand manner, he argues that they can do limited but useful work with practitioners. There is a con-nection between the everyday work practices which are so often the focus of qualitative and particularly ethnographic research and the 'knowledge in action' of practitioners. Practitioners can relate to this kind of research.

Working with practitioners is all the more likely if applied linguists are researching with them. Cameron et al. (1992) argue on both ethical and epistemological grounds for a research *with* paradigm.[1] Such notions as intellectual compatibility and the social distribution of knowledge play an important role. I want to add to this 'research with' an 'act with' dimension. An integrated approach in which research and intervention go hand in hand strengthens our interpretive capacity and establishes relations which allow for more ethnographic depth – what Cicourel (1992) calls 'ecological validity'. It is often only when there is *acting* with as well as *researching* with that we get access to richer interpretations to thicken up the thin gruel of our own analyses.

For example, in analysing an oral exam for membership of the Royal College of General Practitioners (MRCGP), a setting which is used as a case study later in this paper, our interpretation of the data was enriched by views from examiners with whom we were doing on-going practical work:

01	E3	let's go on to something (.) clinical one of your visits was a postnatal visit [(.)] there's no need [to going in to great detail about it] (.) why =
02	C	[uhuh] [no right okay]
03	E3	= do you do a postnatal visit
04	C	um (.) I think one of the (.) reasons ((slightly laughing)) is because you get paid for it (.) um [(.)] (its an item) (.) it's one of your uh (.) =
05	E3	[right]
06	C	= commitments and (.) only if you finish (the whole care of the patient) do you get full pay

Our assumption was that the candidate had committed a sociopragamtic failure since her response was treated as a dispreferred one. We assumed that, from the mass of gatekeeping data we have looked at, a more stylised honest answer, which did not mention money, would be a preferred response. However, the GP examiners, with whom we discussed the data for training purposes, were much more nuanced in their evaluation – stating that the GP practice was viewed as a business and that her response was reasonable if not the best answer.

A third possibility or limitation concerns our involvement with practitioners over time. In acting with practitioners, we can establish more long-term relationships which in turn allows any changes to be incremental. New work practices in industry and in health care settings, for example, show that professional work/knowledge is distributed over many units and disciplines over time and it is the relationship between the new work order and our AL work that I now turn.

The new work order

The new ways in which work is being organised, and the new discourses which both constitute and account for these new ways of working, offer some useful insights when thinking about the research/practice relationship. The NWO is beginning to have a significant impact on discourse research of institutional life. (Gee et al., 1996). It also provides a paradigm for looking reflexively at our work as collaborative AL workers. The NWO:

> Is creating new roles, identities and discourses;
>
> Its defining shape and colour is unpredictable and in a state of often rapid change and so has to be researched over time;
>
> Within it, professionals' everyday practices have to be made more explicit and public;
>
> New subject positions are constructed in the discourse.

Iedema and Scheeres (2003) discuss these new work order practices in relation to a hospital setting where patients' diagnosis and treatment and the management of the hospital more generally, require multi-disciplinary approaches. For example, instead of doctors talking in code to each other or via scribbled notes, they have to meet and talk in multi-disciplinary meetings. Similarly, through the agreeing of clinical pathways for patients, there has to be more description and explanation within an overarching frame of accountability. So, there is more reflective language about work, more meta-discursive language. This means there is more modality and conditionality, less certainty, more respect. So the new work order creates new ways of being. The discourse may be more distant from the here and now but more focused on the immediate work of self and other. In other words, more time is spent on identity politics, on the renegotiation of work and self.

Iedema and Scheeres argue that the new work order has a significant impact on discourse analysts working in professional and workplace settings since 'Discourses are no longer stable objects' but are increasingly complex and unpredictable. It is no longer relevant to look at single events but rather to look at how they are chained together over time.[2] As Iedema and Scheeres say: 'As discourse analysts we may not be well equipped for this new position'.

These arguments have been made in relation to discourse analysts as researchers, not necessarily as those trying to address social problems and contribute to change. But I want to argue that by looking reflexively at what we do as change agents, we are faced with precisely the kinds of new work orders that Iedema and Scheeres are talking about. These differences are thrown into relief when we compare the approach used to relate research to practice in the latter part of the 20th century with the approach we may need to use today.

Working towards the solution of real world problems in the 1970s and 1980s was rather different from similar engagements in the 21st century for the reasons I have just described. But it is also because the rules of engagement were rather different from the way I think they have to be today. If we compare one kind of interventionist work that applied linguists were doing with institutions then – cross-cultural training work in industry and the public sector – with broadly similar work with institutions today, we can see a number of differences. Much of what was done then was one-off interventions, parachuting in and not leaving with much evidence to develop a reflexive account of what we were doing.

A comparison of the two approaches can be summarised as follows:

1970s/80s	2000s
Engineering/enlightenment model (Bulmer, Bloor)	Reflexive/enlightenment model (Bloor, Bourdieu)
Gatekeeping interview	Activities that surround and include gatekeeping
Focus on cultural differences as topic	Focus on practices as topic
Autonomous and one-way	Collective and reciprocal

I want to look in more detail now at how the NWO practices shed light on us as interventionist researchers, drawing on the NWO themes mentioned above:[3]

> Long-term and wide ranging relationships (including on-going and implicit evaluation) within a framework of change;
>
> Having to make explicit and public what we do;
>
> New subject positions;
>
> Engaging in speaking and writing practices not sanctioned by our own field of inquiry;
>
> Being reflexive about our own identities.

The RCGP case study

I want to illustrate these points through a case study of our consultancy research with the Royal College of General Practitioners. So, first a few words about this context. The new work order has begun to creep into even the bastions of medical stability and hierarchy such as the Royal Colleges. There is, increasingly, more accountability to outside pressures of social justice, more change in procedures and practices. We were invited in after several studies by the RCGP had shown that ethnic minority candidates were receiving lower grades than their white counterparts. Our initial relationship was with the exam panel, and later with the oral development group and examiner GPs. Our first goal was a descriptive study of the oral exams which are part of the membership of the Royal College of General Practitioners. Our research focused on the hybrid discourses of the exam: institutional, professional and personal and we argued that this hybridity had the potential to be indirectly discriminatory against those who had not trained in the UK (Roberts and Sarangi, 1999). Since this initial research we have been involved in a number of activities with the RCGP and I will now use the five NWO themes to look at the research consultancy process and our collaborative relationships with the college.

Long-term and wide ranging relationships As I have said, new work orders and organisation of work also means that any aspect of professional life involves long chains of events – so any set of interviews, meetings etc. are only part of an intricate set of interactions which all have a bearing on each other. This argues for long-term relationships with organisations and research sites. This can be illustrated by detailing the range of events which chain together over the period of our involvement. The first chain lists the events within the initial activity of analysing the oral exams:

Chaining within an activity: 1996 – 2000

Negotiating the basis on which the research will be done – joint problematisation;

Observation of how the examiners are selected;

Observation of how examiners are trained (useful because several institutional assumptions made explicit – intense dialogue between examiners and trainers);

Informal discussions with examiner trainers and new examiners;

Semi participant observation of oral exams;

Interviews with candidates;

Examiner and researchers viewing and analysis of videos;

Interim discussion document;

Report;

Jointly authored publication of research in the BMJ;

RCGP comments on discourse book chapter.

The second set of events involve chaining across institutional activities, 1999 – 2002, in other words taking the initial research further into training, activities by examiners based on our work and further consultancy with other Royal Colleges:

Examiner training day;

Preparation for examiner's training day with subgroup of oral development group;

Critique of handouts for the training day;

Trial of materials with the oral development group;

Paper based on BMJ article by co-ordinator of critical essay development group;

Presentation at training day with oral development group as leader analysts;

Evaluation of the day;

Observation and report on simulated surgery;

Comments on communication aspects new examination curriculum (and other ongoing short consultancy work);

Discussion and presentation for the International MRCGP exam;

Consultancy work with other Royal Colleges.

This long-term relationship in which changes were taking place also provided an opportunity for us to be given feedback and evaluated. Our own discourses were coming under scrutiny at every point and our taken for granted ways of seeing things from our own specialism as discourse practitioners was challenged. In fact, the constant evaluation, reflection and meta-discursive activity characterised the whole period and all our work with them. The careful, long-term and highly collaborative tone of the research and action was set by the College – they set the pulse. And we were grateful for that.

Having to make explicit and public what we do This means making ourselves accountable and relevant which involves more metadiscourse as work comes under scrutiny from 'outsiders'. It means having to explain your work and normalise it within a new setting. For example, writing about what Discourse Analysis is for a readership who may be either unfamiliar or sceptical of it.

New subject positions When working over time with professionals from very different discipline backgrounds, the position of the discourse analyst is constantly renegotiated. Our own authority and credibility cannot be taken for granted as it is evaluated by a professional community with different certainties from our own (Roberts and Sarangi, 2003).

For example, in the joint writing of the British Medical Journal (BMJ) article, it was difficult to adopt an appropriate evaluative stance – were we inside and therefore modest or outside and congratulatory? We can compare this with a chapter in a book intended for a discourse/sociolinguistic audience. The example that follows are comments by the Convenor of the Examinations Panel on our article for the BMJ (Roberts et al., 2000) and on a chapter in an edited book for an academic readership of discourse specialists (Roberts and Sarangi, 1999):

> Putting myself in the position of a naive reader ignorant of the background to the study, I gain the distinct impression that the RCGP and the exam have been detected in some form of assessment misdemeanour, and the paper is a gentle rebuke for it. Your preliminary studies showed no overt or intentional discrimination, 'merely' the unwitting linguistic potential discrimination which the paper very elegantly describes. It doesn't come across that the Exam Board, seeking to improve the exam, actually took the initiative in commissioning the study, nor that the RCGP is probably unique among the medical Royal Colleges in having the courage proactively to evaluate its Oral procedures in this way. The more extensive passages on pages 4 and 5 of the chapter text, and its overall tone, give a much more generous perspective. But few people whose opinions matter to us are likely to read the book, whereas many will read the BMJ article,

and I hope by a few judicious re-wordings you could manage to convey a sense that the difficulties you identify with MRCGP are probably endemic in all medical exams using the oral format, and that the willingness of the college to open its exam to scrutiny is something that others might consider adopting.

The example from the BMJ draft paper:

Oral assessments are widely used in medical undergraduate and postgraduate examinations and in the selection procedure for membership of royal colleges such as the Royal College of General Practitioners (RCGP) (1). However their validity and reliability have been the subject of much discussion and the RCGP has a tradition of reflecting on these issues (2,3,4). For example, the College has expended much effort in improving its membership exam through the careful selection and training of examiners, the development of clear questions and criteria for marking and on-going discussion of techniques and problems (5). In parallel with these efforts, the debate about equal opportunities and the possible discriminatory outcomes of the exam has continued. In addition to the college's general concerns about this issue, there had been some anecdotal reports from failed candidates that their lack of success might be due to racial discrimination.

And the example from the book chapter:

The college (RCGP) has a long tradition of developing and evaluating the selection examinations for its membership (Lockie 1990, Southgate and Wass 1992) and in establishing their validity and reliability. The careful selection and training of examiners, the development of clear questions and criteria for marking and the on-going discussion of techniques and problems for examiners have all contributed to this goal. However, the RCGP exam board recognised that, despite the procedures in place, there was the possibility of discriminatory outcomes for certain groups of minority ethnic candidates. The college's concern led to a further study which concluded that the relatively disadvantaged position of this group of doctors stemmed in part from the conditions under which they were working in inner city practices where training opportunities were limited (Wakeford et al., 1992).

The exam board's commitment to equal opportunities led them, then, to consider whether the oral examination, in hidden and subtle ways, might itself contribute to the candidates' relative lack of success. The orals became the focus of concern because a significant number of ethnic minority candidates educated and trained overseas did relatively less well or failed this part of the exam.

When we compare the two texts:

> In the book chapter, the RCGP is represented as a more active agent in tackling the issues of potential inequality. It is the thematic focus of more sentences.

> In the BMJ draft, the inequality issue is presented as a debate with the college as the implied agent only.

> Mention made of anecdotal evidence of possible racial discrimination in the BMJ draft where we wanted to highlight the seriousness of the issue but is less important to the argument of the book.

The retrospective justification for these differences was that we were trying to balance criticism and praise. As the lead authors of the BMJ article, we did not want the medical readership to think we were complacent but for the chapter, we wanted to show the benefits of consultancy research. We saved our generous perspective for the book. But it was the convenor who made us aware of this and forced us to reflect on our own practice.

Engage in speaking/writing practices not sanctioned by our particular field of inquiry
Joint writing of articles for a relatively unfamiliar audience engages the AL in rather different writing practices and these have to be constantly negotiated. In the joint writing of the BMJ article our methods of data collection and transcription impressed as 'science' – making talk visible, pathologising it for scrutiny which fits well with evidence-based medicine. However our basic ontology was frequently questioned and we found ourselves talking up the authority of our analysis in a way which we were not so comfortable with.

We also found our acknowledgement of alternative interpretations, as opposed to taking an authoritative stance, met with some puzzlement. The caution derived from acknowledging alternative interpretations in our writing was criticised as lacking firmness and robustness. What looked like 'dormouse valour' – as Shakespeare put it – to our medical colleagues, was, to us, a healthy plurality.

Being reflexive about our identities and being involved in identity politics
This is what Iedema and Scheeres call 'rewriting organisational', and I would say, 'professional identities.' The unremarkable and naturalised ways of doing and being an Applied Linguist are confronted by the 'Other'- in this case the gatekeepers of the RCGP exam panel and the editors of medical journals. Similarly, the GP examiners in confronting their transparency model of language/meaning are distancing themselves from stable and dominant forms of medical discourses work and metacommunicating about it in ways which engages them in thinking about their authority not only as doctors but RCGP gatekeepers.

The Exam board convenor responded to both the BMJ paper and the chapter for discourse specialists in this way:

> I haven't thought this through, but your text (which by any standards is closed-packed) is itself couched in institutional language, while the bits that are of most direct application to us are expressed at the professional level. Does this imply that the institutional level is in some way more sophisticated (in which case it may be the right level to go for in professional exams)? Or, if utility is greatest at the professional level, should that be one that both we and you should try to stick to?

What we saw as our *professional* AL language (modified to respond to the audience for the BMJ) appeared reified and abstracted to him. So *our professional* discourse was *his institutional* discourse. We had been doing identity work without knowing it! What we thought was a shared set of discourses was actually a means of maintaining the boundary of our profession (see Candlin and Hyland, 1999) and a way of distancing the medical practitioners rather than collaborating with them. And yet the fact that we were having a dialogue about it gave us another social positioning through which, perhaps, some resolution would emerge. Some two years later, when the 120 GP examiners had a training session with us, we were more aware of the need to ground our 'abstractions' in more detail and acknowledge more of the GP perspective which had come through in working with the oral development group on our transcribed data. And this modified discourse was responded to as professional – that is, relevant and usable rather than institutional, abstract and distant.

In the 101 immediate responses from our training session, what came out most strongly was the idea that the language of the oral exams is a topic to be studied in its own right:

> 'The current Orals are a complex game, the rules of which are misunderstood by candidates and not adhered to by examiners. We survive through a combination of ignorance and arrogance. If the future of this part of the exam lies in the interaction between candidate and examiner, then what do we actually want to test? It is clear that our superficial intentions on questioning are not actually what we are assessing. So what are the elements of this orals interaction that we value and have validity?'

> Dessert: Could the co-examiner be woken from their slumbers and asked to assess the interaction and not just the candidate's response?'

This metadiscoursal work suggested a new way of looking at the discourse of the exams and possibly new subject positions in relation this event.

Institutional implications

I want to turn now to some of the institutional implications of the kind of collaborative work which I have been illustrating. Borrowing from Bourdieu's (1992) notion of a 'sociology of sociology', a reflexive account of our discourses and identities could be institutionalised, made part of what ALs do when they address social problems. This reflexivity makes us think about our ways of knowing, talking and writing and so is part of our intellectual labour. It should also help us with the ongoing dialogue with practitioners just as their dialogue with ALs can produce a reflexive habit in us.

So both collaborative research with practitioners and a reflexive account of this collaboration should be part of:

> ESRC and other funding bodies' criteria for AL bids.

> RAE criteria about how we should spend our time and what counts as serious publications. For example one criterion could be the numbers of articles jointly authored with practitioners and/or

published in media read by practitioners.

(One respondent to my email request for details of action-orientated research, told that her appraiser had suggested that 'she give up on all the political, solidarity stuff and concentrate on her career.')

MA and PhD research courses.

Criteria for journal and book reviewers.

A more general encouragement of more detailed and reflexive accounts in papers addressing real world problems.

What might these accounts include?

The goals of interventionist research and its provenance. For example, research that became interventionist, consultant research which started as short term consultancy and grew into research and so on.

How any original goals were re-negotiated to tune with both AL researchers' and practitioners' priorities – i.e. joint problematisation.

Reflections on the collaboration with practitioners in data collection, analysis and writing. For example, struggles over classification, metaphors etc. in co-authored writing.

Reflections on the extent of reciprocity in feedback and evaluation.

Reflexive account of how the whole project fed into an understanding of one's own professional discourse and specialist paradigms and the contribution of this understanding to effective interventions in the future.

Conclusion

However much we insert ourselves within a specialist area, we are also answerable to others, if we are to define ourselves as applied in the sense used here. The melt down of authority and credibility by post-modern influences does not leave us empty handed, even if it makes us cautious. We can, and I would argue, should intervene but we need to do it collaboratively and reflexively working with other professionals from the initial design stage through to mutual critique and evaluation.

Talking to ourselves is all very well, but like looking for hairs on the palms of your hands, it may be the first sign of what Milton called 'a melancholy and moon struck madness'. Sanity lies in talking and acting with others. I wonder if we do enough of it.

Acknowledgement

I would like to acknowledge Srikant Sarangi's contribution to many of the ideas in this paper during our collaborative work together and to thank Ben Rampton for his, as ever, trenchant comments on an early draft.

Notes

1 Cameron et al.'s central argument concerns working with informants who are relatively less powerful than the researchers and finding ways of empowering them. In this paper, I focus on working with informants who may have a relatively strong power base within their own institutions and where researchers and practitioners can work together as equals.

2 This lack of stability and the consequent need to re-design the research/action relationship echoes the work of Alain Touraine on social movements and his method of sociological intervention.

3 This chimes with a BAAL plenary by Ben Rampton in 2000 – that AL can be construed as a late-modern activity, although he was coming at it from a completely different angle.

References

Bloor, M. (1997) Addressing social problems through qualitative research. In D. Silverman (ed.) *Qualitative Research: Theory, Method and Practice*. London: Sage. pp. 221–238.

Bourdieu, P. (1992) Thinking about limits. In M. Featherstone (ed.) *Cultural Theory and Cultural Change*. London: Sage.

Brumfit, C. (1991) Applied linguistics in higher education: riding the storm. *BAAL Newsletter*, 38: 45-49.

Cameron, D., Frazer, E., Harvey, P., Rampton M.B.H. and Richardson, K. (1992) *Researching Language: Issues of power and method*. London: Routledge.

Candlin, C. N. and Hyland, K. (1999) (eds) *Writing: Texts, Processes and Practices*. London: Longman.

Cicourel, A. (1992) The interpenetration of communicative contexts: examples from medical encounters. In A. Duranti and C. Goodwin (eds) *Rethinking Context: Language as an Interactive Phenomenon*. Cambridge: Cambridge University Press. pp. 291–310.

Gee, J., Hull, G. and Lankshear, C. (1996) *The New Work Order: Behind the Language of the New Capitalism*. Sydney: Allen and Unwin.

Iedema, R. and Scheeres, H (2003) From doing work to talking work: renegotiating knowing, doing and identity. *Applied Linguistics*, 24,3:316-337.

Mauranen, A. and Sajavaara, K (1997) (eds) Applied Linguistics across Disciplines. *AILA Review*, 12.

Mey, J. (1987) Poet and peasant: a pragmatic comedy in five acts. *Journal of Pragmatics*, 11: 281-297.

Peräkylä, A. (1995) *Aids Counselling: Institutional Interaction and Clinical Practice.* Cambridge: Cambridge University Press.

Rampton, B. (1997) (ed.) Special Issue: Retuning applied linguistics. *Applied Linguistics*, 7, 1.

Roberts, C. and Sarangi, S. (1999) Hybridity in gatekeeping discourse: issues of practical relevance for the researcher. In S. Sarangi and C. Roberts (eds) *Talk, Work and Institutional Order.* Berlin: Mouton de Gruyter.

Roberts, C. and Sarangi, S. (2003) Uptake of discourse research in interprofessional settings: reporting from medical consultancy. Special issue of *Applied Linguistics*, 24, 3: 338-359.

Roberts, C. and Sarangi, S., Southgate, L., Wakeford, R. and Wass, V. (2000) Oral Examination – equal opportunities, ethnicity and fairness in the MRCGP. *British Medical Journal*, 320: 370-375.

Sarangi, S. (2002) Discourse practitioners as a community of interprofessional practice: some insights from health communication research. In C.N. Candlin (ed.) *Research and Practice in Professional Discourse.* Hong Kong: City University of Hong Kong Press. pp. 95-135.

10 Categorisation practices across professional boundaries: some analytic insights from genetic counselling

Srikant Sarangi*, Angus Clarke**,
Kristina Bennert*, Lucy Howell*
* *Cardiff University*
** *University of Wales College of Medicine*

Abstract

In this paper we begin with a brief overview of the tensions in keeping description and evaluation analytically separate. The tensions are manifest at the level of coding, claims making and so on, and are particularly salient when dealing with interactional data in professional and institutional settings. The categories that discourse analysts draw upon to make sense of the data are often thematically loaded. For example, categories such as risk, responsibility, blame, non-directiveness, advice giving, information giving, are not just linguistic labels of description devoid of evaluative content. Instead, they encode aspects of institutional/professional realities and can be contentious when co-analysing the data. In more specific terms, we will focus our attention on two central categorisations in our ongoing work in the analysis of genetic counselling discourse: counsellors' initiation of therapeutic frames, and clients' normalisation of experience/expectation. Based on a set of illustrative examples, we would like to reflect upon a series of inter-related questions: How do these analytic categories emerge out of the data? Are these categories descriptive and/or evaluative in nature? To what extent do they blind the analyst to alternative modes of description? And, in what ways do co-researchers from different professional backgrounds (here communication/discourse analysts and clinical geneticists) contest the perceived histories of these categories? In the final part of the paper we will revisit some of the core methodological issues surrounding discourse analysis in professional settings. We will reassess the strengths and limitations of loose thematic coding vis-à-vis structural mappings of discourse data and suggest ways in which the latter can be seen as a preliminary step towards thematic generalisations. This will provide an evidential basis for addressing professional practitioners' concerns not just about the variable meaning potential of our discourse-analytic categories but also about the analytic procedure that we implicitly follow in arriving at specific categorisations of data.

Introduction: Categorisation work in professional discourse studies

In this paper we deal with the tensions in keeping description and evaluation analytically separate when categorising, coding or mapping interactional data in professional and institutional settings. Categorisation constitutes a key element in different traditions of qualitative analysis and different categorisation practices can lead to alternative interpretations of the same data. The categories that discourse analysts draw upon to make sense of the data – whether deductively applied or inductively emergent – can be thematically loaded. For example, categories such as risk, responsibility, blame, non-directiveness, advice giving, information giving, are not just linguistic labels of description devoid of evaluative content. Instead, they encode aspects of institutional/professional realities, so embody evaluative content and can be contentious.[1]

Exactly how the categoriser keeps his/her distance from a named category and how such a category is understood by co-analysts and target participants remains a moot point for discourse analysts. A discourse analyst can approach text/talk data armed with linguistic categories (e.g., discourse particles, pronouns) and/or para-linguistic/non-linguistic categories (e.g., rhythm, pause, tone). Certain kinds of categorisation labels may be unproblematic both at the level of analytic coding and at the level of uptake. For instance, identification of turn-taking patterns – opening, closing, opening of closing etc. – in the CA-tradition can often go uncontested. On a descriptive plane, these are universal categories, but they can be evaluative when we ascribe them specific functions and meanings. Does the 'opening of closing' index some kind of power relations? Does the pronoun 'we' suggest inclusiveness or exclusiveness when X says 'we need to consider this alternative'?

In addition to this problematic of the 'evaluative' tone of our categorisation practices, there is also the issue of non-categorisation or mis-categorisation of data because of a lack of adequate knowledge on the part of the discourse analyst in a given professional site (Sarangi, 2002). From a CA perspective this is a non-issue because the analyst is supposed to be only noticing those moments which are made relevant by participants themselves. In the professional setting, the problem of categorisation, however, is not necessarily solved by using the rather abstract notion of 'participant's perspective' or 'members' method'. What if there is a gap in understanding and experience between the analyst and the participant to the extent that what is made relevant by participants is not quite observable by the analysts (Sarangi and Candlin, 2001)? Moreover, if we were to adopt a participant's perspective in analysing professional-client encounters, which of the participants do we become? Collaborative interpretation of data then becomes obligatory.

Collaborative categorisation may not always be a smooth endeavour. It is very likely that the categories discourse analysts deploy to account for the data may be resisted by the professional participants if and when we care to take our analysis to them. Roberts and Sarangi (2003) provide a detailed account of how a distinction they proposed between institutional discourse and professional discourse generated interesting feedback from the medical practitioners. Apart from challenging the clarity and utility of such categorical distinctions, the medical colleagues also questioned the evaluative force of the distinction, e.g., is institutional discourse more powerful and favourable than professional discourse? Does it mean that discourse analysts operate with the higher-order institutional discourse and the medical practitioners are constrained by their professional discourse? There is thus a need for discourse analysts to reflect on the unintended consequences of their categorisation practices.

It is worth stressing that categorisation is central to all professional activity, although different professionals will have recourse to different discursive practices in how they code, highlight and articulate their knowledge and action (Goodwin, 1994). In medical work, for instance, doing a diagnosis is a form of secondary categorisation based on primary categorisation of evidence and symptoms. The evidence is central to arriving at a consensus about the diagnosis. In this respect, non-diagnosis, which is a recurrent feature of genetic counselling, is also a form of categorisation. By extending this medical paradigm, we can revisit the practices of discourse analysts when it comes to labelling events vis-à-vis available evidence.

In what follows, we reflect on this very categorisation process of discourse analytic work, which fits in to the collaborative interpretive scheme. We will illustrate our argument in the context of genetic counselling discourse with two analytic categories:

(i) counsellors' initiation of therapeutic frames;

(ii) clients' normalisation strategies.

We arrived at these two categories by examining what seemed to constitute critical moments in our data corpus in light of how counsellors speak about failed agendas, the unwillingness of clients to engage with the risks of knowing test results etc. In this paper we first offer a brief account of our research site and then we introduce two illustrative examples around the above two categorisations, while raising the following series of inter-related questions:

How do these analytic categories emerge out of the data?

Are these categories descriptive and/or evaluative in nature?

To what extent do they blind the analyst to alternative modes of description?

And, in what ways do co-researchers from different professional backgrounds (here communication/discourse analysts and clinical geneticists) contest the perceived histories of these categories?

Background to the project

The project titled 'Communicative Frames in Counselling for Predictive Genetic Testing' is being carried out in a collaboration between discourse analysts and clinical geneticists and genetic counsellors. The primary data we are analysing in this project are audio-recordings of consecutive counselling sessions (e.g., preliminary appointments, first appointments, results-giving etc.) for predictive testing. Predictive testing, in contrast to symptomatic testing where the test is to confirm a diagnosis of already existing symptoms, is aimed at establishing the at-risk status of people who know that there is a genetic disorder in their family. As can be seen, in the context of genetic counselling, collaborative interpretation can be helpful to permit appropriate distinctions to be drawn (e.g., between different types of genetic tests, different kinds of clinic appointments), which then allows the insights of discourse analytic methods to refer to categories that are relevant to the participants (Sarangi and Clarke, 2002a, 2002b). Here we are already borrowing the categories of different types of genetic testing that are accepted within the genetic counselling profession. In addition to observing and recording what happens in the clinic, our data corpus extends to accommodate medical case notes and ethnographic interviews with a selection of clients and counsellors. The project's overall aim is to examine in detail the extent to which identifiable themes are bound up with certain interactional formats within a clinic session. Our interest also lies in the possible variations across sessions and across different genetic conditions. With the help of the NVivo software, we have begun to map all sessions in their interactional and thematic sequences as a way of building a broader context for our detailed analysis of specific examples.

In terms of communicative frames, genetic counselling is a hybrid activity type (Sarangi, 2000).[2] Unlike mainstream doctor-patient interaction, genetic counselling for predictive testing involves history taking around family trees, educational elements (e.g. explanation about the mechanisms of inheritance) and reflective elements where counsellors encourage clients to think aloud their decision-making strategies and possible implications associated with having a specific test result. Generally speaking, participants constantly shift between these various frames in order to achieve their distinctive, and sometimes conflicting, agendas.

Categorisation 1: therapeutic frames

Given the hybrid nature of genetic counselling as an activity type, one is likely to encounter a range of overlapping discourse types (Sarangi, 2000) that are observable in other settings (e.g., history taking, diagnostic reasoning, self-reflection). Let us consider the case of what we identified and labelled as the 'therapeutic frame'.

There is an established line of research devoted to therapeutic encounters, which has identified distinctive features both at interactional and content levels (e.g., Buttny, 1996; Ferarra, 1995; Gale, 1991; Grossen and Apothèloz, 1996; Labov and Fanshel, 1977; Måseide 1987; McNamee and Gergen, 1992; Miller and Silverman, 1995; Turner, 1972). At one extreme is psychotherapy where talk is treatment, in the sense that language is regarded as both the method of diagnosis and the medium of treatment. In psychotherapy as an activity, clients are encouraged to find solutions to their questions through introspection and self-reflection, while the therapist takes on the role of active listener, giving things a particular 'hearing'. Clearly, in the context of genetic counselling, talk is not accorded a strong therapeutic value, nor does it get equated with treatment. There is nonetheless a therapeutic/reflective frame by means of which clients are encouraged to think about their decision-making processes. Our attention to this frame type was triggered by its routine initiation in almost every counselling session. In terms of content, we found this communicative frame to be tied up with presence or absence of talk about psychosocial coping and adjustment, which is likely to occur when talking about hypothetical scenarios in which responses to possible future test results are considered. With regard to interactional features, the frame is marked by an (attempted) shift of client's and counsellor's interactional roles with the client accepting extended speakership and the counsellor assuming the role of active listener, limiting herself to minimal back-channelling, expressions of empathetic tokens etc.

This communicative frame is initiated by counsellors to facilitate informed, client-centred decisions about the possibility of predictive testing. An attempt is made to engage clients in troubles-telling and encourage them to adopt introspective and self-reflective stances. In this respect, talk is stripped of its informational function as it becomes a way of working things through. This resembles what happens in therapy talk more generally, although it is obvious that several other features characteristic of psychotherapy are notably absent from this therapeutic frame found in genetic counselling (e.g. the use of figurative language or inventing metaphors, probing follow-up questions or long pauses or reformulation to introduce discrepancy and shift the client's perspective as an active intervention). However, to us, the term 'therapeutic frame' seemed appropriate to refer to this mode of talk, and not to imply that genetic counselling and psychotherapy are comparable activity types, or that psychotherapists and genetic counsellors inhabit comparable expert identities.

Let us now turn to example 1, which is taken from a Huntington's clinic,[3] to illustrate how our category 'therapeutic frame' informed our preliminary analysis. The client is a woman in her late 20s, who has an affected mother (MO) and whose siblings have recently been tested negative. The extract starts about 10 minutes into the first of two pre-result appointments. The counsellor (G) is seen as attempting to engage the client (AF1) in the formulation of a post-test scenario.[4]

Example 1

(G = genetic counsellor, AF1 = adult female)

1 G: have you thought about how you would deal with the knowing, 'cause it's a- as you say you're not- you wouldn't expect to have any symptoms for a long time

2 AF1: I haven't thought about it, because I don't know whether I have got it yet so I just deal when I

3 G: mm

4 AF1: find out. it's just like- me I don't deal with anything till I know

5 G: mm

6 AF1: you know I wouldn't worry about it thinking oh I- I gotta do this and do that until I know whether I got it.

7 G: mm

8 AF1: and then I'd deal.

9 G: when you thought about coming forward for the actual testing, then you must (.) have thought (.) that- that the possibility is that as well as coming and finding out that you haven't got the gene? ((pause)) but (..) it's an absolute equal possibility that we can then go and say right 'we're afraid (we've got bad news) we've found the gene

10 AF1: =yeah

11 G: ehm (..) I mean I know it's- it's a sort of- (..) I keep asking the same question in a different way, but in a sense it's (.) I suppose it's because you are so:::: not anxious about the Huntington's, because you have taken being at fifty percent risk so much (.) in your stride or so it seems, and there is so much else (.8) that- that you have that you don't worry about it too much that (.) it's thinking about (.) it suddenly becoming a big focus. (.) you know, that if you have the gene (.) that there will be a time you can't not think about it. and really how you would – how you would cope with that.

12 AF1: right, well, that I don't know until the (.) the time comes.

13 G: mm

14 AF1: basically, I just- (it's nothing like really, no we just)

15 G: mm

16 AF1: fine, you know

17 G: how do you think it would affect you?

18 AF1: well I don't know, it's- I don't think it's changes.

19 G: =mm

20 AF1: = because like it wouldn't- hopefully wouldn't come into effect for another ten- ten odd years you know and-

21 G: mm

22 AF1: I just wait and see what's round the corner.

23 G: mm

24 AF1: it's just people worry about that and then go home and get knocked over by a bus you know? It's just so-

25 G: mm

26 AF1: so many other things can go wrong (.) without worrying about the Huntington's

27 G: mm

28 AF1: but I just think peace of mind and for the children and it's to find out whether I have got it or haven't got it.

Preliminary analysis Drawing upon the interactional and content features typical of therapeutic interaction, we may categorise example 1 as a mismatch between the counsellor's initiation of a therapeutic frame (in turn 1, and especially in turn 11) and the client's failure to take up the invitation to reflect on the hypothetical scenarios (turn 2 where the client could have described how she might cope if she were to be found positive). Instead, she appeals to a rational-factual unfolding of events in a real time sequence: she will think about dealing with things once she knows for certain what the test results are (see turns 4 and 6). The counsellor's suggestion to 'think about' is rephrased by the client as 'worrying about' (turn 6) which she sees as unwarranted. This is a form of normalisation we will return to later – where a therapeutic initiation is responded to by a normalising account, thus aborting the co-production of a successful therapeutic frame.

In turn 9, the counsellor embarks on another attempt to encourage the client to take speakership and produce hypothetical-reflective talk, but the client remains persistent that she will 'just wait and see what's round the corner' (turns 12, 22). Each of her responses is designed as a 'closure', showing an eagerness to hand speakership back to the counsellor. By contrast, the counsellor tries to keep the client in the speaker role by maintaining an active listener role through providing minimal feedback and by refraining from her role as the provider and elicitor of factual information. The fact that the counsellor delivers an account of why she 'keeps asking the same question' (turn 11) can be seen as an explicit recognition of the interactional misalignment. As example 1 illustrates, G's initiation of what we have labelled therapeutic frame is not always taken up by AF1. This results in extended sequences in which G continues to re-initiate the frame while AF1 keeps declining extended speakership.

Secondary analysis (informed by feedback from practitioners) When discussing our preliminary analysis with genetics counsellor colleagues, the use of the term 'therapeutic frame' created some dissonance. The term was seen as misleading if we were to target our discourse analytic findings to genetic counselling professionals, given that 'therapeutic' has a rather well-defined meaning in the healthcare domain. 'Therapeutic frame' could easily be seen as implying an activity role of genetic counsellor as therapist, which is far from the professional self-understanding of genetic counsellors or the professional definitions of genetic counselling. Instead of thinking about their interactions with clients in terms of 'failed' or 'successful' attempts at bringing off therapeutic frames, genetic counsellors are concerned with fulfilling their duty of adequately preparing clients for potentially unfavourable test results, in the absence of normative expectations shared across the profession regarding the mode of talk best suited to accomplish this aim.

We thus had to concede that use of the term 'therapeutic' might obstruct understanding and impede uptake of discourse research by practitioners. Psychotherapy as a comparison was also felt to be inadequate because in the case of predictive testing the client's 'problem' is not necessarily constituted and resolvable in relational terms.

Following further discussion among the research team, we agreed to use a less evaluative notion – reflective frame – which did not bring with it the baggage of therapy as a professional activity and identity. An advantage of this re-labelling was that it allowed us to reformulate our analytic focus in terms of how hypothetical-reflective questions (which might or might not be realised in a quasi-therapeutic style) featured within the counselling agenda across conditions and session types. The resistance generated among genetics

Table I Frequency of hypothetical reflective questions in 24 pre-test clinics

Type of counsellor question	Number of occurrences
Awareness and anxiety	102
Decision-about-testing	63
Impact of result	60
Dissemination	29
Non-specific invite	23
Other	15

professionals to the use of the category label 'therapeutic frame' thus led to a re-examination of the range of routine topics addressed by such open-ended counsellor questions (Table 1).

Categorisation 2: normalisation of experience/expectation

If we go back to example 1, there are several instances in AF1's talk which we can categorise as 'normalisation of experience/expectation'. In fact, we were tempted to claim that it is such 'normalisation strategies' which did not help the counsellor in realising the reflective frames. For instance, formulations such as 'I don't deal with anything till I know' and 'I wouldn't worry about it' suggest a kind of normalisation of AF1 as a person first, and this is then used as a rationale for dealing with the at-risk status only secondarily. Indeed it is this kind of generic normalisation that is seen as inappropriate by the genetic counsellor for its lack of genetic context-sensitivity (cf. turn 276).

In this instance, with the help of Nvivo software, we collated clients' 'normalising' responses to counsellors' initiation of hypothetical-reflective frames. We identified up to 11 strategies/themes in clients' responses. Table 2 shows the different types of 'normalisation strategies' and their frequency of occurrence across 24 Huntington's Disease (HD) clinics.

We felt that clients could be seen to 'normalise' counsellors' threatening scenarios by playing down the exceptionality of being at genetic risk and claiming the maintenance of their pre-test identities, e.g., through emphasis on agency or emotional strength. As can be seen from Table 2, the two most

Table 2 Frequency of types of normalisation themes clients orient to in post-test scenario

Themes	Number of occurrences
'other things can go wrong in life'	16
'allows me to make choices'	15
'it's a long way away'	10
'have to get on with life'	10
'enjoy normality while it lasts'	10
'still able to function'	09
'will learn to cope'	08
'certainty will bring normality'	06
(8) 'for my children's sake'	04
'grown up with the disease'	04
'there may be future treatment'	03

prevalent themes in clients' normalising responses were emphasising on the ability to prepare and adapt to life with the disease (theme 4: 'allows me to make choices'), and pointing out that a diagnosis of HD is not the only threat to a happy healthy life (theme 9: 'other things can go wrong in life'). Further common themes included a foregrounding of the time-lag between being found to carry the gene and the actual onset of symptoms (theme 2: 'it's a long way away'), combined with assertions that knowledge of positive status would allow the client to make the most of life before onset (theme 10: 'enjoy normality while it lasts'). However, when we considered our data examples in more detail we realised that even though client's responses looked deceptively similar on the surface level of theme, closer attention to how individual responses unfolded clarified that surface themes could not be easily equated with a particular degree of engagement.

Let us now examine some of these normalisation strategies in their interactional context. Consider example 2, taken from another Huntington's clinic, to illustrate our point. The client is a woman in her thirties, who has grown up with an affected father and whose brother has recently been diagnosed with HD. The extract starts about 25 minutes into the second of three pre-test appointments.

Example 2

(G = genetic counsellor, AF2 = adult female)

1 G: did it ((AF2's brother testing positive)) did it make your fifty fifty
            risk feel any different for you or
2   ((pause))
3 AF2:   =[[no]
4 G: =[[or] more determined to know [or]
5 AF2:   [just] the luck of the draw, isn't it, you know (.) I mean you can't
            make it less and you can't make it more you can't do anything, you
            know, it just is (.) isn't it, you know I mean I know that it's clicked
            in my head and I know (.) what it is
6 G: mm
7 AF2:   you know, whatever- if I was born with the gene I was born with
            it, if I wasn't I wasn't (.) of course I'm hoping that I haven't got it
            'cause I'm a human being, I want to survive (.) I'll probably smoke
            myself to death anyway ((laughs)) (.) you see how stupid that is (.)
            ridiculous
8 G: so aside from the decision making issues (.) the whole issue about
            relationships and children (…) have- have you (.) thought about (.)
            actually just living with (.) certainty
9 AF2:   yeah, yeah (.) I could- I could just sort of- 'cause I don't want no
            one looking after me. I'd rather go into a home. I can prepare those
            type of things ahead of time […] ((AF2 goes on to formulate plans
            of how she can maintain her maintain her independence))
10 G: there u- (.) in one sense, what strikes me is that's a long way in the
            future so in one sense that's very like (.) your mum (.) in that (.) it's
            the practical [(.) it's ::the]=
11 AF2:   [((starts to laugh))] =yeah, I am practical
12 G: pragmatic, it's the [let's] put everything in place
13 AF2:   [yeah] also emotional and all that (.) (^^^) to find out
14 G: yes
15 AF2:   I'll probably cry. (..) 'cause I cry at anything now (.) but I'll
            probably cry 'cause I don't want it (..) initially my initial reaction
            (..) .hhhh and then (…) I'll just .hh I'll just get up next day and
            take one day at a time (..) that I mean I'll probably go down. (.)

then I just come back up again 'cause you know
16 G: mm
         ((pause))
17 AF2: 'cause that's my (.) that's part habit that I (.) you know that's part of
         my- you know, if I get bad news I go down a bit, then I come up
         (.) and I'll just go with the flow then (.) 'cause that's who I am

Preliminary analysis The extract begins with the counsellor probing whether
the client's feelings about her at-risk status have changed in any way by
having access to her brother's test result. However, the client does not
respond on the same level. She seems to reject the idea of a personalised risk,
something that bears a special subjective meaning for her and thereby would
single her out from the crowd. Instead, she constructs her genetic status as
part of life's lottery, something that is arbitrary and disconnected from her as
a person. Her formulation 'I'm a human being, I want to survive' can be
heard as a claim to normality, emphasising that she is just like everybody else
(turn 7). As AF1 in example 1 ('it's just people worry about that and then go
home and get knocked over by a bus you know?', turn 24), the client, in
example 2, deflates the threat of Huntington's Disease by contrasting it with
a mundane 'everyday risk' ('I'll probably smoke myself to death', turn 7).
Interesting here is the shift from a position of no control over her genetic
status to the active engagement in the risk behaviour of smoking: a risk she
can choose to take. Furthermore, the choice of such an extreme case
formulation, followed by laughter, can also be seen as an attempt on the part
of the client to undermine the grave tenor of the interaction, but this is not
taken up by the counsellor. Up to this point it seems then that both the
client in example 1 and the client in example 2 use the normalisation
strategy – 'other things can go wrong in life' – to avoid engagement with
their genetic at-risk status.

After being prompted further by the counsellor (turn 8), AF2 still glosses
over the issue of living with the certainty of future disease as a currently
healthy person and instead picks up on what she would do once she begins
to show symptoms. Here, as in example 1, 'knowing' in itself is not
constructed as problematic by the client. Rather, it allows her to ensure
future normality by preparing for things ahead of time (turn 9). The client
gives an idiosyncratic and concrete description of how she envisages her
future as affected by HD. A sense of normality here is constructed by stressing

her determination to maintain what is important to her current self in her future life.

However, the counsellor persists in refocusing the client on the more immediate future after receiving a positive test result (turn 10), and this time the client aligns with her efforts and starts to describe her hypothetical coping process (turn 15, 'I'll probably cry'). The client then goes on to contextualise this hypothetical account of her emotional response as part of her general coping routine for traumatic events ('part habit [...] if I get bad news'). Here post-test normality is constructed by presenting the worst case scenario of receiving a positive test result as an order of events she is already familiar with ('getting bad news'), and therefore equipped to handle, using her personality as resource and explanation (turn 17, 'that's who I am').

Secondary analysis (informed by feedback from practitioners) As was the case with 'therapeutic' frame, the discourse analytic category 'normalisation' was also perceived by practitioners as highly evaluative and negative – as carrying overtones of trivialisation and not adequately describing (some of) the psychosocial adjustments that clients articulated in their responses. Some of the talk that we labelled as 'normalisation' was regarded by practitioners as being in fact a display of clients' adjustment and coping strategies. In this case, the different perspectives led to a reconsideration and subsequent abandonment of the original analytic category. Similar to our previous experience, we agreed on a less evaluative category – engagement – in order to explore how clients differed in the way they engaged or did not engage in the assessment of risks associated with knowing their genetic status. We realised that the one and the same topic might be talked about with different degrees of engagement, ranging from the statement of generalised 'truths' (such as 'it's about making choices', 'it's just the luck of the draw', 'life goes on', 'worse things can happen') through individualised references to personality and routines ('that's who I am', 'that's what I do when I get bad news') to much more concrete, descriptive and experiential accounts of concerns and scenarios (not included in the data examples presented here). While 'normalisation' could sometimes be seen as a way in which the client could reassure herself, minimising the possible problems of having a predictive test and permitting a degree of denial (as in example 1), this did not provide an adequate account of all such statements (as in example 2).

By dropping 'normalisation' as an over-arching category, we arrived at a new differentiation of data examples along a continuum of degrees of engagement that were previously grouped together under the same theme (McAllister, 2002; Sarangi et al., 2003). This led us to consider the various axes along which clients formulate their accounts (see Figure 1). We identified accounts as mapped alongside an axis of time, recruiting past experiences or projecting themselves into the more or less distant future. In addition to this time axis, clients also bring in their wider social and familial networks (parents, partners, children or friends) to account for their decision to have testing (in example 1, for instance, the client goes on to shift the focus onto her children: 'but I just think, peace of mind and for the children and it's to find out whether I have got it or haven't got it'). As we have already seen, counsellors' attempts to focus clients on a particular site along these axes might not always be taken up successfully, leading to some misalignments (as in example 2 where several attempts are needed before the client moves from her account of preparing for the distant future to her

Figure I The temporal and social axes which mediate counsellor's questions and clients' accounts

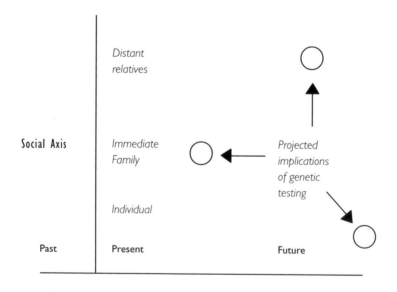

more immediate reaction on receiving the result).

In the case of therapeutic frames, it was the label of the category – therapeutic frame – that caused difficulties in communicating the discourse analytic insights, but there was little disagreement about the kind of phenomena being alluded to. In the second example, discussion about the label – normalisation of experience/expectation – prompted a reclassification of the data according to a different criterion – engagement – which led to an analysis of temporal and social frames.

Conclusion

In this paper our primary focus has been one of the core methodological issues of categorisation when dealing with discourse data in professional settings. Although we have used the concepts of therapeutic frame and normalisation of experience, our discussion is not meant to be exhaustive except for pointing to the methodological controversies that have practical analytic consequences.

The genetic counselling site and the two analytic categorisations have been used here to illustrate the tensions inherent in matching analysts' and participants' perspectives (Sarangi and Candlin, 2001). In other words, this is a testing of discourse-analytic interpretations. As we have tried to show, discussions between discourse analysts and practitioners have led to changes in our analytic practices. Pariticipants in this setting also include the clients and their families. So far we have not touched on clients' insights – which no doubt will add another layer of complexity to this analytic puzzle. We aim to tune into the clients' perspective for checking our remaining analytic biases. In a post-clinic interview, a client outlines (reflectively!) her orientation to the purpose of talk in the clinic:

> HD6: we'd be going down ((to the clinic)) for (.) some kind of counselling which- we paid several visits down there ((pause)) before the test was done (.) three at least (.) three maybe and the fourth (.) you you're given time to think very carefully about what you're going to do and (.) they were <u>very</u> helpful (.) didn't try to sway in anyway at <u>all</u> and (.) they listened to anything we had to say (.) er there was nothing they could say to me have it done or don't have it done, naturally I knew that, but I think they gave me the strength in the end to go through with it

This client describes her series of genetic counselling appointments as providing welcome opportunities to talk about her feelings and anxieties regarding predictive testing with professional experts. While she recognises that the counsellors ultimately can't take away the burden of decision-making from her, she accomplishes the idea that they are there to listen and to support her during this difficult process. This orientation towards genetic counselling as serving not just informational but also psychotherapeutic goals is not shared unanimously among clients (as data example 1 demonstrates). Our analysis, however, shows how some clients, especially if they have long-standing knowledge about the disease in the family, might align with a notion of counselling as a 'talking cure' rather than as an information-focused service. These divergent orientations among clients will lead us to analyse incidents of 'reflective frames' in our data corpus in terms of how these frames are initiated, how they are responded to, and what are the interactional moments of misalignment which obstruct the successful realisation of counselling agendas.

At the outset of this paper, we had mentioned coding and mapping alongside categorisation of interactional data. The question remains as to how we approach the mass of transcribed data, and how we pull out and analyse a selected set of examples for the purposes of uncovering useful patterns of interaction that would be useful for our target participants. Central to this of course is our labelling of categories in particular, and our language of analysis in general, which has been the main point of attention in this paper. It seems to us important that we bear in mind the strengths and limitations of ad hoc thematic coding vis-à-vis structural mappings of discourse data (Roberts and Sarangi 2002). The mapping can then be seen as a preliminary step towards thematic generalisations. This will provide an evidential basis for addressing professional practitioners' concerns not just about the variable meaning potential of our discourse-analytic categories but also about the analytic procedure that we implicitly follow in arriving at specific categorisations of data.

Acknowledgement

This paper is based on the project titled 'Communicative Frames in Counselling for Predictive Genetic Testing', funded by The Wellcome Trust (2000-2004).

Notes

1   For a detailed discussion of institutional versus professional modes of talk, see Sarangi and Roberts, 1999.

2   The notion of frame is taken from Goffman (1974:21) to denote 'schemata of interpretation' that enable participants (here counsellors and clients) 'to locate, perceive, identify, and label' occurrences and events within their everyday (professional and family) life spaces.

3   Huntington's Disease is an inherited late onset degenerative neuropsychiatric disorder which affects both body and mind. The pattern of inheritance is autosomal dominant, i.e., there is a 50% chance that the child of an affected parent will have inherited the disease-associated mutation. The discovery of the HD gene in 1993 has made it possible to test at-risk individuals for Huntington's disease before symptoms occur, although uncertainties remain with regard to the exact age of onset and the way in which the disease will manifest. There is currently no effective treatment or cure available for HD and clients typically die from the condition some 10 to 15 years after onset.

4   We have used the following simplified transcription conventions: (.): micropause; (..): pause up to one second; (...): pause exceeding one second; question mark [?]: rising intonation; period (.) falling intonation; comma (,) fall-rise); colons after vowel [so:::]: vowel stretch; underlined text: special emphasis; [text in square brackets]: overlapping speech; (text in round brackets): transcriber's guess; ((text in double round brackets)): description or anonymised information.

References

Buttny, R. (1996) Clients' and therapist's joint construction of the clients' problems. *Research on Language and Social Interaction*, 29, 2: 125-153.

Ferrara, K. W. (1994) *Therapeutic Ways with Words*. New York: Oxford University Press.

Gale, J. E. (1991) *Conversation Analysis of Therapeutic Discourse: The Pursuit of a Therapeutic Agenda*. Norwood, NJ: Ablex.

Goffman, E. (1974) *Frame Analysis*. London: Penguin Press

Goodwin, C. (1994) Professional vision. *American Anthropologist*, 96, 3: 606-633.

Grossen, M. and Apothèloz, D. (1996) Communication about communication in a therapeutic interview. *Journal of Language and Social Psychology*, 15, 2: 101-132.

Labov, W. and Fanshel, D. (1977) *Therapeutic Discourse: Psychotherapy as Conversation*. New York, London: Academic Press.

Måseide, P. (1987) The permanent context construction: A neglected dimension of therapeutic discourse. *Text*, 7, 1: 67-87.

McAllister, M. (2002) Predictive genetic testing and beyond: A theory of engagement. *Journal of Health Psychology*, 7, 5: 491-508.

McNamee, S. and Gergen, K. J. (1992) (eds) *Therapy as Social Construction*. London: Sage.

Miller, G. and Silverman, D. (1995) Troubles Talk and Counseling Discourse. A Comparative Study. *The Sociological Quarterly*, 36, 4: 725-747.

Roberts, C. and Sarangi, S. (2002) Mapping and assessing medical students' interactional involvement styles with patients. In K. Spelman-Miller and P. Thompson (eds) *Unity and*

Diversity in Language Use. London: Continuum.

Roberts, C. and Sarangi, S. (2003) Uptake of discourse research in interprofessional settings: reporting from medical consultancy. Special issue of *Applied Linguistics*, 24, 3: 338-359.

Sarangi, S. (2000) Activity types, discourse types and interactional hybridity: the case of genetic counselling. In S. Sarangi and M. Coulthard (eds) *Discourse and Social Life*. London: Pearson. pp. 1-27.

Sarangi, S. (2002) Discourse practitioners as a community of interprofessional practice: some insights from health communication research. In C. N. Candlin (ed.) *Research and Practice in Professional Discourse*. Hong Kong: City University of Hong Kong Press. pp. 95-135.

Sarangi, S. and Candlin, C. N. (2001) 'Motivational relevancies': some methodological reflections on the social theoretical and sociolinguistic practice. In N. Coupland, S. Sarangi and C. N. Candlin (eds) *Sociolinguistics and Social Theory*. London: Pearson. pp. 350-388.

Sarangi, S. and Clarke, A. (2002a) Constructing an account by contrast in counselling for childhood genetic testing. *Social Science and Medicine*, 54: 295-308.

Sarangi, S. and Clarke, A. (2002b) Zones of expertise and the management of uncertainty in genetics risk communication. *Research on Language and Social Interaction*, 35, 2: 139-172.

Sarangi, S., Bennert, K., Howell, L. and Clarke, A. (2003) 'Relatively speaking': Relativisation of genetic risk in counselling for predictive testing. *Health, Risk and Society*, 5, 2: 155-170.

Sarangi, S. and Roberts, C. (1999) *Talk, Work and Institutional Order: Discourse in Medical, Mediation and Management Settings*. Berlin: Mouton de Gruyter.

Turner, R. (1972) Some Formal Properties of Therapy Talk. In D. Sudnow (ed.) *Studies in Social Interaction*. New York: Free Press. pp. 367-397.

11 Quantifying non-sexist language: the case of Ms

Juliane Schwarz

Lancaster University

Abstract

After implementing Ms as alternative to Mrs and Miss in non-sexist language guidelines, a lot of research on the title quantifies its distribution and documents socio-economic backgrounds in which Ms users are most likely to be found. More recent research draws on (real or hypothetical) Community of Practice to theorise different title choices of women. In this paper, I will briefly identify the merits and shortcoming of these two approaches and which of their aspects I incorporate in my research: its aim to work towards change and the assumption that different choices are not neutral from the former; the research method (focus group discussions) and analysis (looking for metalinguistic awareness of non-sexist language) from the latter. I will discuss how my research participants report on their own practice of Ms, their evaluation of the title, and concepts they associated it with, such as 'Ms as alternative choice', 'Ms as indication of certain marital statuses and non-disclosure of marital status', "Ms as indication of being a feminist or being a lesbian' and 'Ms as an indication of age'. I will show which of these concepts are foregrounded in the three groups which were made up by participants of different age groups and whether differences in the three groups can be traced back to the different age of the participants.

Introduction

From the late 1960s and early 1970s, sexist language was a focus of critique for the new Women's Movement. Sexist language was seen as rendering females invisible, or as insulting, trivialising and/or defining them. Feminists have seen the two traditional English titles of Mrs and Miss as examples of the last point. Since they reveal information about a women's marital status, they define females in relation to men, whereas the male equivalent does not reveal a man's marital status (Kramarae and Treichler, 1985; Lakoff, 1975; Spender, 1980). To remedy this inequality, feminist language reformers suggested various alternatives (Pauwels, 1998):

a) Replace Miss and Mrs altogether with a new title (replacement option);

b) Extend the semantic field of one so that it can function as a title for all women independent of marital status, and avoid the other one (extension option);

c) Replace Mr by two different titles indicating marital status or revive master as a title for an unmarried man;

d) Introduce only one title for adult women and men together;

e) Abolish title.

For English, guidelines have promoted Ms (Miller and Swift, 1991; Pauwels, 1998).[1]

Thirty years after the topic was identified as an obstacle to gender equality, I try to gain some understanding about its relative success in replacing the two older titles in British English (Romaine, 2001). In this paper, I will discuss findings of my research about Ms, how it is talked about now, and how it is used and understood.

Background to the study

In recent research on Ms, two strands can be identified:

a) Studies on the distribution and spread of the title;

b) Studies on how identities are constructed through the choice of titles.

In strand (a), researcher analyses questionnaires data (Chiles, 2003; Pauwels

2001) or English language corpora (Holmes, 2001; Romaine, 2001) to document quantitatively whether and how Ms has succeeded in replacing Mrs or Miss. Various social factors of Ms users are compared to those of non-users.

Strand (b) can be observed in recent discussions of female titles and married women's surname choice. Sara Mills (2003), for example, discusses how her research participants, feminist academics, chose different titles to accommodate different (real or hypothetical) CoPs, for example, use Ms to stress their allegiance to a hypothesised feminist CoP whereas use Mrs to stress their commitment towards their husbands which might be important in a CoP valuing traditional (marital) ideas. In another article (Mills, 2003b), Mills discusses potential problems with this kind of approach, an approach she describes as *Third Wave Feminist Linguistics.*[2] In focusing on studies of the local and describing discrimination in certain CoPs, it is difficult for Third Wave feminists to refer to global, structural and systematic forms of discrimination and to argue for change. I would add that it is also prone to the potential danger of being understood as different choices i.e. using Ms or Mrs, or keeping or changing the woman's surname after marriage are equally valid.[3]

In my research, I combine various elements of strand (a) and strand (b). I am interested in why some non-sexist language campaigns, e.g. Ms replacing Mrs and Miss, were only relatively successful.[4] In assuming that people belong to different CoPs, i.e. 'an aggregate of people who come together around mutual engagement in an endeavour' (Eckert and McConnell-Ginet, 1992), and that the implicit or explicit acceptance of Ms might vary within these different CoPs, I do not look, however, for quantitative evidence for the distribution of Ms as in strand (a). The aim of my research is to look for metalinguistic awareness of my participants, i.e. how they report on their own practice, how they evaluate non-sexist language reforms and what concepts they associate with them. This kind of qualitative method places me in strand (b), an approach which does not assume that attitudes are cognitive processes which are fixed but seen as being negotiated locally as discussed in Discursive Psychology (Potter, 1996; Potter and Wetherell, 1987). Yet, the aim of my research is to identify potential factors which might help render certain linguistic items less sexist[5], and I work with the premise that there are choices which are better in a feminist sense than others, e.g. using Ms.

The data used in this article comes from three focus group discussions[6] with female undergraduate students from various disciplines who are all native speakers of British English.

Late Teen Group: age 18 – 19 (Kelly, Emma, Abi, Lisa)

Mid 30s Group: age 35 – 37 (Rebecca, Louise, Kate, Gemma)

Over 50s Group: age 52 – 64 (Anne, Helen, Elizabeth, Chris)

The groups were moderated by myself. In each group, there was one other person in the room who assisted me and helped with the recording. To even out the age imbalance between the moderator (33 years old) and the participants, the assistants were roughly the same age as the participants.

Participants' reported practice of Ms

One of my questions concerned the participants' own practice in relation to Ms. The only participants to report using Ms as a title for themselves are in the Mid 30s Group. Two of them, Rebecca and Kate, make it clear that they use Ms. Kate does not give any reasons for her choice, but Rebecca discards Mrs and Miss. She associates Miss with younger females: 'I'm not a Miss (.) I'm not a girl anymore', and Mrs only with married women: 'and Mrs is wrong (.) cos I'm not married' (Rebecca, Mid 30s Group, 113). She thus relates her choice to use Ms in relation to marital status and age.

This supports quantitative findings on the distribution and spread of Ms which indicate that age is an important factor in choice of title and that it is most widely used by women who do not fall into traditional categories of 'married' and 'single/unmarried' (Chiles, 2003; Pauwels, 2003, 2001, 1998). Pauwels claims that Ms is, however, increasingly used by women within these traditional categories in Australia (Pauwels, 2003: 566). This positive evaluation of the title's success is not, however, supported by my own data from the Over 50s Group, in which all the participants are married and claim not to use Ms, and the Late Teen Group, in which all the participants are unmarried and claim to use Miss.[7]

The possibility that the usage of Ms is spreading within the community of women who are married and therefore would traditionally use Mrs can, however, be found in the response of another participant in the Mid 30s Group. Louise indicates that she utilises different titles in different CoPs. She distinguishes between using Ms professionally and Mrs in private: 'professionally (.) if I was a (.) like a chair or whatever (.) I'd go neutral (.)...

but being married (.) I suppose you use (.) I use Mrs' (Louise, Mid 30s Group, 125). The strategy of choosing different titles appropriate to different CoPs is also discussed in Mills (2003). Mills shows that her (feminist) participants do this, but, she sees this choice as a potential site of tension and struggle for them, indicating different potentially conflicting affiliations. Louise, however, seems to make her choice on pragmatic grounds and does not identify any tension.

In the same turn, Louise raises another important issue which might shed light on the relative success of Ms. Although she indicate that she uses the titles differently in different CoPs, the way she explains her usage of Mrs in private suggests that it is this title which she identifies most closely with: 'I use Mrs cause that's **what I am**' (Louise, Mid 30s Group, 125). Being married seems to be the most important identity for this married woman, and the title Mrs is important to her.

The connection between female titles and marital status can also be found in a response of another Mid 30s Group's participant. Gemma recently separated from her husband and seems to find it hard to identify an appropriate title.

121	G	I'd rather just use a name (..) just my first name as opposed to using (.) I'm separated (.) so (.) rather not say Mrs or Miss or anything (.) there is too much story there [laughter]
122	J	what do you tick (.) when you (.) when you tick a form
123	G	oh (..) I don't know (.) it's just a recent thing (.) cos I'm undecided at the moment so (.) I just leave it blank [laughter]

Conversely to Louise, it seems that Mrs is so strongly connected with her married identity, that being separated (and not even divorced) the title does not seem to be available for her anymore.

Later in the discussion, Gemma and Louise discuss how they were treated differently when they were married and were addressed as Mrs:

140 G   I think (.) you're treated differently (..) being a Mrs (.) I
            noticed this when I very first got married (.) completely
            different in shops and everything [J really] yeah (.) cause
            you're a Mrs (.) it's (.) I don't know (.) it's a subtle (..)
            underlying (..) change (..) you're more accepted as more (.)
            I don't know (..) there's a difference (.) I think (.) definitely
            (..) I don't know about the Ms thing or the Miss thing yet
            (.) but I'll let you know (.) [J laughs] if there is any subtle
            change on that (.) I think you see (.) tend to get treated
            more (.) em (.) grown up (.) or something
141 L   yeah (.) a bit more like a responsible adult (.) [S mm] I
            suppose (.) so (.) like if you go to the bank (..) I don't
            know (.) if you're 20 and not married (.) they wouldn't
            have taken me seriously (.) as go in (.) being married and
            settled down and (.) you know (.) because you get a family
            then and (.) you're more secure (.) I suppose (.) aren't you
            (.) but I think (.) the perception of Miss is like (.) wayward
            child (.) they're not gonna (..) be as responsible

These participants describe a link between Mrs and ideas about maturity and
'being grown-up' which is evaluated very positively (see also Mills,
2003:102). As a consequence, it seems to be quite natural for them that being
a Mrs becomes an important identity for a married woman which in turn
makes Mrs a very prestigious title. This might be one reason why Ms was not
very successful in replacing Mrs as a title for married women in Britain.[8]

Participants' evaluation of Ms
Ms seems to be quite negatively evaluated when the participants are asked
directly about it. Anne in the Over 50s Group uses the word 'hate' when she
speaks about Ms:

> well I think (.) it is (.) but I think most divorced women do (.) my
> daughter is divorced (.) and she uses Ms (.) and I **hate** it (.) and I said
> (.) why [laugh] why are using Ms (.) (Anne, Over 50s Group, 211)

Anne does not give any reasons for why she feels so strongly about Ms. The
same is true of Helen, another participant in the Over 50s Group:

I think (.) it's good (..) when this came up (.) **I don't like M** (.) **S** (.)
either (.) but I was very pleased (.) cause I always found it offensive (.)
when I was a teenager (.) the Mrs and the Miss (.) why should men
just be Mr [De yeah] and why should we be Mrs or Miss (.) I always
hated that (Helen, Over 50s Group, 348)

Although Anne seems to be very pleased to have an alternative to Mrs and
Miss, she still indicates a dislike for the new title, as though it were important
to distance herself from it, yet does not make clear why.

Kate in the Mid 30s Group also indicates that, although she identifies
herself as a Ms user, she does not like the title. She says she finds it difficult to
pronounce: 'me (..) officially (.) Miss or Ms (.) em (..) I use (.) M (.) S (.) but
I hate that word (.) cause I can barely say it' (Kate, Mid 30s Group, 116). Kate
refers to a general problem related to the pronunciation of the title Ms: It
constitutes of a consonant cluster /mz/ which is unacceptable in English and a
vowel needs to be inserted to make it acceptable. Pauwels indicate that there
is, however, no agreement on the quality of this vowel which should be
inserted, resulting in various phonological variants of Ms. Pauwels makes it
clear that this might lead to confusion and misunderstanding (Pauwels
1998:137), a problem Kate addresses quite candidly: 'I sound like a demented
being (.) when I say it' (Kate, Mid 30s Group, 116).

The question of a title for women which does not indicate marital status
therefore seems to be expressed in terms of two extreme poles in the two
older groups. On the one hand, there are strong negative feelings expressed
towards the term. On the other hand, availability of a title not indicating
marital status seems to be considered important.

This is different in the Late Teen Group, the group with the youngest
participants. None of them indicate any feelings towards the title directly. The
underlying attitude seems to be informed by the idea that 'it's good that
there is a choice' (Emma, Late Teen Group). On the other hand, none of the
Late Teen Group's participants reports using Ms. When I ask them about
their own practice, all of them indicated they use Miss.

The way in which Ms is discussed within the Late Teen Group suggests a
detached mild curiosity about a phenomenon which seems to have little or
nothing to do with their own lives. They discuss Ms mainly in connection
with women's marital status. Being married does not seem to be an option
for the participants of the Late Teen Group yet: 'but (.) our age obviously (..)

you're not gonna be married (.) or something' (Emma, Late Teen Group, 141). Their main examples of Ms users are their former school teachers, which does not seem to add to the popularity of the title for this young group.

Participants of the two older groups seem rather to show ambivalent yet strong feelings about Ms. This youngest group does not seem to share these strong feelings. They seem to take a distancing stance towards the title relating it to certain practices, i.e. marriage and certain people, e.g. teachers, but not to themselves.

Conceptualisation

In the three groups, Ms is discussed in relation to the following concepts: Ms as an alternative choice, certain marital statuses and non-disclosure of marital status; Ms as indication of being a feminist or being a lesbian; and Ms as a indication of age.

Ms as an alternative choice Ms as an alternative choice is discussed by Deborah Cameron as a positive outcome of non-sexist language reforms (of which she is otherwise rather critical): 'Choice has altered the value of the terms and removed the options of political neutrality' (Cameron, 1999: 119).

The concept of having an alternative to Mrs and Miss is spontaneously brought up in all three groups. The idea of having a choice itself is seen to be important and rather positive for the participants, e.g. in Helen's (Over 50s Group) and Emma's (Late Teen Group) arguments as discussed above. However, the more political idea of 'not only having a choice but it being non-neutral' is not found directly in my data.

In the Mid 30s Group, Louise makes a slightly different point. Whereas Helen and Emma discuss the title as an alternative which is good to have, Louise points out that a woman using Ms might be perceived as somebody making an active choice and therefore sees Ms as a tool to convey agency and strength:

'I think Ms (..) gives (..) the idea that **you choose** (.) to be that… if you choose to be Ms (.) then **you've** decided that (.) and that's what **you** want to be' (Louise, Mid 30s Group, 154). She compares Ms to Miss: '…whereas Miss (.) you don't choose (.) because you just haven't been saved by a man (.) do you know (.) it's that (.) isn't it (.) it's like (.) if you stay at Miss (.) then (..) you're lacking something (.) because

somebody else hadn't come and changed you (.) your name...'
(Louise, Mid 30s Group, 154).

Another participant in the Mid 30s Group describes how she has to defend
herself when she introduces herself as a Ms. She makes it, however, quite
clear that she has the right to choose the title which she things best:

> 'when I (.) when I do say Ms (.) to some (.) some different groups (.)
> it's particularly older men (.) they (.) they normally go off on one [J
> and they do what] and I have to defend (.) why I'm saying Ms (.) and
> I have to explain to them the whole history behind it (.) and than
> eventually (.) they'll say (.) oh right (.) yeah (.) I guess you have a right
> to call yourself that of course (.) I've got a right to call myself anything
> I bloody want [laughs] but they have the attitude (.) that I have to
> really defend it' (Rebecca, Mid 30s Group, 160).

Ms as indication of certain marital statuses and non-disclosure of marital status
In the Over 50s Group and the Late Teen Group, the first reaction to the
question about Ms is that the title is used by divorcees: 'because there are so
many (.) erm (.) divorced ladies now (..) who prefer that...' (Anne, Over 50s
Group, 206) and 'for me (..) em (..) the people who I know who use that are
usually divorced women' (Kelly, Late Teen Group, 121).

Anne's idea that Ms is used mainly by divorced women is immediately
challenged by Elizabeth in the Over 50s Group. Elizabeth does not seem to
believe that Ms is a title for divorced woman but that 'it was a symbol of (.)
er (.) somebody who (.) refused to say (.) whether they were married or not'
(Elizabeth, Over 50s Group, 209). Anne justifies her assumption by referring
to her own experiences. Her daughter is divorced and uses the title.

The participants of the Late Teen Group suggest four more groups of
people who might use Ms, in addition to those given above:

> Women who are not married but cohabiting;

> Women who do not want people to know whether they are relying
> on men;

> Women who feel too old not to be married (and who are embarrassed
> about it);

> Women who might think that they would be regarded differently

whether they are married or not.

Ms as indication of being a feminist or being a lesbian Some studies suggest that the new title Ms is associated by hearers with certain social identities of its user. As shown above, one such could be that Ms users are identified as being divorced. There are, however, other concepts which the title may convey in different CoPs, e.g. being a feminist or being a lesbian (Ehrlich and King, 1992; Pauwels, 1998, 1987).

The concept that Ms is an indicator of a feminist can be found in the utterance of just one of the participants. She makes it clear, however, that this is not the opinion of the participant herself, but of certain groups of people who construct Ms users negatively:

> but if you use Ms as well (.) I mean sometimes as you say that (..) especially to men (..) they did (.) sometimes it's like (.) you know (.) they've got that knowing look like (.) you know (.) bra-burning (.) **feminist** (.) bolshy (..) you know (.) manic-type person (Kate, Mid 30s Group, 157)

The association between Ms use and feminists is not made anywhere else in the discussion groups. Feminism itself, however, is brought up in the Late Teen Group in relation to Ms. One of the participants refers to feminism and Ms in three different turns. None of the others mention it but do seem to support Emma (yeah) when she argues that Ms is 'like a feminist thing'.

> I think (.) that's **like a feminist thing** [some: **yeah**] (..) to me (.) I don't know (.) that's like (..) a couple of teachers were like Ms so and so and (.) that was (.) I think (.) that was (.) **a feminist thing** (.) because they don't wanna (..) [sb yeah] they didn't want people to know whether they were married or not (.) because the fact that whether or not (.) they were (.) like (.) relying on their man (..) [J laughs] it's irrelevant (.) and it's like that (..) to me (.) that's **like a feminist thing** (Emma, Late Teen Group, 124)

Not disclosing one's marital status seems to be a 'feminist thing' for Emma because overtly married women might be seen as relying on their men. Feminism is brought up again by Emma when I ask the group whether 'there might be any point abolishing Mrs and Miss altogether'. After a pause, Emma indicates that 'there is a feminist argument for that;' for her, however,

it is not necessary to abolish Miss and Mrs since neither of these titles seems
to be negative.

147 E   yeah (.) I could see (.) that there's **like a feminist
             argument for that** [J yeah, yeah] but in (.) in reality I
             don't (..) think that that's necessary
148 J   you don't think (.) it's (.) it's important
149 E   E no (.) cause I don't think either of them are negative (.)
             are they [J pardon] I don't think either of (..) either of the
             Miss or Mrs are negative terms (..) if they were (.) then
             yeah (.) maybe that should be abolished (.) cause (..) but I
             (..) like I say (.) there is (.) **there is a feminist argument
             for it** (.) but in reality (.) I don't think it's necessary (.)
             that's my opinion

Emma constructs herself as aware of a feminist argument which supports the
substitution of Ms for Mrs and Miss. She makes it clear, however, that this is
not her own personal opinion. She distances herself from this argument by
claiming that the two older titles are not negative. She constructs the
'feminist argument' as unrealistic by inserting a contrastive structure '**there is**
a feminist argument for it (.) **but** in reality' (Atkinson, 1984), which indicate
that the abolishing of the two older terms is not an endeavour correspond
with reality.

Unlike findings of other studies (Pauwels, 1987), Ms in this study is
associated more with feminism and feminist ideas, than as an indicator of
being a feminist. Similar observations can be made in relation to the concept
'Ms as indicator of being a lesbian'.

Ms as indicator of being a lesbian is mentioned only once but, as in 'Ms
being a feminist', it is not the participant's own opinion but rather a
hypothetical position against which she has to defend herself. In the Mid 30s
Group, Rebecca lists some assumptions associated with the title by some
different groups (particularly older men): 'is it because I'm a **lesbian** (.) and
stuff like that (.) and there is a whole assumption that I'm a man hater'
(Rebecca, Mid 30s Group, 160). Neither Rebecca nor the other participants
themselves seem to associate the use of Ms with being a lesbian. There seems
to be some metalinguistic awareness, however, that some groups of people do

make this connection.

Ms as an indication of age As indicated above, age is identified as an important factor of Ms usage by Pauwels (2003, 2001, 1998). Age is conceptualised in relation to the title in the Mid 30s Group and the Late Teen Group. In the Mid 30s Group, Rebecca explains why she prefers using Ms instead of Miss by identifying the second title as one for younger women 'I'm not a Miss (.) I'm not a girl anymore' (Rebecca, Mid 30s Group, 108).

In the Late Teen Group, age seem to be a bigger issue. It is mentioned three times and mainly in connection of being old and not married.

> some people I know (.) they use it (.) cause like (.) they **feel they're quite old not to be married** (..) but if (.) if they call themselves Miss (.) they think of elderly (.) spinster type (Abi, Late Teen Group, 125)

> yeah (.) you more (.) not want people to know if you weren't married (.) so you might use Ms (.) but (.) **our age** obviously (..) you not gonna be married (.) or something (Emma, Late Teen Group, 141)

> it's good that there is a choice (.) cause if women like (..) are embarrassed about the fact that they are **older and still not married** (Emma, Late Teen Group, 143)

Age thus seems to be an important concept in the choice of a female title in the youngest discussion group along with marital status. The title is seen mainly in relation to these two concepts. It is worthwhile remembering that the whole group agreed that they were non-Ms users. This implies that their present title choice, Miss, is as a temporary option which might change in the case of marriage and/or when they get older.

Conclusion

Reported practices, evaluations and conceptualisations of Ms vary quite dramatically in the three different focus groups. The discussion shows, however, that these variations are not linear, i.e. that the younger the participants, the more they use non-sexist language; or that the more they have witnessed the feminist movement, the more they are open to suggested change. Various other aspects are foregrounded rather differently in the three groups.

In the youngest group, the participants agree that they do not use Ms at all. Their attitude towards the title does not, however, seem to be negative. They appear to appreciate and even share some (quasi-) feminist arguments, e.g. it is good to have a choice. On the other hand, they seem to regard Ms as something which has little to do with their own lives, and relate to it mainly in terms of (lack of) marital status and (non-young) age.

In the group with the oldest participants, the discussion about Ms is relatively short; it revolves mainly around the concept of choice and whether Ms is a title for divorcees or for women who do not want to reveal their marital status. The first possibility is seen as rather positive, although the attitudes towards Ms are rather negative.

The participants of the Mid 30s Group foreground the concept of choice. They describe a Ms user as a person who is seen as making her own choices. The right to do so seems to be important. The discussion about Ms indicates a further aspect in relation to female titles: how being a Mrs seems to be an important identity for married women. As a consequence, the married title Mrs seems to accrue considerable prestige. This might be one of the reasons why Ms has not been successful in replacing Mrs for married women.

Notes on transcription conventions

(.) aspiration pause
(..) longer pause
[remarks] remarks and back-channelling in square brackets
[laughter] more than one person is laughing
[laughs] speaker laughs or it is indicated who it is
(Anne, Over 50s Group, 154) speaker, group and turn in round brackets

Notes

1 In other languages, for example Dutch and German, feminist language reformers have promoted the 'extension' option, i.e. they have not invented a new neutral title but have extended the referential potential of the title for married women (*mevrouw* in Dutch, *Frau* in German) to a title for all women.

2 They are also identified as postmodern feminist linguistic (Swann, 2002).

3 This might be one reason why Sara Mills was constructed by a moderator of the BBC radio programme *Woman's Hour* (11.4.2002) as supporting the idea that women should change their surname to that of their husbands when they marry.

4 In addition to Ms, I am also interested in other 'classical' sexist terms and concepts such as 'generic' he, -person compounds –ess suffixes, girl used for an adult woman as well as how non-sexist language intervention is judged.

5   This is, of course, not the only aim of a feminist linguist (see the discussion on sexist discourse in Cameron, 1992).

6   I conducted these for research for my PhD thesis on attitudes towards non-sexist language.

7   The amount of data in my research is, of course, not big enough to make a quantitative claim for British English.

8   Studies in Dutch and German suggest that the 'extension' strategy seems to be much more successful (Pauwels, 1996).

References

Atkinson, J. (1984) *Our Master's Voices: The Language and Body Language of Politics*. London: Methuen.

Cameron, D. (1992) *Feminism and Linguistic Theory*. London: Macmillian.

Cameron, D. (1995) *Verbal Hygiene*. London: Routledge

Chiles, T. (2003) 'Titles and Surnames in the Linguistic Construction of Women's Identity.' *New Zealand Studies of Applied Linguistics*, 9.

Eckert, P. and McConnell-Ginet, S. (1992) 'Think Practically and Look Locally: Language and Gender as Community Based Practice.' *Annual Review of Anthropology*, 21: 461-490.

Ehrlich, S. and King, R. (1992) 'Gender-Based Language Reform and the Social Construction of Meaning.' *Discourse and Society*, 3, 2: 151-166.

Holmes, J. (2001) 'A Corpus-based View of Gender in New Zealand.' In M. Hellinger and H. Bussmann (eds) *Gender Across Languages: The Linguistic Representation of Women and Men*. Amsterdam: Benjamins. pp. 105-114.

Kramarae, C. and Treichler, P. (1985) *A Feminist Dictionary*. London: Pandora Press.

Lakoff, R. (1975) *Language and Woman's Place*. New York: Harper.

Miller, C. and Swift, K. (1991) *Words and Women: New Language in New Times*. New York: Harper Collins.

Mills, S. (2003) 'Caught between Sexism, Anti-Sexism and 'Political Correctness': Feminist Women's Negotiations with Naming Practices.' *Discourse and Society*, 14, 1: 87-110.

Mills, S. (2003b) 'Third Wave Feminist Linguistics and the Analysis of Sexism.' *Discourse Analysis Online*, 2, 1.

Pauwels, A. (1987) 'Language in Transition: A Study of the Title Ms in Contemporary Australian Society.' In A. Pauwels (ed.) *Women and Language in Australian and New Zealand Society*. Sydney: Australian Professional Publications. pp. 129-154.

Pauwels, A. (1996) 'Feminist Language Planning and Titles for Women: Some Crosslinguistic Perspectives.' In U. Ammon and M. Hellinger (eds) *Contrastive Sociolinguistics*. Berlin: Mouton De Gruyter. pp. 251-169.

Pauwels, A. (1998) *Women Changing Language*. London: Longman.

Pauwels, A. (2001) 'Spreading the Feminist Word: The Case of the New Courtesy Title Ms in Australian English.' In M. Hellinger and H. Bussmann (eds) *Gender Across Languages: The Linguistic Representation of Women and Men*. Amsterdam: Benjamins. pp. 115-136.

Pauwels, A. (2003) 'Linguistic Sexism and Feminist Linguistic Activism.' In J. Holmes and M. Meyerhoff (eds) *The Handbook of Language and Gender*. Oxford: Blackwell. pp. 550-570.

Potter, J. (1996) *Representing Reality. Discourse, Rhetoric and Social Construction*. London: Sage.

Potter, J. and Wetherell, M. (1987) *Discourse and Social Psychology. Beyond Attitudes and Behaviour*. London: Sage.

Romaine, S. (2001) 'A Corpus-Based View of Gender in British and American English.' In M. Hellinger and H. Bussmann (eds) *Gender Across Languages*. Amsterdam: Benjamins. pp. 153-175.

Spender, D. (1980) (1985) *Man-Made Language*. London: Routledge and Kegan.

Swann, J. (2002) 'Yes, but is it gender?' In L. Litosseliti and J. Sunderland (eds) *Gender Identity and Discourse Analysis*. Amsterdam: Benjamins. pp. 43-67.

12 Interaction in the literacy hour: a case study of learners with English as an additional language

Catriona Scott
University of Bristol

Abstract

This paper reports the findings of an exploratory case study which looked at interaction during guided group work in the Literacy Hour, focusing on learners with English as an Additional Language (EAL). The National Literacy Strategy is considered by the DfEE (1998) to have benefits for learners with EAL as it provides opportunities for collaborative learning and guidelines for teaching practice which implicitly advocate negotiation of meaning and of form. It has been suggested that this may facilitate language acquisition (see, for example, Ellis et al., 1994 and Mackey, 1999). However, in the EAL context, Cameron et al. (1996) consider that there is a tendency for teachers and pupils to collude in developing strategies which avoid negotiation. Through an analysis of secondary data from an ESRC-funded research project on classroom assessment it appeared that, whilst negotiation of form was more prevalent than negotiation of meaning, generally Cameron et al.'s (1996) scepticism would appear to be well-founded.

Introduction

The case study discussed here explored opportunities for negotiated interaction during guided group work with the Class Teacher (CT) or Language Support Coordinator (LSC) in the Literacy Hour and focused on primary school learners with English as an Additional Language (EAL).[1] Secondary data was analysed for interactional modifications or negotiation sequences, drawing on Pica and Doughty (1985) and Mackey (1999).

Second language acquisition (SLA) research has suggested that negotiated interaction, in which the learner or the teacher signals a difficulty which is resolved through negotiation, has potential benefits for linguistic development. However, research into negotiated interaction has typically been undertaken in EFL or adult settings, in contrast to the EAL context in which children are engaged in language learning across the curriculum in mainstream classrooms.

The study discussed in this paper focused on the Literacy Hour, part of the National Literacy Strategy introduced by the DfEE[2] in 1998 to raise standards of literacy in primary schools. The strategy provides objectives for each year and term in phonics, spelling and vocabulary, grammar and punctuation, comprehension and composition. These objectives are to be met through dedicating an hour a day to literacy, divided into segments as shown in Figure 1.

The DfEE (1998: 106) suggests that the National Literacy Strategy (NLS) has a key role in meeting the linguistic needs of EAL learners, stating that it 'can help pupils to make more rapid progress in learning with EAL than

Figure 1 How to divide the hour: drawing on the National Literacy Strategy Framework for teaching, DfES, 2001: 9

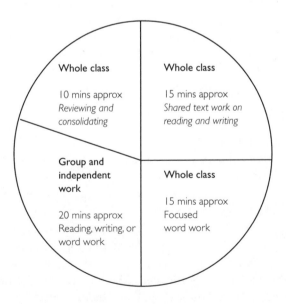

might otherwise be the case'. Within the Literacy Hour, group work is considered by the Teacher Training Agency (TTA, 2000: 47) to be of particular value as 'Well-structured group work and opportunities to work collaboratively are particularly effective in helping pupils with EAL to learn English, since they allow pupils to test their ideas and understanding, and ask questions to clarify their understanding, in a supportive environment'.

The DfEE (1998) and TTA (2000) advocate teaching practices consistent with the promotion of negotiation of meaning and of form in emphasizing the importance of opportunities for EAL learners to ask questions to clarify understanding and of 'focused attention to language learning' (DfEE 1998: 106). However, the extent to which proposals match practice is far from certain. As Sylva (1997:13) points out, 'Even when working to a shared National Curriculum and within a relatively small geographical area, within one LEA, teachers' delivery is remarkably diverse at the classroom level'.

This study aimed to provide an in-depth picture of what happens in the classroom, considering findings from SLA research in terms of the implications for negotiated interaction in the Literacy Hour with EAL learners.

Negotiated interaction and the implications for learners with EAL

Long (1996:453) states the need for caution in advocating negotiated interaction, pointing out that the Interaction Hypothesis '…involves a mix of well and less well-established L1 and L2 acquisition research findings, some rather high inference interpretation, and some speculation'.

However, Mitchell and Myles (1996) maintain that there is considerable intuitive support for the Interaction Hypothesis and that research evidence for it is building.

Researching the impact of negotiation of meaning on comprehension, Loschky (1994) and Ellis et al. (1994) found that unmodified input with negotiation has greater impact on comprehension than pre-modified input which has been adjusted to be comprehensible to the learner.

However, a number of factors may limit negotiation of meaning. Foster (1998), studying dyads and groups in an EFL classroom, found that the amount of negotiation depended on the approach taken by individual learners to the task. In the dyads, some learners adopted strategies such as extracting information, rather than waiting for their partner to supply it. In the groups, some learners dominated the interaction, whilst others contributed little or nothing. Foster (1998) concludes that whilst teachers can present learners with opportunities for negotiation, they cannot force the learners to take them and negotiation may not happen even in a task specifically designed to encourage it. In addition, Aston (1986) points out that frequent or lengthy interruption for negotiation of meaning may become frustrating and that learners can feign comprehension hoping all will become clear later.

In negotiation of form, linguistic code is highlighted through negative feedback to promote noticing of a gap between the learner's interlanguage and the target language. However, Swain (1995) suggests that rather than promoting noticing through input by flooding (increased instances of the form) or enhancement (highlighting the form in some way), there needs to be a focus on output:

> [Swain] ... has argued convincingly that learners may need access to 'pushed output' in order to advance to higher levels of grammatical proficiency. She suggested that pressure to produce language that is concise and appropriate may help learners test hypotheses about the L2 and encourage them to engage in syntactic as opposed to semantic processing (Ellis, 1994:456).

The feedback necessary to induce pushed output can be overt (apparent to the learner) or covert. Teachers may use a combination of both, for example repetition followed by a recast in which the teacher reformulates the utterance. Lightbown (1998) points out that recasts are a common form of feedback, but when used in isolation without explicit or overt negative feedback, they can be heard as a continuation of the conversation rather than as corrective feedback:

> S: I don't speak very well English.
> T: You don't speak English very well
> S: No.

> The student's response is conversationally appropriate but shows no evidence that the corrective feedback has been noticed (Lightbown 1998:192).

This study considered both overt and covert feedback in promoting noticing of form and the implications in terms of how the pupils may perceive the feedback.

There are several possible benefits for EAL learners in negotiating meaning and form, namely that:

input can be at a level that maintains cognitive complexity, an important factor in integrating EAL learners into the mainstream classroom (School Curriculum and Assessment Authority [SCAA] 1996 and the National Association for Language Development in the Curriculum [NALDIC] 1998);

meaningful interaction involves reciprocity (Malamah-Thomas, 1987) which makes the prediction of comprehension problems necessary for pre-modified input unworkable; with negotiated interaction, prediction is not necessary as problems are dealt with as they arise;

negotiation of form has the potential for helping learners to notice gaps between their interlanguage and target language (Mackey, 1999);

through 'pushed output' learners are encouraged to produce more target-like utterances (Swain, 1995).

However, in addition to the factors which might limit negotiation noted above, in mainstream classrooms where language is taught through curriculum subjects, Cameron et al. (1996:224) comment that negotiation of meaning may be inhibited, since 'Subject classrooms seem to be prone to the joint construction by teachers and pupils of coping strategies that reduce communication problems by reducing demands and responses'.

This study therefore aimed to explore negotiation of meaning and of form in classes with EAL learners during the Literacy Hour to see whether guided group work does provide an environment conducive to negotiated interaction.

The study
The findings from the case study reported here are based on analysis of secondary data from an ESRC-funded project focusing on classroom assessment[5] which aimed to explore opportunities for and instances of negotiation of meaning and form.

Audio data from four guided group work sessions in the Literacy Hour, each lasting approximately 20 minutes, were transcribed and analysed; for three sessions video data were also available. The sessions selected were from

Table I Selected sessions from Key Stage I

Session	Audio	Video	Led by
A I – Thunderbird			LSC
A2 – Fisherman			CT
BI – Mr Crunchy Crisp			LCS
B2 – Moon			CT

two classes at Key Stage 1 containing a high proportion of EAL learners; in each class one session was led by the Class Teacher (CT) and one by the Language Support Coordinator (LSC) (Table 1).

Instances of negotiation of meaning were explored using Pica and Doughty's (1985) *Interactional modifications in the negotiation of meaning* and the data were analysed for clarification requests, confirmation checks, comprehension checks and self- or other-repetitions. Foster (2001) warns that there is a danger of finding what you are looking for and that a repetition may be coded as negotiation when in fact it simply indicates that the speaker was listening. Coding was therefore checked with a peer for reliability and the audio and video recordings were used to provide additional information and aid interpretation.

The data were analysed for negotiation of form by looking for covert feedback, for example in the form of a clarification request:

NNS: He pass his house.
NS: Sorry?
NNS: He passed, he passed, ah, his sign.

(Nobuyoshi and Ellis, 1993:204)

and for overt feedback, for example through repetition and/or recast:

S   He's in the bathroom.
T   Bathroom? Bedroom. He's in the bedroom.

(Lightbown and Spada, 1999:105)

In addition, the role of negative feedback was considered in terms of whether it promoted reformulation by the learner and the data was analysed for instances of 'pushed output' (Swain, 1995), continued negotiation until a target-like utterance is produced.

Findings
The findings from the analysis of each of the four guided group work sessions are illustrated using extracts from the data which highlight particular episodes showing negotiated interaction. The context for each session is given briefly at the beginning of each section.

Thunderbird session Six learners and the LSC were grouped in a circle, reading 'Thunderbird' from *Toys and Games* and the focus of the session was on prediction. It began with a discussion of what was happening in the story based on the pictures. The learners then read individually, with the LSC supporting each learner in turn (this part was not recorded). After reviewing the story so far, the LSC asked the learners to predict what might happen next. The LSC then read aloud with the learners following in their books to see if their predictions were borne out. The session concluded with a review in which the LSC elicited what had happened.

Early on in the session, there was an opportunity for negotiation of meaning, shown in Extract 1 (below). The learners had their books open at a picture of a boy looking at a toy car in a shop window. The extract shows the LSC trying to elicit 'shop window' in turn 3, and Gin supplying 'The window' in turn 4. The LSC seeks clarification in turn 5, beginning a process of negotiation through the subsequent turns:

Extract 1

3	LSC	Rah, we're not going to read yet
		Right, you can see that–
		Can you see that blue car on the box that the boy's–
		What do you think he's looking through?
4	Gin	Can you see him looking?
5	LSC	The window
		The window
		The window of what do you think it might be?
6	Rah	Car
7	LSC	He's not looking through the window of a car
		What's he looking through the window of?
8	Mat	Um, the (screen)

9   LSC Looking through–
                    The boy?
                    Can you see that boy there?
                    He's going like this
                    Can you see him in the picture?
                    He's looking
                    What's he looking through?
                    Somebody said the window

The LSC's elicitations and the extended attempt at clarification in turn 9 do not elicit 'shop window' and the LSC eventually abandons the negotiation, providing the answer and 'framing' a shop window with her hands.

This episode raises issues about coding, since I originally considered it an extended misapprehension and an opportunity for negotiation which was missed. Perhaps, though, it is more a question of what is being negotiated and by whom. The questions in this episode come from the LSC, rather than the learners attempting to clarify their understanding, which the TTA (2000) asserts is an opportunity afforded by group work in the Literacy Hour. We do not discover which window Gin meant in turn 4 since a different learner responds to each elicitation; there is no reciprocity in terms of an individual learner and the teacher, but between the group as a whole and the teacher, which perhaps differs from the building of a conversation envisaged by Malamah-Thomas (1987).

In addition, this extract shows the limitations of transcripts, as the video data show another learner, unseen by the LSC, pointing to the picture in his book during turn 9 and apparently indicating the shop window, although he does not say anything.

Turning next to negotiation of form, there were several instances of recasts, as in the following episode taken from later in the session when the LSC is eliciting information about a picture which shows the same boy at school, drawing the toy car:

Extract 2

38   LSC   He's at school, all right
                 What's he doing?

39	Avt	He's try to draw a car
40	LSC	Right, you think he's trying to draw a picture of that Thunderbird car
		Page seventeen, then, let's look at that–
		no, no

In turn 40 the LSC reformulates and expands on Avt's response of turn 39 and then moves on. In this episode and the other three instances of recasts during the 20 minute session, the LSC's reformulations are not accompanied by explicit negative feedback and at no point are they repeated by the learners. As a result, it is not clear whether the recasts are taken by the learners to be corrective feedback or a social move, in other words whether the gap between interlanguage and target language is noticed (Lightbown, 1998).

In practical terms, however, eliciting repetitions from the learners would lead to frequent interruptions in the flow of the session which could prove disruptive rather than helpful (Aston, 1986) and I interpret the modelling of the target language without explicit negative feedback as consistent with a focus on the meaning of the story rather than on linguistic code features.

Fisherman session In this session, four pupils led by the CT worked on creating a suitable ending for a story involving an enchanted fish which granted wishes. The session began with a review of the story so far and the CT reminded the learners of plot structure before asking them to suggest how the story might end.

There was a single instance of negotiation of meaning in the session, but this came from the CT rather than a learner. At this point, the CT was eliciting what might happen next in the story and in the extract given below a learner suggests 'They all might jump off the roof'. It is not clear who might jump and the CT requests clarification in turn 80, given by the learner in turn 81:

Extract 3

79	Px[6]	They all might (jump off the roof)
80	CT	Who might?
81	Px	the fish– the fish might kill himself so they can't have no more wishes

> 82 CT The fish would kill himself?
> Hmm

Interestingly, the learner's explanation contains an error, '...they can't have no more wishes', which goes uncorrected. The lack of correction here I interpret as indicating a continued focus on meaning, the CT responding with a doubtful 'Hmm' as she considers the validity of the learner's suggestion.

As in the Thunderbird session described above, there was more negotiation of form than of meaning, with reformulations by the CT which again were not repeated by the learners, raising the issue of whether the corrective feedback was noticed (Lightbown, 1998). An exception in which the CT gives overt negative feedback is shown in the following extract. The learners are reading aloud (indicated by capital letters) and read 'went' as 'wife'. The CT interjects in turn 28 and the learners read the word again correctly. The CT then repeats the entire phrase before the learners continue reading:

Extract 4

> 27 PP[6] THE FISHERMAN WIFE
> 28 CT No-/
> 29 PP WENT
> 30 CT THE FISHERMAN WENT
> 31 PP TO SEE THE ENCHANTED FISH (★★★) FISH (★★★)

Not all errors were corrected, however, and it is not clear what criteria the CT used in determining whether an error went unchecked or not. Given that the focus of the session was on generating ideas for the story ending, it could be that the CT did not correct utterances in which a linguistic problem did not impede meaning, as I would suggest is the case below:

Extract 5

> 40 CT Go on then Ade
> 41 Ade The waves was coming
> 42 CT Yes
> 43 Ade The sky was going darker and darker

Although there are errors in both of Ade's utterances, his meaning is clear and the ideas are accepted by the CT. However, I was unable to check my interpretation with the CT and the interpretation is therefore high inference.

Mr Crunchy Crisp session The focus of this session was on phonics and in the first part of the session, the seven learners worked individually to create sentences containing as many /cr/ sounds as possible which they wrote in their Have-a-Go books, with the LSC providing help where necessary. In the final part of the session, the learners matched pictures to the initial sounds of the words (/c/, /cl/, and /cr/).

In terms of negotiation of meaning, the matching task in the final part of the session led to several comprehension checks and clarification requests, as in the following extract in which the LSC is describing a picture to the learners who are to draw a line from the picture to the initial letter of the word, in this case 'cape'. Nal, pointing to her paper (apparent from the video recording), requests confirmation in turn 261, and the LSC reiterates the word 'cape' in turn 263:

Extract 6

260	LSC	There's a little boy, or a little girl running and there's an arrow pointing to something, and it's pointing to a–
		Cape
		Cape
261	Nal	That?
262	Px	(cloak)
263	LSC	Cape
		Not cake
		Cape, cape

From the unidentified learner's interjection of 'cloak' in turn 262, it is apparent that the picture prompt could validly be linked to either /c/ or /cl/ as the initial sound, since there seems to be no reason why 'cloak' would be any less acceptable than 'cape'. This contribution was not taken up; it is unlikely that the LSC heard it, since on the audio recording the interjection was very quiet and she was dealing with the query from Nal at the time.

There are several cases of negotiation of form. Extract 7 (below) is taken from the earlier part of the session in which the learners are thinking of sentences to describe what Mr Crunchy Crisp could be doing; the sentences are supposed to involve as many /cr/ sounds as possible. Here, Ehi makes a suggestion which is reformulated by the LSC with explicit corrective feedback in turn 91. There is, however, no indication that Ehi notices the correction; his focus has moved to sharks, which unfortunately do not meet the task criteria:

Extract 7

90	Ehi	Miss, I know one-
		(★★) swimming on the water
91	LSC	I don't think he could be swimming on the water
		Have him swimming <u>in</u> the water-
		But we're looking for the /cr/ words
92	Ehi	Sharks are (★★★★)
93	LSC	Yes, we know sharks are different, but we're looking for the
		/cr/ words, okay?
		/cr/, /cr/

In addition, there is an instance of pushed output (Swain, 1995) in this session. In the following extract, the LSC pushes the learner to produce the plural morpheme in turn 105, leading to a self-correction in turn 106:

Extract 8

104	Nal	[/o/ and /f/
		/o/, /f/
105	LSC	/o.f./
		MISTER CRUNCHY CRISP HAS LOTS OF CRISPS
		You've got <u>crisp</u>
106	Nal	Has he only got one crisp or has he got more than one?
107	LSC	/s/
		Yep, that's right, another /s/

Although there was more negotiation of meaning in this session than in either the Thunderbird or Fisherman sessions, in my opinion it was still not a major feature of the interaction. As in the previous sessions, negotiation of form was more prevalent than negotiation of meaning and the explicit focus on form I ascribe to the focus on phonics.

Moon session The final session involved five pupils and the CT. Using word makers, they were making words containing /oo/, either suggested by the CT or by a learner. Rather like Scrabble, the learners placed letters on word racks to form the word which was then checked by the CT.

In terms of clarifying misunderstanding, there were two examples of negotiation of meaning. Early in the session, on completion of a word, the CT instructs the learners to remove the letters from their word racks. In turn 46 Aal requests confirmation of the instruction from the CT:

Extract 9

46	Aal	Take this off?
47	CT	Mm?
48	Aal	Take this off?
49	CT	Yeah, put them back in the thing

Later in the session, a learner seeks help from the CT with 'I can't find it' in turn 337, but it is not clear what is missing and the CT requests clarification in turn 338. The learner's reply in turn 339 is followed by a confirmation check from the CT in turn 340:

Extract 10

337	Mav	I can't find it
338	CT	What can't you find?
339	Mav	N
340	CT	A /n/?

The extracts show negotiation of meaning occurring naturally in the course of the conversation, but relating to the task rather than inability to comprehend input. Indeed, in extract 10, it is the CT who makes the clarification request not the learner, but I interpret the question as genuine rather than a pedagogic tool.

Throughout this session, the learners were encouraged to reflect on the words they and their peers had constructed in order to correct their errors and it yielded many examples of negotiation of form. In the extract shown below, Uza is trying to make the word 'balloon'. The CT indicates a problem at the end of turn 194 and follows this up in turn 196, negotiating until Uza finds the right letter after a final prompt from the CT in turn 200:

Extract 11

194	CT	Are you ready with that /oo/ sound?
		Soon, Aal
		Oh, still haven't quite got that first sound for balloon, have we?
195	Px	Soon
196	CT	What's that sound there?
		What have you put in there?
197	Uza	O.U.
198	CT	No, that's fine, all that's fine
		But that sound, what's that sound?
		It's not /p/
199	Uza	/n/
		/b/
200	CT	Is that a /b/?
		Are you sure?

The CT gives overt negative feedback with a tone of genuine enquiry. In turn 229 the CT looks at the word Aal has made which is incomplete and in turn 231 exclaims 'Ooh, what's missing?'. A response is given by another learner in turn 234, confirmed by the CT in turn 235:

Extract 12

228	Aal	I done it
229	CT	Let's have a look then
230	Nuh	I done it
231	CT	[Ooh, what's missing?
232	Px	[Room
233	Px	[Mr P?
234	Nuh	/oo/

235   CT   You've got no /oo/ in there
              You've got /sn/
              You haven't got–

Negotiation, particularly of form, occurred spontaneously in the inter-action, with explicit negative feedback from the CT and learners helping to correct each other's work, as in the above extract when Nuh interjected with '/oo/'. There was also pushed output (Swain, 1995), with the negotiation continuing until the correct spelling was produced, as in extract 11.

In my view, this session with its focus on phonics lent itself to negotiation of form, as did the Mr Crunchy Crisp session. In both these sessions, the focus on form was more explicit than in the Thunderbird and Fisherman sessions, in which there tended to be covert feedback through recasts.

Discussion

Negotiation of meaning Bearing in mind Foster's (2001) comments concerning the danger of finding what you are looking for, I was wary of ascribing negotiation of meaning too readily. However, this research provided little evidence of negotiation of meaning, with only single instances in the Thunderbird and Fisherman sessions, despite the fact that these focused on stories and might have been expected to provide more negotiation of meaning than either the Mr Crunchy Crisp or Moon sessions which addressed phonics.

In the Thunderbird and Fisherman sessions, it may be that the co-construction of understanding and/or the story line alleviated the need for negotiation, as the learners were expressing ideas using language of their choice rather than dealing with potentially complex input. Equally, it could be that teachers and learners are involved in just the collusion of which Cameron et al. (1996) warn. There are also time constraints and there is much to tackle in only twenty minutes. In the Thunderbird session, the CT abandoned negotiation (see extract 1) perhaps because continued attempts to elicit 'shop window' were becoming frustrating as suggested by Aston (1986) or due to insufficient time.

Such evidence as there was of negotiation of meaning did not involve EAL learners using negotiation to clarify their understanding as envisaged by the TTA (2000); instead, learner initiations gave rise to questions from the

CT or LSC (see extracts 3 and 10). Queries from the learners seemed to me to arise in terms of the task ('what am I supposed to be doing?') rather than as a result of difficulty in comprehending input (see extracts 6 and 9), which may have been the result of the types of activity that they were engaged in. In the *Mr Crunchy Crisp* session, the learners were creating their own sentences, with the LSC helping to provide ideas and in the *Moon* session, the aim of spelling out words which contained /oo/ was accomplished using familiar vocabulary.

It would have been interesting to have analysed the independent reading section of the Thunderbird session, which unfortunately was not recorded. In this the interaction between the teacher and the individual learners as she listened to them read might have given rise to negotiation of meaning in the sense that the TTA (2000:47) consider valuable to 'make explicit those meanings which are embedded within sentences, or implied through context', input being provided by the book rather than being mediated by the teacher. On the other hand, it may be that, as Conteh (2000) suggests, learners collaborate fully only without the inhibiting and constraining presence of the teacher and that there would be more negotiation of meaning in the groups working independently.

Negotiation of form All the sessions, particularly Moon and Mr Crunchy Crisp, showed a greater propensity for negotiation of form, which is not surprising considering the focus on phonics. However, in the latter the teacher tended to give the answer, rather than using negotiation. In the Moon session, on the other hand, there was considerable negotiation of form perhaps reflecting the more explicit focus inherent in phonics instruction in the NLS with its emphasis on 'focused attention to language learning' (DfEE, 1998:106) for pupils with EAL.

The use of recasts as implicit negative feedback raises the question of whether the learners recognize the feedback as corrective (Lightbown 1998). However, in sessions with a predominant focus on meaning rather than linguistic code, which I suggest is the case in the Thunderbird and Fisherman sessions, it seems to me that more explicit feedback would prove disruptive to the flow of the session. Explicit negative feedback was used in the Mr Crunchy Crisp and Moon sessions, so it would seem that teachers amend their feedback to suit different teaching aims, whether consciously or unconsciously.

Conclusion

In this case study of negotiated interaction during guided group work in the Literacy Hour with EAL learners, there was little evidence of negotiation of meaning. This would seem to support Foster's (1998) scepticism concerning the spontaneous use of negotiation of meaning in the classroom arising from research in the EFL context and also Cameron et al.'s (1996) doubts about the extent to which meaning is negotiated in the EAL context.

There were differences between the classes, and similarities within those classes, in terms of the feedback given by the CT and LSC, with more explicit negative feedback occurring in the sessions with a focus on phonics. However, in this study it is impossible to know whether the sessions studied typified interaction in the classes directed by those teachers or to what extent the task type impacted on the patterns of interaction. Such issues would have to be the subject of longitudinal study involving the same participants in Literacy Hours with a range of aims. It might well be the case that negotiation of meaning is more a feature of small group interaction independent of a teacher, as suggested by Westgate and Hughes (1997) and Haworth (1999), which might prove fruitful areas for future research.

On the other hand, there was greater negotiation of form in all four sessions, although with varying degrees of explicitness in the feedback given to learners which I would argue is perhaps due to the different purposes of the sessions. The NLS documentation, with its emphasis on 'focused attention to language learning' (DfES, 1998) for EAL learners, seems to me to present an opportunity for focus on form through scaffolding and collaborative learning, although to what extent this is being implemented in classrooms at present remains an open question.

Notes

1   EAL is defined as the descriptive term '…used for pupils who are in the process of learning English on entry to school … The presence of languages other than English in pupils' home backgrounds does not always mean that these pupils are 'bilingual'. The term EAL is intended to recognize that in learning English, not as an option, but as the prime language of instruction, pupils are adding to their existing linguistic skills' (SCAA, 1996a:2).

2   Although now the DfES, references in this paper are made using the name in use at the time when the documentation was published.

3   NALDIC is an organization which promotes the development of policy, practice and research related to the teaching and learning of EAL and provides a professional forum for

discussion of issues.

4   Classroom Assessment of English as an Additional Language in Key Stage 1 Contexts, ESRC Award No. R000238196.

5   Px – an unidentified learner.

6   PP – entire group in chorus.

References

Aston, G. (1986) 'Troubleshooting interaction with learners: the more the merrier?' *Applied Linguistics*, 7: 128-143.

Cameron, L., J. Moon and Bygate, M. (1996) 'Language Development of Bilingual Pupils in the Mainstream: How do Pupils and Teachers Use Language?' *Language and Education*, 10, 4: 221-236.

DfEE. (1998) *The National Literacy Strategy: Framework for teaching*. London: DfEE.

DfES. (2001) *The National Literacy Strategy: Framework for teaching*. 3rd edition. London: DfES.

Ellis, R. (1994) *The Study of Second Language Acquisition*. Oxford: Oxford University Press.

Ellis, R., Tanaka, Y. and Yamazaki, A. (1994) 'Classroom interaction, comprehension, and the acquisition of L2 word meanings.' *Language Learning*, 44: 449-491.

Foster, P. (1998) 'A Classroom Perspective on the Negotiation of Meaning.' *Applied Linguistics*, 19, 1: 1-23.

Foster, P. (2001) *Task-based learning*. Talk given at the Graduate School of Education, University of Bristol, 13 June 2001.

Haworth, A. (1999) 'Bakhtin in the Classroom: What Constitutes a Dialogic Text? Some Lessons from Small Group Interaction.' *Language and Education*, 13, 2: 99-117.

Lightbown, P. M. (1998) 'The importance of timing in focus on form.' In C. Doughty and J. Williams (eds) *Focus on form in classroom second language acquisition*. Cambridge: Cambridge University Press.

Lightbown, P. M. and Spada, N. (1999) *How Languages are Learned*. 2nd edition. Oxford: Oxford University Press.

Long, M. H. (1996) 'The Role of the Linguistic Environment in Second Language Acquisition.' In W. C. Ritchie and T. K. Bhatia (eds) *Handbook of Second Language Acquisition*. San Diego: Academic Press.

Loschky, L. (1994) 'Comprehensible Input and Second Language Acquisition: What is the Relationship?' *Studies in Second Language Acquisition*, 16: 303-325.

Mackey, A. (1999) 'Input, Interaction, and Second Language Development.' *Studies in Second Language Acquisition*, 21: 557-587.

Malamah-Thomas, A. (1987) *Classroom Interaction*. Oxford: Oxford University Press.

Mitchell, R. and Myles, F. (1998) *Second Language Learning Theories*. London: Arnold.

NALDIC Working Party. (1998) *Provision in Literacy Hours for Pupils Learning English as an Additional Language: NALDIC Literacy Papers*. NALDIC Publications.

Nobuyoshi, J. and Ellis, R. (1993) 'Focused communication tasks and second language acquisition.' *ELT Journal*, 47, 3: 203-210.

Pica, T. and Doughty, C. (1985) 'The Role of Group Work in Classroom Second Language Acquisition.' *Studies in Second Language Acquisition*, 7: 233-248.

SCAA (1996) *Teaching and learning English as an additional language: new perspectives* (SCAA Discussion Papers: No. 5). London: School Curriculum and Assessment Authority.

Swain, M. (1995) 'Three functions of output in second language learning.' In G. Cook and B. Seidlhofer (eds) *Principle and practice in applied linguistics: Studies in honour of H. G. Widdowson*. Oxford University Press: Oxford.

Sylva, K. (1997) *Observing practice in the 'Literacy Initiative for Teachers' (L.I.F.T.) and comparison classrooms*. Paper presented at the British Educational Research Association Annual Conference September 11-14 1997, University of York.

TTA (2000) *Raising the Attainment of Minority Ethnic Pupils: guidance and resource materials for providers of initial teacher training*. London: Teacher Training Agency.

Westgate, D. and Hughes, M. (1997) 'Identifying 'Quality' in Classroom Talk: An Enduring Research Task.' *Language and Education*, 11, 2: 125-139.

13 Is the university a community of practice?

John M. Swales

University of Michigan

Abstract

Much recent research, such as Hyland (2000), has uncovered important differences in written rhetorical and linguistic patterns from one disciplinary cluster to another. We also know that particular written genres are differently valorized across those clusters. However, it is much less clear whether academic speech as a whole is as distinctive or as contentious or as subject to disciplinary variation as might appear at first sight. In this paper I use the Michigan Corpus of Academic Spoken English (MICASE) to investigate the extent to which academic/research oracy reflects and constitutes a more general community of practice or a tribalized coterie of disciplinary dialects. To study this issue, the paper focuses on three graduate-faculty spoken genres from across a range of disciplinary settings: Research group meetings, departmental colloquia and dissertation defences. Study of their structure, pragmatic patterning, linguistic usage and various other features all suggest, at least in one large institution in the American Midwest, that there is a greater homogeneity in research speech than previously thought.

Introduction

This paper, in line with the conference theme, asks the apparently simple question as to whether universities, the institutions wherein most applied linguists work, can individually be conceived of as constituting 'communities of practice' (Lave and Wenger, 1991). There are of course many ways of tackling this question; one might be historical, another epistemological, a third might examine shared norms and values. However, as might be expected, the focus here will be mostly on linguistic and discoursal features. And here I will be suggesting (modestly) that different answers will likely be forthcoming depending on whether the focus of inquiry falls upon *academic text* or *academic talk*, and that this itself sheds its own light on the concept of community of practice, at least in so far as it manifests itself in the academic and research world – and perhaps in other universes of discourse in which texts are important, such as the law.

At first sight, of course, the university today looks like a totally fissiparous institution, impelled by some 19th century Big Bang scenario whereby divisional constellations are hurtling further and further away from each other, and wherein disciplinary planetary systems are drifting further and further apart so that communications across these extending voids become increasingly difficult. As is well known, the university has reacted to these exigencies by first dividing itself into constituent faculties or colleges – in Michigan's case 19 of them – and then into smaller and smaller units. And even within my own college of Literature, Science and Arts, there are three different tenure and promotion committees: one for the humanities, one for social sciences, and one for the sciences themselves. These collegial committees use very different criteria as they come to examine the CVs and written work of the candidates, and the evaluation letters written on their behalf. In the humanities, scholarship and style are all, with little attention to how well known an applicant's work has or has not become. Impact is rarely important (especially with junior scholars), while co-authorship raises quizzical eyebrows and where an odd kind of mathematics predominates in which half of the authorship of a paper usually equals a quarter of a publication. In the social sciences, citations in the Social Science Citation Index loom large with much lesser attention to the quality – or otherwise – of the actual writing. Finally, in the sciences, a sufficiently steady stream of research grants to sustain laboratory enterprises takes on major importance. In both of these last two areas co-authorship is just fine. These differences also reflect different hierarchies of genres in different areas. And these, to some extent, carry over into research speech, but to a lesser degree. After all every department invites its short-listed job candidates for what Americans succinctly if rather brutally call 'job talks'.

Variation in academic texts

As is well known, there has been much activity over the last twenty years, much of it driven by valid applied linguistic concerns, to show that distinctive textual conventions operate within particular disciplinary areas. The research or scholarly paper, described by Montgomery as 'the master narrative' (1996:6), has been a prime locus of investigation here, ranging from informally written papers by single figures in philosophy, engaging – as Bloor nicely puts it – 'in mind-to-mind combat' (1996:34), to major medical multi-national surveys involving whole rafts of authorial contributors. The world record for a scientific paper is, as far as I am aware, 246 co-authors.

The first of two quick examples of written disciplinary variation concerns the part-genre of the Methods section in research articles. Accounting for methods may be brisk and enigmatic in the hard sciences, with much citational or procedural shorthand, and is increasingly being downgraded to smaller and smaller print, or even to appearing in an appendix (Berkenkotter and Huckin, 1995). This produces an effect that looks decidedly strange in our own field. Here is a brief invented extract:

Methods of collection were essentially those of Sinclair[1]. Items were tagged with a modification of Biber[2], data-based and then subjected to a KWIC concordancer. Collocation outcomes were derived by adapting procedures from Stubbs, Partington and Aston[3-5]. Statistical procedures utilized the Wordsmith package[6], while Thurston and Candlin[7] provided a basis for the collocational line display used in the matched- guise think-aloud protocol experiments.

This account is of course far from replicable – given its allusions to 'essentially', 'modification of' and 'adapting procedures from'. Among other features, it contains a string of verbs (with gapping), an unexplained acronym in the second sentence, and a complex NP at the end of the fourth. More generally, the use of superscripts deprives the reader, at least on initial perusal, of any sense of chronological development (or 'depth perception') into the field. There are no justifications or explications and the focus is heavily on the procedures with little said about the subjects or objects of analysis (Bloor, 1999). As Thompson says of this kind of text, 'There is little sense that one part of the text motivates or is motivated by other parts of the text' (2002:155).

If this is under-specification, then consider this short extract from a paper from *The American Journal of Botany* (my emphases):

To detect groups among the specimens and extract the variables that best diagnose these groups, we used Principal components analysis. Before conducting the analysis, we standardized all measurements so each variable would have a mean of 0 and a standard deviation of 1. For the PCA, we included only continuous characters. *To avoid weighting characters*, we excluded characters that are probably genetically redundant, as revealed by high values for the Pearson correlation coefficient between all possible pairs of characters. (Naczi et al., 1998:435)

This is part of a 34-sentence Materials and Methods section, with as many as six of those sentences *beginning* with a justification for the action taken, as in the italicized fragments above – and none occurring in any other position in the sentence. These pre-justifications are, of course, designed to close down queries that might otherwise arise in the reader's mind as to the rationale for particular methodological choices. As one of the authors (Reznicek) explained in a text-based interview: 'you know we typically had such good arguments for things...so we put them up front and brought them out ourselves...ah, it's a way of anticipating and avoiding criticisms from reviewers'.

The second of the two mini-forays into written disciplinary variation involves having a look at differences in citational patterns. Hyland (e.g. 2000) has investigated, for example, disciplinary variation in research papers across eight fields – variation that goes considerably beyond whether MLA or APA style is chosen or whether a name-date system operates or one involving superscripts, such as whether the item being referred to is part of the sentence or is just a parethetical addition. The former so-called integral citations (Swales, 1990) range from low of around 10% in biology to a high of around 65% in philosophy. Further important differences lie in the propensity for or possibility of direct quotation, especially in indented blocks. Sociologists have a well-known tendency toward what is sometimes known as *foundational citation*; and this invoking of the giants of the field (Durkheim, Weber, Bourdieu) makes them very prone to block quotation. However, research articles in another social science, psychology, hardly ever employ direct quotations, both short and long . In applied linguistics itself the picture is interestingly mixed, block-quoting appearing quite commonly among those with a more humanistic/pedagogical orientation, but much less frequently in the papers of those who align themselves with experimental approaches.

Variation in research speech

In contrast, disciplinary variation in academic speech has been little investigated. There is of course some anecdotal evidence for such variation. I once heard Tony Becher tell the splendid story of a colleague who began his academic career as a philosopher and as a dutiful department member went to hear the speaker at the weekly seminar (or colloquium). After the talk, he was wont to observe 'I didn't quite understand what you said about...'. At which point, the room fell into an awed hush at what the audience took to be a profound observation. Somewhat later in life, Becher's friend changed fields, moved across to comparative literature and went once again to the weekly talk; after which he expressed his customary rumination, 'I didn't quite understand what you said about...', but this time everybody in the room looked at him as though he were totally stupid.

Here is a second anecdote. An ex-colleague is now head of a modern languages department in Britain. Some years ago, this department was looking for a senior lecturer in German, and the external member of the appointments board was a professor of engineering. One of the candidates gave a presentation on his dialectological studies tracing isoglosses among a constellation of rural villages somewhere in Germany. At the close of this fine-grained sociolinguistic presentation, the engineer leant across to my friend, and remarked sotto voce, 'But surely all this stuff about these villages is just a hobby.'

These anecdotes have the additional value of preparing the way for some more general points. Academics tend to listen more widely than they read. Few of the people whose work we read most closely work at our own institutions, but are widely scattered elsewhere and form the well-known Mertonian concept of 'invisible colleges'. On the other hand, we often turn up for our departmental colleagues' talks. Telephoning aside, academic and research talk also tends to be more local and more communal than academic writing, and one of the several reasons for this is that it is often directed toward advising, which brings us back to the 'legitimate peripheral participation' aspect of communities of practice (Lave and Wenger, 1991). Second, research talk (at least at conferences) may be less differentiated by language than by the type and frequency of the supporting visuals (Ventola et al., 2002). Naturally enough there will always be what Mätikalo and Säljö (2002) call *categorial terms* (such as *subaltern* in cultural studies) that puzzle outsiders; further, levels of metaphorical usage of certain terms shift across disciplines, such as the literal use of *black hole* in astronomy as opposed to its widespread figurative use in other fields (Mendis, 2002).

The MICASE research sub-corpus To go beyond the anecdotal and the incidental with regard to disciplinary variation in research talk, I now turn to the Michigan Corpus of Academic Spoken English (MICASE), and in particular to the 36 speech events in the MICASE Research Sub-corpus. This latter consists of such genres as colloquia, advanced doctoral student seminar classes, research group meetings and dissertation defences, spread across the four official divisions of Arts and Humanities, Social Sciences and Education, Biological and Life Sciences, and Physical Sciences and Engineering.

Since disciplinary differences in citational patterns in research articles have already been aired, this will serve as an appropriate entry point. As might be expected, full name and date citations are rare in the MICASE data; more interestingly, they do not seem to vary much, either in terms of frequency or in terms of formulation, according to the disciplinary or divisional area. Below are four examples (my emphases):

1　...one of the tools that uh comes from this definition then is the Nursing Work Index, **it is developed by Kramer and Hafner back in nineteen eighty-nine**.

2　you remember i mentioned um, that uh **Sir William B. Hardy, in nineteen twenty-five or thereabout, uh did** an experiment dropping fatty acid on water...

3　uh the first results, that i know of were from a mathematician **named Glickfield in nineteen nineteen who showed** that you can fill at most eighty-eight percent, of space, and then somebody el- then he proved eighty-threepercent and then **Rankin in forty-seven did eighty-two percent** and then Rodgers in fifty-five seventy-seven-point-nine percent, and then...

4　turns out that this relationship, though people have noticed it for approximately eighty eighty-five years, was first **quantified in nineteen seventy-nine by Jack Wolfe**, using East Asian data.

Valle (1999), in her diachronic survey of the life science article, comments on the emergence of contemporary citation practice as follows: 'Where earlier the reference was to a personal writer, who performed actions in and by means of texts (as expressed by reporting verbs) now it is the text itself, labeled with a combination of name and year, which seems to perform these actions...'(p. 376). Most interestingly, we can note here that rather than reporting verbs per se, we seem, in research speech, to be reflecting an even earlier area of accounting for previous work than Valle refers to – one in which people *did* things, or *developed them* or *first quantified* them.

Colloquia A second levelling factor is the matter-of-fact informality and casualness of research speech at Michigan. Very few of the primary speakers in the MICASE research corpus speak like a book, engage in the rapier-like cut-and-thrust of the academic discussions we have come to expect from novels set in universities, or indulge in vicious critical outbursts. Instead, the great majority of contributions have the flavour of this opening monologue at an ecology colloquium:

> what we plan to do here is uh i'll talk for a little bit, um, about sort of the underlying theoretical framework that we think we are operating under here, and then when i finish that, that'll be just five minutes or so, and then i'll talk about the work that we're doing in Nicaragua, and when i finish talking about the work that we're doing in Nicaragua, why Ivette will talk about the work that we're doing in Mexico, and then finally when fe- she finishes why i'll come back up here to talk uh, um a little bit s- more reflective about how the, uh theoretical framework fits into the work that we're doing and what we plan to do in the future and how other people might be, might b- uh be wanting to join us, okay?

There are a number of observations to be made about this text. It is clear, for instance, that this elaborate road-map is couched in very informal, almost casual terms, since the speaker and his co-presenter are just going to 'talk a little bit' (rather than *discuss* or *describe*) about 'the work' (rather than, say, *research projects*). Indeed, *work* is repeated four times in this short extract. The only exception – and one which consequently stands out – is the repeated phrase 'theoretical framework', but note also that its first use is mitigated by a 'sort of' hedge and by the cautious post-modifier 'that we think we're operating under here'. Mauranen (2001) raises the question of why this kind of prospective move should turn out to be so hedged, and answers it by saying, 'This imposing of the speaker's order on other participants involves using power and therefore calls for mitigation, for redressing some of the power balance' (p. 175). In fact, there are more than 20 instances of first person pronouns followed by the 'talk★ a little bit about' cluster in the research sub-corpus. At the other end of the formality cline, the verb *address* certainly also occurs in the database, but there are only a handful of first person singular uses and these mostly by graduate students talking about their own research. Rather, it turns out that *addressing issues/problems/questions* is something that other researchers have done or something that other entities, such as the university or the government, need to do.

In this climate, one might have expected that this Midwestern politesse would lead to much commendation and congratulation of the colloquium speakers, so that when it came to question/discussion time, we might find prefaces of the type 'Thank you for your interesting presentation, but I do have a question...'. However, the data suggests otherwise (Table 1).

In this admittedly small section of data, it is striking that only one of the 75 questions or comments is opened with a commendation. In addition, and as can be seen from the right side of the table, presenters only rarely prefaced their responses with a commendation on the question or comment, even though such a move does additionally offer some opportunity to temporarily play for time and collect one's thoughts. It seems then that Midwestern reticence extends as far as not making complimentary prefacing remarks. It also appears that the MICASE data does not fit well with Tracy's (1997) account of the colloquia in the two departments of communications that she studied. As far as I can see, the MICASE colloquia are much less afflicted than hers with dilemmas, tensions, status conflicts and contradictions. There are, in my data, no naked antagonisms and no total confusions; there are

Table 1 Commendatory prefaces in four MICASE colloquia

Event	Q/Cs Total	Prefaced	Responses Total	Prefaced
Ecology	11	0	19	3
Science Panel	7	0	20	1
Education	19	0	21	0
Philosophy	28	1	28	0
Totals	75	1	88	4

many instances of laughter, but no descents into distracting hilarity.

Research Group Meetings Four of which we have recorded as part of the MICASE project, but, for space reasons, here I will focus on the AI research group meeting, in which a student rehearses his presentation for his prospectus defence, and is therefore similar in activity to the 'dry-runs' studied by Jacoby (1998). The group director here, in contrast to the one in Jacoby's group, evinces fairly massive epistemic uncertainty:

> you know i i think, uh of course the reallocation is interesting but i, wouldn't necessarily, um, trivialize the initial, allocation, in the first place, you might wanna just say, you know how we come up with this original solution...

It is also interesting that one of MICASE research assistants transcribing this file made the observation that 'you know in this one you can't tell who's the prof and who are the students'. Further evidence of this comes from the fact that of the 42 times the speaker was interrupted with comments, questions or suggestions, the advisor initiated under half. Here are the allocatable speaker turns in the AI research group meeting:

Bob (defender)	172
Advisor (male)	94
Student A (male)	83
Student B (male)	43
Student C (female)	3
Student D (male)	1
Student E (male)	6

We can note here that the advisor is only marginally the most frequent commentator and the two most loquacious senior graduate students (A and B) together considerably outnumber the advisor's turns at talk.

So far then we have seen that research speech at Michigan would seem to be informal, indeed casual in its extempore expression; it tends to be highly hedged; deferential rather than confrontational; guarded and reticent rather than highly evaluative; unpretentious in its choice of words and in its avoidance of name-dropping, Latin tags, obscure references; overall, tending toward the collegial and the demotic, rather than preserving the pose of the intellectual. And these features seem widely distributed across the disciplinary spectrum.

Dissertation defences Finally, I would like to turn to the dissertation defence. There is the earlier sociology defence analyzed by Grimshaw (1989) and Grimshaw and Burke (1994), to which we can now add Michigan defences in AI, cross-cultural social psychology, musicology (jazz), and biology (fossil plants). Of the many interesting features of this speech-genre, I will focus here on the role of humour. Laughter, both individual or general, turns out to be quite common in these speech-events, there being an average across the four defences of a laughter episode some every three minutes. Although, for reasons of space, I will concentrate on the general laughter episodes in the social psychology defence, it is important to point out that there are at least three such episodes close to the beginnings of all the four other defences. It seems as though Grimshaw's opening 'settling in' segment encourages participants to maximize opportunities for humour as a way of relaxing tension, establishing some kind of interactional framework, and/or 'deformalizing' the ceremonial aspects of the genre.

The social psychology defence actually has a laughter episode right at its beginning:

Chair: okey-doke, uh well Incheol was gonna do another, very brief
      summary of what he's up to. uh to bring it all up on our screens…

Cand: alright, um/first of all i'd like to thank all of you, for agreeing to
      be on the committee, reading the draft, and coming to the defence,
      being with me at, my last moment of, graduate school.

S3:   <LAUGH> such optimism

      <LAUGH SS>

We can see here that the chair of the committee begins very informally ('okey-doke'; 'what he's up to'), and follows up with the highly contemporary metaphor of 'bringing it up on our screens'. In contrast, the Korean candidate opens gracefully with a more formal expression of appreciation to his committee, the last part of which leads to S3's witty sally at the candidate's expense. The sally is successful because of the faint chance that the candidate might in the end fail his oral examination and have to do it all over again, and this 'fiction' is maintained by the chair who then says 'if he doesn't pass he told me he's gonna drop out.' It might be thought that this kind of joking banter is only permissible for those in authority, but toward the end of the defence this particular candidate can turn the tables, as it were. The necessary context is that earlier the chair, who is in late middle age, had failed to remember the second part of a question he wanted to ask:

Chair:...how can you put, those, drive all three of those things from
         the same, core notion?

Cand: i mean, i was surprised that um, you, do not see the connection.
        <LAUGH SS> that was <funny

Chair: yes>, we've been talking about the aging problem

      <LAUGH SS>

Cand: (actually) to me, <to me

S3:   it's obvious>

      <LAUGH SS>

The three instances of general laughter here have very different origins, but work together to create a delightful exchange. The first occurs in response to the candidate's (possibly tongue in cheek) expression of surprise at his advisor's apparent obtuseness; his advisor then rises to the occasion, turning the joke on himself by referring to his incipient senility; and when the candidate begins to respond, a quick-witted committee member completes his utterance with a very forthright 'it's obvious', thus extending the jocularity at the chair's expense.

More generally, it might appear on casual observation that several of these humorous episodes are somehow 'off-topic'. Indeed, Fillmore (1994) notes:

> Since a dissertation defense is not primarily an entertainment, the kinds of humorous episodes that occur during it will mostly be **diversions** from the ritual's main purpose. (p. 273, original emphasis)

However, when we recognize that the candidate's dissertation in cross-cultural psychology deals with how members of Korean culture and American culture deal with unexpected events, most of the humorous exchanges can be considered as certainly more pertinent than 'diversions'. For example, there are extensive discussions among participants about cross-cultural perceptions of politeness, wherein the German committee member gets a laugh by saying, after the candidate has observed that the German way of responding to speakers 'looks quite impolite', 'yes, i learned that i i'm trying to improve'. The German committee member also comments on the big differences between recommendation letters in Germany and the USA and gets another laugh when he notes with reference to North America 'at this point we only have genius graduate students'.

There is a tendency for discourse analysts, when focusing on a particular feature, to overdramatize the pragmatic significance of that feature. To counteract any such tendency in this case, let me emphasize that USA dissertation defences are not in the end instances of a Bahktinian carnival (Bahktin, 1968), where the committee members variously play the roles of the rogue, the clown and the fool. However, in another work, Bakhtin does make the highly pertinent comment that laughter 'demolishes the fear and piety before an object' (1981:23). In our case, of course, that object is the defence speech-event, that ultimate rite of passage that university institutions require of their doctoral students, and within that context, humour (along with informality and other features) emancipates by reducing tensions and by moderating the pious insistence of institutional regulations.

Conclusions

In this paper I have tried to indicate disciplinary differences in research talk at Michigan are fewer than we might expect, presumably largely because of its general conversational flavour. And when they do occur, they seem well motivated. Poos and Simpson (2000), for example, have shown, that hedges of the 'sorta/kinda' type are commoner in the social sciences and the humanities, but ascribe this difference to the nature of the discipline. A physicist is unlikely to say 'this is sort of a molecule', while an anthropologist might well say 'this is sort of a cultural issue' and indeed purposefully use that hedge as part of a disciplinary acculturation in which a concept like culture can be shown to be problematized.

This is not to say that so-called ordinary words and phrases are not recontextualized in research settings and become categorialized, as discussed by Mäkitalo and Säljö (2002). One example of many. Recall the colloquium speaker who in his opening remarks states 'I'm going to talk a little bit about our work in Nicaragua'. We understand what this categorial use of work is going to mean in this research speech-event. So when we meet acquaintances at conferences and inquire 'well, what are you working on now?', we do not expect such answers 'my garage', or 'my stamp collection' or even 'next year's departmental budget'.

The talk that occurs in USA research settings was characterized by Grimshaw in 1989 as a mixed style because of its combination of conversation-like clauses and some technical lexis. However, this style is too common, too accepted and too pervasive to be given such a hybridizing label. In Swales (forthcoming) it is described as open and as such it can be suitably technical, especially in terms of noun groups, but casual in its co-ordinated structures and heavy use of deictics. This openness is at least partly derived from the fact that research speech is little legislated, regulated, or explicitly taught. Further, like casual conversation, there is likely to be some overt orientation toward consensus (Eggins and Slade, 1997).

And so, finally, to my opening question. I suggest that our perception of the university has been strongly pressured by the weight of its texts, by its libraries and its groaning bookshelves, which exert a strong and permanent influence around us, and which reify our perceptions of disciplinary differences. Further, it is research writing that is coached, revised, reviewed, copy-edited and generally co-constructed and, finally, it is research and scholarly writing that prevails in research assessment exercises and the like. When we turn to research speech across the disciplines, we see at least in the USA Midwest, a much greater homogeniety in verbal performance, if not in visual support. Of course, the university – in its academic spoken modes – is clearly not a single community of practice in any sensibly tight definition of that somewhat Utopian concept, because only small percentages of its members actually do research talk together. However, the discoursal barriers to cross-disciplinary oral communication are lower and the potential for various kinds of rapprochement greater, and the discoursal and rhetorical facilitators of cross-border communication (informality, lack of obscure allusions, the important role of humour) more recognizable.

References

Bakhtin, M. M. (1968) *Rabelais and his world*. Cambridge, MA: MIT Press.
Bakhtin, M. M. (1981) *The dialogic imagination: Four essays by M.M. Bakhtin*. Austin: University of Texas Press.
Berkenkotter, C. and Huckin, T. N. (1995) *Genre knowledge in disciplinary communication: Cognition/culture/power*. Hillsdale, NJ: Lawrence Erlbaum.
Bloor, M. (1999) Variation in the methods sections of research articles across disciplines: The case of fast and slow texts. In P. Thompson (ed.) *Issues in EAP writing research and instruction*. The University of Reading: CALS. pp. 84–106.
Bloor, T. (1996) Three hypothetical strategies in philosophical writing. In E. Ventola and A. Mauranen (eds) *Academic writing: Intercultural and textual issues*. Amsterdam: John Benjamins. pp. 19–43.
Eggins, S. and Slade, D. (1997) *Analysing casual conversation*. London: Cassell.
Fillmore, C. J. (1994) Humor in academic discourse. In Grimshaw and Burke (eds) pp. 271–310.
Grimshaw, A. (1989) *Collegial discourse: professional conversation among peers*. Norwood, NJ: Ablex.
Grimshaw, A. and Burke, P. (1994) (eds) *What's going on here? Complementary studies of professional talk*. Norwood, NJ: Ablex.
Hyland, K. (2000) *Disciplinary discourses: Social interactions in academic writing*. Harlow: Longman.
Jacoby, S. W. (1998) *Science as performance: Socializing scientific discourse through the conference talk rehearsal*. Unpublished PhD dissertation, UCLA.
Lave, J. and Wenger, E. (1991) *Situated learning: Legitimate peripheral participation*. Cambridge: Cambridge University Press.
Mauranen, A. (2002) Reflexive academic talk: Observations from MICASE. In R. C. Simpson, and J. M. Swales. (eds) *Corpus linguistics in North America: Selections from the 1999 symposium*. Ann Arbor, MI: University of Michigan Press. pp. 165–178
Mäkitalo, A and Säljö, R. (2002) Talk in institutional context and institutional context in talk: Categories as situated practices. *Text*, 22: 57–82.
Mendis, D. (2002) *The functions of idioms in MICASE*. Presentation at the ELI, The University of Michigan, December.
Montgomery, S. L. (1996) *The scientific voice*. New York: The Guilford Press.
Naczi, R. F. C., Reznicek, A. A. and Ford, B. A. (1998) Morphological, geographical, and ecological differentiation in the Carex willdenowii complex (Cyperaceae). *American Journal of Botany*, 85: 434–447.
Poos, D. and Simpson, R. C. (2000) *Hedging and disciplinary variation*. Presentation at the American Association of Applied Linguistics. Vancouver, March.
Swales, J. M. (forthcoming). *Research genres: Explorations and applications*. Cambridge: Cambridge University Press.
Thompson, S. (2002) 'As the story unfolds': The uses of narrative in research presentations. In E. Ventola et al. (eds) *The language of conferencing*. Frankfurt: Peter Lang. pp. 147–168.
Tracy, K. (1997) *Colloquium: Dilemmas of academic discourse*. Norwood, NJ: Ablex.
Ventola, E., Shalom, C. and Thompson, S. (2002) (eds) *The language of conferencing*. Frankfurt: Peter Lang.

Contributors

Kristina Bennert is Research Associate at Cardiff University on the Wellcome Trust project in genetic counselling. Between 1999 and 2001 she worked as Leverhulme Research Fellow on 'Press Representations and Individual Perceptions of Middle Age' at the University of Wolverhampton. Her ESRC-funded doctoral research was a discourse analysis of workplace interactions between trainees and their co-workers in the context of vocational placements. Currently she is editorial associate of the interdisciplinary journal *TEXT*. (bennert@cf.ac.uk)

Angus Clarke is Professor and honorary consultant in Clinical Genetics at the University of Wales College of Medicine. He studied genetics and then clinical medicine before specialising in paediatrics and subsequently clinical genetics. He has research interests in Rett syndrome, ectodermal dysplasia, newborn screening programmes and neuromuscular disease. He also has a particular interest in the social and ethical implications of developments in human genetics and collaborates in this interdisciplinary area with a range of social scientists and philosophers. (clarkeaj@cf.ac.uk)

David Crystal is Honorary Professor of Linguistics at University of Wales, Bangor. He is editor of the Cambridge 'family' of general encyclopaedias. A former editor of several linguistics journals and series, his research interests have included intonation, grammar, stylistics, and in the application of linguistics to religious, educational and clinical contexts. Recent publications include the second editions of *The Cambridge Encyclopaedia of Language* and The Penguin *Dictionary of Language, Language Play, Language Death* and *Language and the Internet*. (crystal@dial.pipex.com)

Esther Daborn is a Lecturer in the English as a Foreign Language Unit at the University of Glasgow. Her work and publications are in the area of World English, discourse analysis, and the use of corpora for developing academic literacy skills. She has worked on communication skills with Electronic and Electrical Engineering students for a number of years. (e.daborn@efl.arts.gla.ac.uk)

Susan Dray is a part-time research associate at Lancaster University working on a project investigating the relationship between literacy and health. She is currently completing a PhD at Lancaster, investigating vernacular writing practices and constructions of literacy in a Creole-speaking society (Jamaica). Her research interests include aspects of Critical Discourse Analysis, language education, literacy and sociolinguistics. She is also interested in the use of photography as an ethnographic research tool. (s.dray@lancaster.ac.uk)

Sandra Harrison is Head of Communication, Media and Culture at Coventry University, where she teaches professional and technical writing and information design. Her recent research applies techniques from the analysis of spoken conversation to the discourse of email discussions, investigating the occurrence of politeness strategies and of metacommunication, and using conversation analysis to illuminate turn sequences, utterance pairs, and repair. A current project investigates the use of ICTs in a local government environment. (sandra.harrison@cov.ac.uk)

Georgina Heydon is a lecturer in English Linguistics at the University of Aarhus, Denmark. She completed both her undergraduate and doctoral degrees at Monash University in Australia where she has also worked as a forensic linguist. Her primary research interests are the critical analysis of discourse, in particular police institutional discourse, and the identification of institutionalised beliefs surrounding discourse practices, such as police-suspect interviews. (enggh@hum.au.dk)

Lucy Howell is a Researcher at Cardiff University on the Wellcome Trust project in genetic counselling. Her doctoral research involved an investigation into talk and text about the process of diagnosis and non-diagnosis in genetic counselling. She is Co-ordinator of the Health Communication Research Centre and editorial associate for the new journal *Communication and Medicine*. (howelll@cf.ac.uk)

Emma Marsden is currently an ESRC funded PhD student in the Centre for Language in Education at the University of Southampton. She has worked as a language teacher in the UK, France, Spain and Chile. Her research interests include input processing and attention in Second Language Acquisition, morphosyntactic development in classroom learners, grammar pedagogy and foreign language education policy. (e.j.marsden@soton.ac.uk)

TJE Miller is Professor of Electrical Power Engineering, and founder and Director of the SPEED Consortium at the University of Glasgow. He is the author of over 100 publications in the fields of motors, drives, power systems and power electronics, including seven books. He is a Fellow of the IEEE, and Fellow of the IEE. (t.miller@elec.gla.ac.uk)

Rosamond Mitchell is Professor of Education at the University of Southampton, and Chair of the Centre for Language in Education. Her research interests include foreign language education policy, classroom second language learning and teaching, and the corpus based study of interlanguage development. (r.f.mitchell@soton.ac.uk)

Florence Myles is Senior Lecturer in French and Linguistics at the University of Southampton. Her research interests are in the area of Second Language Acquisition, especially of French. She is particularly interested in theories of language learning and their empirical implications, and in the interface between linguistic theory and cognitive approaches to the learning of second languages. (fjm@soton.ac.uk)

Celia Roberts is Senior Research Fellow at King's College, London. Her research interests are in interactional sociolinguistics and institutional and urban ethnography. Among her publications are: *Language and Discrimination* (with E. Davis and T. Jupp), *Achieving Understanding* (with K. Bremer et al.) and *Talk, Work and Institutional Order* (with S. Sarangi). For the past five years she has been working in the area of medical communication, with a focus on intercultural issues. (celiaroberts@lineone.net)

Sarah Rule completed her PhD in 2001 and has subsequently worked as a research assistant at the University of Southampton. Her research interests lie in Second Language Acquisition based in a generative framework. She also teaches on Linguistics courses, particularly syntax, in the School of Modern Languages. (sjr1@soton.ac.uk)

Srikant Sarangi is Professor and Director of the Health Communication Research Centre at Cardiff University. His research interests are in discourse analysis and applied linguistics; language and identity in public life and institutional/professional discourse studies (e.g., healthcare, social welfare, bureaucracy, education etc.). He has published widely in these areas, including four books and five journal special issues. He is currently editor of

TEXT: An Interdisciplinary Journal for the Study of Discourse, founding editor of *Communication and Medicine* and (with C. N. Candlin) of *Journal of Applied Linguistics*. He is also general editor (with C. N. Candlin) of two book series: *Advances in Applied Linguistics* and *Communication in Public Life*. (sarangi@cf.ac.uk)

Juliane Schwarz is currently finishing her Ph.D in the Department of Linguistics, Lancaster University. Her research focus is non-sexist language change and how qualitative research methods (interviews and focus group discussions) can inform the study of linguistic sexism. She was a co-organiser of the Second International Gender and Language Association Conference (IGALA2). She is also an active member of the Gender and Language Research Group which she is currently co-ordinating. (schwarz@lancaster.ac.uk)

Catriona Scott worked as a TEFL teacher abroad for almost 10 years. On returning to the UK, she became interested in English as an Additional Language whilst studying for an MEd in TEFL at the Graduate School of Education, University of Bristol and she is still there. She is now doing a longitudinal case study of washback from National Curriculum assessment at Key Stages 1 and 2 in the EAL context for an ESRC-funded PhD. (Ktscott55@hotmail.com)

John Swales is Professor of Linguistics at the University of Michigan, Ann Arbor, and from 1985 to 2001 he was Director of the English Language Institute. His current interests focus on a corpus-based approach to academic speech, genre theory, and genre-based approaches to teaching academic communication. His forthcoming book *Research Genres: Explorations and Applications* is a successor volume to *Genre Analysis: English in Academic and Research Settings* (1990), both published by Cambridge University Press. (jmswales@umich.edu)

Theo van Leeuwen is Professor and Director of the Centre for Language and Communication at Cardiff University. His main research interests are in media discourse, critical discourse analysis and multimodality. He coordinates the Leverhulme programme on Language and Global Communication. He has been a founding editor of the journal *Social Semiotics*, and from 2001 co-edits the new journal *Visual Communication*. (vanleeuwent@cf.ac.uk)